The Ethical Use
of Data in Education

Promoting Responsible
Policies and Practices

EDITED BY

Ellen B. Mandinach
Edith S. Gummer

TEACHERS COLLEGE PRESS
TEACHERS COLLEGE | COLUMBIA UNIVERSITY
NEW YORK AND LONDON

WestEd.org

Published simultaneously by Teachers College Press,® 1234 Amsterdam Avenue, New York, NY 10027, and WestEd, 730 Harrison Street, San Francisco, CA 94107-1242.

Library of Congress Cataloging-in-Publication Data are available at loc.gov

ISBN 978-0-8077-6603-3 (paper)
ISBN 978-0-8077-6604-0 (hardcover)
ISBN 978-0-8077-7991-0 (ebook)

Printed on acid-free paper
Manufactured in the United States of America

This book is dedicated to those who know fact from fiction, know to use data responsibly, and believe in the value of scientific evidence.

I, Ellen, dedicate this book to my husband, Eli, who fact-checks me on a daily basis and understands the foundations and ethics of decision-making. And to Houdi, my devoted feline research assistant, who sat on my notes and by my keyboard and exercise bike while I was writing this book. They both were my muses for the book.

I, Edith, dedicate this book for the preparation of future educators everywhere. You are the next generation of teachers and administrators who deserve our support for taking on this most challenging of professions. And to my current teachers—my grandchildren Kayla, Jackson, and Wren—who teach me something every day.

Contents

Acknowledgments

When Brian Ellerbeck from Teachers College Press approached us at the American Educational Research Association conference in New York in 2018 with an idea for a book proposal, we never envisioned how the landscape of education and the world, more generally, would change so drastically. Brian discussed the need for a book on data ethics in education. Brian, you were prophetic! As we conceptualized what such a volume might look like, we debated what data ethics mean in various educational venues. We thought about the pertinent regulations, such as FERPA, and broadened our notion of data ethics. With that grounding, we considered what components of the educational landscape impact and are impacted by data ethics, and we subsequently laid out a potential outline. Knowing what we wanted represented in the book, we considered the best possible experts who could write to those components. We think we have amassed a thoughtful group of authors who have contributed valuable insights into data ethics. We would like to thank all the authors for their contributions. For many, data ethics have been part of their work and required their thinking to be expanded and explicit, particularly in terms of posing recommendations for future practice.

We would be remiss if we did not mention the current landscape that has challenged the use of data, information, and evidence on a daily basis, even to the point of denial and the rejection of scientific processes. In some way, writing the volume in the midst of the COVID-19 pandemic, where people have been bombarded with data and interpretations that challenged even the most sophisticated consumers of information, has more deeply established the need for using data responsibly and ethically. The situation has made the volume all the more timely and critical. We have made every attempt to be balanced in our statements and examples, but admittedly, there were some challenges in that process. It is not our intention to make any political statement or offend, only to use examples of events that illustrate ethical data use.

For Ellen, her work with the Future of Privacy Forum on the data privacy/data ethics scenarios has been a fabulous learning experience, particularly working with Juliana Cotto, Emilia Rastrick, Jo Jimerson, Jeff Wayman, Amelia Vance, and Jim Siegl. Ellen also appreciated the input from

Amanda Datnow, Cheryl Forbes, Jori Beck, Mark Girod, Alicia Wenzel, and Jo Jimerson, who helped us think about how data ethics might be integrated into educator preparation programs. Jori Beck, Andrea Lash, and Eli Gruber also helped Ellen think through some of issues of data use in diverse fields, particularly around codes of ethics. For the chapter on professional development, a thank you to Kathy Boudett for her willingness to share information about Data Wise. And thank you to Alicia Wenzel for planting the idea about data ethics badging. Ellen would like to acknowledge Susan Mundry and Saroja Warner of WestEd who have pushed her thinking about data literacy as the construct has transitioned to culturally responsive data literacy to move the messaging to an asset model and a whole child perspective. Ellen would like to acknowledge all the colleagues and educators who have impacted her thinking about data use more generally and helped her to think about what it means to use data effectively and responsibly, especially Jan Anderson, for her collegiality, friendship, and humor. Finally, Ellen would like to acknowledge Kathy Fishman for her friendship, her support, and being a kindred spirit about so many things, as well as Holly Barone and Catherine Dunik for their like-mindedness about their love of our fur-babies.

For Edith, her work as the executive director of data strategy at the Mary Lou Fulton College at Arizona State University gave her the opportunity to engage with faculty in multiple education preparation programs across the college as they engaged in the effort of program redesign. Ensuring that the educator preparation programs have the knowledge, skills, and dispositions to include ethical data literacy across the curriculum is a daunting task, and she has appreciated the time working with multiple clinical and tenure-track faculty as they have sought to do so under the guidance of Nicole Thompson. The opportunity to learn about Principled Innovation with its foci on multiple ethical and character traits supported by Cristy Guleserian has been instructive on so many levels.

We want to acknowledge all the educators who are consumed by a plethora of data, data technologies, and data regulations that impact their practice at every turn, from moment-to-moment data collection to more long-term data, from data for continuous improvement to accountability and compliance data. Educators are literally drowning in data. And with the development of more diverse data, more sophisticated technologies and apps, and the complexities of student contexts, there are increasing risks to inadvertent and innocent misuses of data. The objective of this volume is to bring awareness to the educational community, alert where needed, raise questions and challenges, and provide potential future steps to mitigate problems.

We want to thank Danny Torres for navigating the contractual process. And we want to thank Brian Ellerbeck for identifying the need and letting us run with our ideas.

The Ethical Use
of Data in Education

Data Ethics

An Introduction

Ellen B. Mandinach and Edith S. Gummer[1]

DEFINING THE LANDSCAPE

We begin the exploration of data ethics by grounding the examination from a perspective of what data are and are not, posited by Spiegelhalter (2019): "Numbers do not speak for themselves; the context, language, and graphic design all contribute to the way the communication is received" (p. 69). Data are based on an evidentiary process, given meaning by context to transform them into information and then into useable knowledge (Mandinach et al., 2008). To make sound decisions, educators need data that are valid, reliable, and of sufficient quality. Thus, the study of data and data ethics is complex.

This book provides a landscape of educational data ethics. We use a broad definition of *data ethics*. Data ethics are more than the protection of student privacy and confidentiality as outlined in the Family Educational Rights and Privacy Act (FERPA), which governs the use and protection of student data, as well as associated regulations such as the Children's Online Privacy Protection Act (COPPA), the Children's Internet Protection Act (CIPA), the Protection of Pupil Rights Amendment (PPRA), and the Health Insurance Portability and Accountability Act (HIPAA). The *Forum Guide to Strategies for Education Data Collection and Reporting* (National Forum on Education Statistics [NFES], 2021, p. 6) notes the following: "While laws set the legal parameters that govern data use, ethics establish fundamental principles of right and wrong that are critical to the appropriate management and use of education data." Privacy is essential but so are fairness and the understanding of the consequences of data use (Casola, 2020). For advanced data use, data ethics are "the intersection of moral, methodological, and practical concerns" and their balance in data use (Hoffmann as cited in Casola, 2020, p. 71). For governmental workers, the General Services Administration (2020) defines data ethics as "the norms of behavior that promote appropriate judgments and accountability when collecting, managing, or using data, with the goals of protecting civil liberties, mini-mizing risks to individuals and society, and maximizing the public good" (p. 5). We further define data ethics in education to be synonymous with responsible data use grounded in a set of skills and knowledge known as data literacy. The chapters contained in the book focus on various interact-ing components that impact responsible data use. We first turn to relevant research, theory, and professional organizations' codes of ethics to inform our view of data ethics. We then provide an examination of data ethics in other disciplines to extract illustrative parallels. We conclude with a section on skepticism and denial, followed by an overview of the book.

We recognize the complexities of educational decision-making, particu-larly throughout the COVID-19 crisis. There are and were no easy decisions or definitive answers to issues raised in the pandemic, which significantly impacted education and decisions about the safest and best mechanisms for instruction. It has been an evolving landscape of data, with best guesses based on the best available data.

Where appropriate, we touch on the data ethics that surround the tran-sition to virtual and hybrid learning environments made necessary by the pandemic. Educators have been working in unchartered territory, and there is much unknown about how to provide safe, efficient, and effective instruc-tion online while also protecting the privacy of data. Good data are essential to inform the decisions that were made during the pandemic and the conse-quences for children's lives and educational opportunities that follow.

Informed by Research, Theory, and Professional Organizations

When we were asked to write this book, we never imagined that we would be living in a time where data and evidence are so conflicted. When Lee Cronbach (1988) noted that validity rests in the interpretations made from the data, not just the property of a test, he could not have foreseen the cur-rent state of the use of data and evidence. Nor could Sam Messick (1989), who spoke of consequential validity and the intended and unintended social consequences resulting from the interpretation and use of results. Messick cautioned about using measurement and the resulting data for alternative purposes for which they were not originally intended. Aspects of validity are based on collecting evidence that can be verified, and interpretations are not "alternative facts." Interpretations are drawn from evidence and can be contested based on context and points of view. We live in times when data and evidence are assailed, and, at the same time, the education community is advocating strongly for the use of research evidence to inform policy and practice decisions (Farley-Ripple et al., 2020). It is a time when the ethics of data use are increasingly important.

We look to Kahneman and Tversky (1983, 1984; Tversky & Kahneman, 1971, 1974, 1983) whose groundbreaking work on decision-making is relevant. Decision-making is not just about statistical or instrumental validity as noted earlier (Cronbach, 1989; Messick, 1988); it is about the underlying assumptions made to support the decision-making process. Kahneman and Tversky's work on fallacies, illusions, biases, and unfounded assumptions relate to how ethics, beliefs, and preferences impact judgment and decisions. Their work discusses decisions made based on beliefs that are not supported by data but are founded on misconceptions of the laws of chance and heuristics that can cause systematic errors leading to biases of intuition and errors of judgment and choice (Kahneman, 2011). As Tversky and Gilovich (1989) state, people "tend to 'detect' patterns even where none exist" (p. 21).

Kahneman and Tversky's work is salient as it pertains to decision-making based on beliefs and intuition rather than sound and valid evidence. Kahneman (2011) distinguishes between two forms of thinking, one slow and one fast, and how those forms relate to decision-making based on differing types of evidence and cognitive processes. Slow thinking is "deliberate and effortful" (p. 13), whereas fast thinking is automatic and uses intuition, heuristics, impressions, beliefs, and memory. Kahneman also notes the importance of expertise and experience, referencing Simon's (1992) work on experts in which Simon examines the intuition of experts, demonstrating their ability to immediately recognize patterns and base decisions on those patterns by accessing stored information and calling on knowledge and expertise. But experts can also make less consequential decisions through intuition using situational actions. Spillane and Miele (2007) note that experts can identify complex patterns that novices do not notice. Schildkamp and Poortman (2015) note that the use of data is more effective than intuition in educational decision-making. Vanlommel and colleagues (2021) find that educators may privilege some data while disregarding other types. They articulate the complexity by which educators ignore or integrate different types of data to inform decisions. These approaches to examining phenomena and making decisions help us to understand our examination of data ethics.

Decision-making experts are susceptible to the fallacies mentioned by Kahneman and Tversky as well as other sources of bias. Drawing from the cognitive sciences, Dror (2020) notes that bias can enter into decisions by having either too much contextual information or not enough, as well as from having expectations based on the information. Bias also can emerge from the types of data being used, the analytic methodology employed, and the interpretations and conclusions drawn from the data.

Many forms of bias are relevant to educational data use, also known as data fallacies. For example, cherry-picking is one such source of bias where results may be excluded that do not conform to the desired outcome. Another fallacy is to make conclusions or interpretations based on incomplete data, basically data that have "survived" decision-making rules. There is a bias known as the McNamara fallacy, which comes from military data uses. Bias here occurs when a data user focuses only on certain metrics that provide a limited view of a complex situation. In education, this is seen in decisions based solely on annual summative test scores due to the overreliance on summary metrics. Decisions based solely on total test scores may introduce inaccurate interpretations and decisions (Geckoboard, n.d.).

Prominent British statistician David Spiegelhalter (2019) states the following:

> Statistics can bring clarity and insight into the problems we face, but we are all familiar with the way they can be abused, often to promote an opinion or simply to attract attention. The ability to assess the trustworthiness of statistical claims seems a key skill in the modern world. (p. 17)

He comments further on the need for data ethics to avoid conflict of interest, overenthusiasm, distortion, and inaccurately framing arguments by ensuring that data are examined by balancing the technical with the societal context.

The American Statistical Association (ASA, 2018) addresses data ethics in its guidelines found in *Ethical Guidelines for Statistical Practice*, which are intended to facilitate ethical decision-making. According to ASA:

> Because society depends on informed judgments supported by statistical methods, all practitioners of statistics—regardless of training and occupation or job title—have an obligation to work in a professional, competent, respectful, and ethical manner. Good statistical practice is fundamentally based on transparent assumptions, reproducible results, and valid interpretations. In some situations, guideline principles may conflict, requiring individuals to prioritize principles according to context. However, in all cases, stakeholders have an obligation to act in good faith, to act in a manner that is consistent with these guidelines, and to encourage others to do the same. Above all, professionalism in statistical practice presumes the goal of advancing knowledge while avoiding harm; using statistics in pursuit of unethical ends is inherently unethical. (p. 1)

The guidelines outline eight topics of which the following six are particularly relevant:

- The use of appropriate and relevant data that can produce valid results without prejudice
- The disclosure about issues with the data and the analytics in terms of reliability and quality
- Making valid inferences through transparent analytics
- The consideration of possible explanations and the notion that it is plausible to draw differing explanations from the same data

- The need to use sound methods
- The obligation to maintain objectivity

The American Psychological Association (APA, 2020) and the American Educational Research Association (AERA, 2011) have codes of ethics that include the ethical use of data, mostly in terms of protecting privacy and confidentiality. AERA, APA, and National Council on Measurement in Education (2014) specify appropriate design and use of tests and test results that guide the field of education. But none of these resources address actual data ethics as explicitly as ASA. The National Education Association's (n.d.) code of ethics has little mention of data other than the disclosure of information. We raise these issues because they relate not only to the practice of education but to research as well.

Educational research is also controlled by Institutional Review Boards (IRBs), which ensure that data are protected and that research is conducted properly and ethically. Yet, there are still instances of irresponsible research, including poor management of data, data disclosures, falsification of data, manipulation of data sets, bad reporting, or no reporting at all. Some of these violations have been noted in the public media; others have been dealt with by professional organizations and funding agencies. However, most researchers conduct their work responsibly.

We highlight several key tenets to responsible research: (1) data and the ensuing reporting must be properly fact-checked; (2) the data and the instrumentation must be used for their intended purposes; (3) researchers must not rush to publication; (4) researchers must use appropriate statistical procedures and ensure that certain data points, such as outliers, are included in their analyses; and (5) researchers should not use representations that skew, distort, obfuscate, or mislead, nor should they selectively identify which results to report.

The General Services Administration (2020) outlines several tenets of data ethics for governmental employees that generalize to education: (1) adhere to applicable statutes and regulations, (2) act with integrity, (3) be accountable, (4) be transparent, (5) be informed by advances in technology and data science, (6) protect privacy and confidentiality, and (7) be respectful to the public. The report further outlines the benefits of data ethics, which include risk mitigation, transparency, consistency, enhanced public trust, consideration of potential impacts, and improved decision-making.

Cooper (2016), on behalf of the APA, addresses research ethics and presents guidelines for the proper collection, handling, analysis, and management of data. Cooper provides guidance on how to properly collect data, protect the confidentiality of data from the research subjects, and determine what to consider as proprietary data. Cooper addresses how to store and protect data, as would be addressed by the typical IRBs; the need to encrypt data; who has access to data; data retention; and data disposal. The book then provides salient examples about data falsification, data fabrication, modifying data, and fact or error checking. Cooper also addresses pitfalls of statistical analyses, noting that proper analytic techniques must be used. The quest for significant results must not be abused. Methods that should not be used include performing premature or incomplete analyses (e.g., the "eyeball" test), using data that are only moderately relevant, and including large numbers of subjects to ensure significance that overstates the effects. Lastly, Cooper addresses proper interpretations and reporting. The message from this volume is that the guidelines are generalizable to data use well beyond research.

DATA ETHICS IN OTHER DISCIPLINES

As we turn to an examination of other fields to see how they address data ethics, we need to consider some caveats. First, much has been written elsewhere about ethics in these disciplines, but perhaps not specifically about data ethics. Second, it is our intention to describe ethical issues that have arisen in the practice of these disciplines and link them explicitly to data ethics. Third, these examples may or may not be representative of the range of issues, but we hope they will provide illustrations of the ways data have been manipulated in other fields.

Our intention is for these examples to show that education is not unique in the ways data can be used for inappropriate means. We do not assert that our coverage is complete. Many of the examples have been drawn from topics that have been addressed in the news and have had broad public exposure, but have not had scholarly treatment. Other examples have been drawn from the unfortunate circumstances of the Coronavirus and how the data ethics around use of data and evidence have been questioned and brought into the public light. The purpose of drawing from these diverse disciplines is to illustrate the ways data ethics can play out across domains. Finally, we make no pretense to being data ethicists in these fields.

Business

Businesses are guided by data and data analytics about production, inventory, costing, distribution, and almost every aspect of the supply chain. Companies can inflate profit reports to influence investors (Friedman, 2020). Hotels may advertise a room rate that has multitudes of hidden costs, including several kinds of taxes and resort fees, even if guests are not using the services. People in loyalty programs end up paying for items twice, such as free Wi-Fi or newspapers to which the status entitles them, because of the resort fee. The same airline seat may have many different prices, depending on status, time of purchase, availability, and other criteria. Some airlines have hidden charges that mislead customers, whereas others are quite up front about their fares. After customers complete their transactions, they may incur additional charges such as for baggage or a seat. The ethics of these examples are based on calculations derived from data.

Manufacturers may take shortcuts and release products with insufficient testing, poor quality control, or known defects where actuarial calculations determine that there is less financial loss potential from lawsuits than correcting the problem. Such calculations are based on data and probabilities but are not ethical. The use of inappropriate and inadequate data in conjunction with the use of products for unintended purposes is more than problematic. Companies may prematurely release a product in the rush to market to gain an advantage without adequate supporting evidence. Companies sometimes use inaccurate data and inadequate information on product FAQs with the intention of misleading customers.

No company seeks to have its data systems hacked, but Marriott, Target, and Neiman Marcus are among the major companies that had personal information inadvertently released. These are the businesses that rely on underlying algorithms to track purchase histories for their own marketing strategies or release those data to other companies. Additionally, there are incidences such as the profiling used by Cambridge Analytica, which was about the misappropriation of digital information (Herman, 2018; Lapowsky, 2019). Applications on smart devices, such as health apps, regularly take personally identifiable information. These ethical issues pertain to data security, data use, and data interpretation, but they are mostly about some companies either misleading consumers or having a sole focus on corporate profits by taking shortcuts and providing misinformation to the public for financial gain.

Sports

A recent trend in athletics is to use sophisticated data for performance analytics. The analytics of baseball, as seen in *Moneyball* (Lewis, 2004), prompted a new reliance on data. For example, the media reported on the signal-stealing scandal that rocked baseball in 2017 (Vigdor, 2020). Catchers sending signals to pitchers is a major form of data that has existed for a long time and is based on predetermined and data-driven strategies from performance trends. Signal and play stealing also occur in football, which is not illegal (Forde, 2020). Although signal stealing is technically legal, it is unethical. What is illegal is using videotaping to capture the signals. Armed with sophisticated data analytics, the level of detection and use of this information has significantly escalated, stimulating more sophisticated means of stealing the signals through technologies and human creativity.

Illegal coaching has come into the news, particularly in the wake of a highly publicized incident at the 2018 U.S. Open. Communicating information about what a player should be doing, from coach to player, is illegal. In fact, tennis has been slow to become data driven, thinking that coaches prefer to use observations and experience instead of data (Robson, 2015). Robson calls this a "data dinosaur" (p. 1). Observations are a source of data, but less systematic and analytic, as shown by Gilovich and colleagues (1985). Data analytics are important and have become a part of tennis for players who use the services of the analytic software companies. These companies use sophisticated analytics to examine data trends based on performance patterns, strokes, strengths and weakness, and other key indices. The ethical issue is that some players can afford the technologies and others cannot. They therefore have a distinct advantage, causing an inequity in a financially based digital divide based on the use of data and analytics.

Advanced analytics are used in other sports as well. Sophisticated analyses have been conducted on rugby matches, identifying key actions (Legg et al., 2012). These analyses produce visualizations of what is called "real-time" performance analyses. Because of the level of sophistication, we are mindful of Wang's (2021) caution that the data used in analytics can be fraught with error and potential bias based on the underlying algorithms. Such potential bias is echoed by Pasquale (2015), who calls for "transparency, equity, and fairness in automated decision-making" (Tene & Polonetsky, 2018, p. 134).

Other issues and misconceptions about data use in sports may or may not pertain to data ethics. Tversky and Gilovich (1989; Gilovich et al., 1985) provide evidence to dispel the notion of the "hot hand" phenomenon, using data to analyze the validity of giving the ball to the player who is on a hot streak. The belief is based on a cognitive illusion and is engrained in coaches, players, and fans. It impacts game strategy. Similar beliefs can be seen in tennis with what is called "the zone," when a player goes on a streak and simply cannot miss.

In college sports, coaches have had schools or recruits manipulate their grades for college admission. Common cheating scandals occur when athletes get tutored, and professors are pressured to alter grades simply because the students are athletes (Tracy, 2019). A big cheating scandal occurred when coaches accepted bribes from parents whose students did not even play their sport (Korn & Levitz, 2020).

Additionally, sports performance data have been manipulated to enhance salaries and recruitment, not to mention covering up or lying about drug use for performance enhancement and better statistics. Modifications are made to uniforms based on physics data for swimming, skiing, and other speed sports that are meant to enhance performance that sometimes skirt the rules. The technical improvements may or may not be unethical, but they do advantage and disadvantage some athletes. And, of course, there is betting that involves inside information from coaches and players, or even players tanking a tennis match, boxers taking a fall, or other athletes throwing games.

A final sport-related data ethics issue that also crosses into the area of law and jurisprudence is the legal action filed by the Women's National Soccer Team (WNT) against the U.S. Soccer Federation. The WNT claims that the players were denied equal compensation, including equal benefits, accommodations, medical treatment, and support. In a court decision in May of 2020, a federal judge dismissed the claim of inequality (Dias, 2020) based on flawed calculations. The WNT were at the height of excellence, having won the World Cup, receiving bonuses and endorsements. In contrast, the men's team was in an opposite situation. It had not attained any of the metrics for which players would have been compensated at a much higher rate than the WNT. The retrospective period also facilitated flawed calculations. The judge may have been within legal rights, but the decision certainly was unethical data-wise.

Medicine

Many parallels exist between education and medicine in terms of the data cycle: collect data, analyze the data, make a diagnosis, determine a course of action, evaluate the outcome, and potentially start anew. Clearly, modern medicine relies on data, both current and historical, to analyze and then aid in diagnosing and determining a course of treatment. Medical professionals must abide by strict codes of ethics that protect the privacy and confidentiality of patients, guided by HIPAA. In the *American Medical Association Code of Ethics* (2001), there is a section about working with patients to make informed decisions through communication and consent. Processes and protections are provided for disclosing and sharing information. Medical professionals also abide by the Hippocratic oath to do no harm. Hospitals have medical ethics committees to help professionals navigate challenging situations and medical dilemmas.

Medicine is a scientific and data-driven discipline that is also informed by experience. Simon (1992) notes how medical experts call on knowledge, experience, heuristics, and even intuition to make diagnoses and determine courses of action, and they know when to access additional information. Every time a patient is seen, the doctor collects and links data to the patient's history. But there can be problems. Because of insurance pressures, doctors' time is at a premium, and there can be a rush to move from patient to patient. In the quest to get to the point, some doctors can be quick to judgment, look for the obvious, overlook root causes, and simply make mistakes. Part of it may be how a patient describes the situation, a doctor's carelessness, or limited knowledge or lack of specialization on the part of the doctor. Doctors can be quick to treat in ways that the data do not support. For example, a doctor might fail to carefully examine an X-ray or test, make a snap judgment, and miss the root cause of a problem; that is, they may work from incomplete data or no data at all. Doctors may make global decisions rather than treating the individual with specific needs (e.g., "All patients like this treatment so you will too"). Patients are unique cases with unique data and histories that require individual approaches. The lesson here is about the need to combine expert knowledge with the triangulation of many relevant data sources, not just the obvious answer but uncovering root causes as well.

Other examples of doctors and data ethics are salient. Doctors may manipulate insurance claims to their advantage, they may double bill, or they may add procedures they did not perform. Doctors are implicated in the opioid epidemic by overprescribing drugs for which they receive kickbacks. They may untruthfully claim that they are an in-network doctor, and only later do unsuspecting patients get hit with huge bills. They may invite other doctors into procedures, not for consults, but so they too can bill (Rosenthal, 2014). Mandinach has been in multiple public places where she overheard doctors on a plane bragging about overbilling older patients through Medicare or on an Amtrak train where a doctor used a patient's name out loud when talking about his erectile dysfunction—both clearly ethical violations.

Messaging in medicine can be based on not only the underlying data but calculations around and perceptions of how the data will be interpreted. The interpretation of results can be affected by manipulating the messaging. Kahneman and Tversky (1984) discuss how the formulation effect impacts public health communication. They note that there are significant differences between talking about a mortality rate as opposed to a survival rate by saying "lives saved" or "lives lost." According to Kahneman and Tversky (1984), "Formulation effects can occur fortuitously, without anyone being aware of the impact of the frame on the ultimate decision. They can also be exploited deliberately to manipulate the relative attractiveness of options" (p. 346). The underlying data are the same, but the findings relate to levels of risk aversion and risk seeking.

Medical professionals participate in research where data ethics come into play. Perhaps the most notorious medical experiments were those conducted by Dr. Mengele in the Nazi concentration camps and the Tuskegee Study of Untreated Syphilis in the Negro Male (Paul & Brookes, 2015). These are extreme examples, but, more recently, there are salient examples such as doctors who may use nonrepresentative samples from which to draw conclusions about groups beyond those tested.

Finally, there are the issues surrounding the Coronavirus. Luckily, much of the medical profession has held a tight line about not rushing to promote potential treatments that have not been adequately vetted through the scientific process or using treatments intended for other diseases in the hopes they have positive effects. The consequences of using evidence and data responsibly are tantamount to malpractice. Without such ethical practices, people can unnecessarily suffer and even die.

News, Media, and Advertising

We live in a time when the media are being attacked for "fake news." Not that long ago, venerable news anchors were considered to be the sources of truth. Now it is the opposite, with questionable practices occurring, such as delivering stories without sufficient due diligence for evidence, using inaccurate or uninformative graphics and visualizations, framing stories in overly positive or negative ways to skew interpretations, exaggerating and manipulating results, and failing to provide interpretive notes about certainties or alternative views (Spiegelhalter, 2019).

When asked about the ethics of news reporting, Cooper (2021) commented about the importance of fact-checking by the news media and how there must be several layers of quality assurances. Even with quality processes in place, errors still can occur, usually followed by apologies. Yet, some people support selective presentations and the suppression of truth through skewed evidence, unbalanced presentations, withholding information, and misrepresentation of fact—all to promote their own perspective. Reporters may run with stories without proper fact-checking, all in a race to be the first to release a news item. Some news outlets make no pretense about the lack of fact-checking; they are proud to present their own versions of reality. A Dilbert cartoon provides a parody on fact-checking (Adams, 2020a), in which Dilbert says, "I need a quick decision on this, but I don't have time to compile the relevant facts." The Boss replies, "Without facts, I would be guessing." Another Dilbert cartoon is equally relevant (Adams, 2020b): The Boss says on a virtual call, "Is this data accurate?" Dilbert argues, "You don't go to war with data you need. You go to war with the data you have." The Boss replies, "Did you just make it sound noble to use bad data?" Dilbert responds, "And heroic." The point is perfectly made in both strips. Further, graphical displays in visual and print media can distort findings. They may be geared to the general public for easy take-away messages, but they just as easily can distort the validity of the data by how they are displayed.

In the wake of the pandemic, Bursztyn and colleagues (2020) examined the impact of how news reporting affected beliefs and behavior around the Coronavirus. Their analyses yield clear evidence of how various television news shows reported the virus and how the seriousness with which they treated the topic influenced viewers' behavior, such as social distancing and abiding by the stay-at-home orders. The report notes that the findings are not unique to the pandemic but that news reporting impacts the belief and preparation for natural disasters and weather-related events such as hurricanes as well as voting and social justice behavior. Thus, reporting with credible information is impactful.

Data ethics are relevant to other media too. Advertising can be similarly misleading. Deceptive advertising can mask details in the fine print. Through such advertising, stores may use bait-and-switch tactics to attract potential buyers. Pharmaceutical ads may put ideas in patients' minds that they want a certain drug and then pressure their doctor to prescribe, without having sufficient knowledge regarding whether the drug is right for them.

Encyclopedias were once considered a veritable source of information. One would consult the *Britannica* or the *World Book*. Their writers and editors would meticulously fact-check. Now people consult the Internet, Wikipedia, and other sources that may not be properly vetted for accuracy.

Our point is that there are many ways that data can be used to an advantage, be skewed, and be distorted. It is incumbent on the general public to be good consumers of information, understanding what is true and what is a distortion. Biased news sources and advertising rely on peoples' inability or unwillingness to discern fact from fiction or not question the "news." The term "alternative facts" becomes particularly relevant, given the public's lack of ability to make the distinctions. People may exhibit confirmation bias and hear what they want to hear or believe what they want to believe. When an authority figure says something once, then repeats it multiple times, people may tend to believe that it is true.

Politics and Government

The ethics of data use in government has been a concern for decades, yet more recently it has been especially called into question. Nancy Pelosi (2020) was accurate when she said "the plural of anecdote is not data." The voting rights issues are an example. Politicians on both sides may use data to their advantage, trying to outgame the other side by manipulating numbers, gerrymandering, ousting eligible voters, redistricting, and even throwing away valid ballots. A reprehensible action is instilling fear in the validity of the entire voting process, which is in essence the most important data collection activity in a democracy.

Other common forms of ethical violations based on data and polling include the failure to recuse oneself when there are clear conflicts of interest, blind loyalty and approval of unethical behavior despite contradictory evidence, skewing and misrepresenting polls and ratings for political gain, and blatantly rejecting scientific facts and evidence for political expedience. One example is the data scandal from Cambridge Analytica (Herman, 2018). The overarching theme is the rejection and minimization of the need for evidence and science.

Without question, the most recent distressing and public misuse of data is the promotion of disinformation and untested cures for the Coronavirus pandemic. Evanega and colleagues (2020) examined misinformation in what they called the "infodemic." The study found that the biggest source of misinformation by far was former President Trump who accounted for 37.9%. The study also found substantial identifiable misinformation threads and conspiracies (46.6%). There were statements about possible cures, all without a scientific and evidential basis. Examples include the use of a drug for other purposes being held up as a promising cure, premature and inadequate testing of a drug, and the use of UV light and disinfectant treatments. These promotions of untested treatments were posed without evidence or validity, and killed people seeking help under dire circumstances (Nierenberg, 2020). There is evidence that the number of people who were tested was manipulated in order to change the percentages of those infected and suppress the numbers of those who were infected and died in an attempt to lessen the impact (Alwine & Goodrum Sterling, 2020). Hundreds of press conferences provided skewed interpretations of data, recommendations for untested "cures," and disregard for best practices such as social distancing and wearing masks. Businesses were opened, closed, and reopened despite violations of recommended safe practices ignoring relevant data. This is an example of agendas determining which data to pay attention to and which to ignore, pitting economics against public health. Schools and universities have been caught in the crossfire, with administrators trying to adopt safe practices for their students and educators based on available data and recommendations.

Statements were made by both sides of the issues, and the segments of the media then promoted misinformation. Relying on assumptions, beliefs, and misinformation is not science nor the ethical use of data and evidence. Further, the failure to admit to errors simply serves to compound problematic actions. When recommendations and guidelines, based on scientific evidence, are proffered by experts, it is ethically challenging when politicians reject those recommendations based on the politics of the situation. In this distortion, one side indicates that including nontested cases inflates the numbers artificially, whereas the other side denies this accusation. Either way, manipulating the data for political purposes is an ethical issue. When lives depend on having reliable and valid evidence, using data in such a manner is not only unethical but also reprehensible.

The Legal System

If we rely on television portrayals of lawyers, one would come away with horrible impressions of how they play games, manipulate the truth, and violate the ethics of the profession to win cases. Perhaps the practices that are depicted in the media do not cross legal boundaries, but they may stretch the ethics. The American Bar Association has a strict code of ethics that governs practice, and law schools have rigorous courses on what is evidence and guidelines for the use of evidence. The legal professional must strictly adhere to protecting the privacy and confidentiality of their clients. However, some lawyers do take advantage of loopholes and deal with evidence in less than ethical ways that are not illegal but are problematic.

Lawyers can hide crucial evidence by burying it in scads of irrelevant evidence. They can withhold data and skew evidence. They can cherry-pick data and frame evidence in biased ways. They may provide irrelevant information or distort evidence and the truth to throw the jury and opposing lawyers off track. They may fail to use reliable and trustworthy evidence. The selection of jurors has become a scientific discipline in which lawyers and trial scientists gain explicit and implicit insights into the thinking of potential jurors and try to load the jury with those favorable to their client. They may play on the emotions of the jury by manipulating facts as they pose their legal arguments, all in an effort to influence interpretations and the decision-making process.

We are all aware of high-profile legal cases featuring withheld evidence, lies, and ethical breaches. The ethics also extend to juries, not just legal professionals. We see the guilty being released or pardoned and innocent people being convicted because juries cannot differentiate fact from fiction and do not know how to properly vet data. We also see law enforcement officers making false arrests and traffic stops based on stereotypic profiling, whether by the type of car or the color of skin. All of these are examples of how the use of evidence can be easily skewed within the boundaries of ethics and of legal professions.

SKEPTICISM ABOUT DATA AND EVIDENCE USE

We live in a time where data and evidence are questioned, eschewed, and rejected, and where expertise is questioned. Another Dilbert cartoon (Adams, 2020c) is apropos here. The Boss says, "I can't approve your plan until I know what the experts say." Dilbert replies, "I can save us some time by talking to the people who bribe the experts. I'll get the same answer faster." The Boss responds, "Ouch! The truth hurts!" Finally, Dilbert soothes him with, "Take a deep breath. It will pass."

In this section, we explore why data have come under scrutiny, and why there is skepticism and even denial. We address this topic here because it is relevant to current educational practice, and examples are used from education and beyond education so that educational decision-making can be better understood.

Admittedly, data-driven decision-making is difficult, even when people are data literate. Decisions are not clear cut, and they have consequences and, therefore, consequential validity. One can question if there are "right" interpretations. Experts in psychology and relevant fields have taught us a great deal about the cognitive processes that underlie decision-making, the heuristics and different approaches, and the kinds of conscious and unconscious errors that people make (Kahneman, 2011; Kahneman & Tversky, 1983, 1984; Simon, 1992; Tversky & Kahneman, 1971, 1974, 1983). Yet, decisions, even those grounded in scientific evidence, are not made in a bubble, and therein lies the conundrum.

Denial, the use of truth, and evidence have become topics of great interest in the media, in the scientific community, and in education. A special issue of *Educational Psychologist*, for example, examines "post-truth" in education and addresses the "infodemic" (Brazilia & Chinn, 2020, p. 107). The authors define *post-truth* as "the range of current threats to people's abilities to know what is true or most accurate in media- and information-rich societies" (p. 107). This is an essential concept that includes the ethical use of data, information, and evidence. It addresses the emerging trends to challenge and discredit credible evidence, while prompting inaccuracies, rumors, and falsehoods. It further addresses the use of misinformation, disinformation, and "malinformation."

We describe some hot-button topics that directly and indirectly impact education where evidence is being questioned and even denied. We provide an overview of the issues surrounding the skepticism and criticisms of data use. We address denial and then explore some of the strategies and cognitive components that come into play with the skepticism. We cover the role of technology, media, and social media and how they contribute to the skepticism issue. Finally, we address how politics and policies affect decision-making and can promote skepticism. These discussions are illustrated with topics where there is rejection of data, evidence, and science. The topics are included in curricula, and their coverage is impactful in education.

Topical Examples

Holocaust denial has occurred since Hitler's initial actions, and denials persist even today. With few survivors left to provide testimony, the denial may become more vocal. Lipstadt (2006), a historian specializing in the Holocaust, chronicled her trial in England where a British historian brought a libel lawsuit against her. He accused Lispstadt and her publisher of libeling him as a Holocaust denier. The burden of proof was on Lipstadt because the legal process occurred in Great Britain where she had to prove that the Holocaust existed. Part of the issue here was where the burden of proof laid, the onus for proving or disproving a phenomenon or activity, as well as what constitutes proof. Lipstadt prevailed with incontrovertible proof, but obtaining what constituted acceptable proof was not trivial. Despite the verdict, deniers continue their quest.

A principal in Florida was accused of denying the Holocaust and was fired in 2019 (Diaz, 2020) but reinstated after a judge ruled in his favor. He had communicated to a parent through email the lack of evidence for the Holocaust. His comment, "I can't say the Holocaust is a factual, historical event." He further said, "I do allow information about the Holocaust to be presented and allow students and parents to make decisions about it accordingly. . . . I do the same with information about slavery." Issues like this call into question the role of educators in perpetuating the denial of historical events where their personal beliefs differ significantly from and deny the veracity of evidence. Although the district board members were disgusted by the principal's position, he was reinstated to a different position with the judicial decision saying he should never have been fired.

Another issue, climate change, has become a major controversy in which scientific evidence is discarded. The controversy began with businesses that had financial gain at risk, and it quickly morphed into a political issue. There is significant scientific evidence in peer-reviewed journals affirming the effects of climate change, yet deniers and skeptics abound. Research has found that 20% of Americans believe that climate change is a hoax (Lewandowsky et al., 2013). Media attention has provided a false equivalence based on coverage and giving credence to deniers. Activists reject the evidence as distorted and dispute its accuracy (Theel et al., 2013). The basis of the denial is unclear and may be based on beliefs or divergent pseudoscience. It may also be based on identity protection and the high level of environmental risk acceptance in certain demographics (McCright & Dunlap, 2011). Denial may be promoted by business interests that run counter to the evidence. Denial is fueled by certain media outlets as well as energy-related businesses, politics, and policies. Take, for example, the United States' 2017 withdrawal from the Paris Climate Agreement during the Trump administration that rejected science in favor of the administration's economic policies and goals.

Evolution has been hotly debated and has emerged as a contentious topic in education by those who believe that creationism, creation "science," or Intelligent Design have a rightful place in curricula. Creationism casts aside the theoretical science from scientists starting with Charles Darwin that developed into multiple lines of evidence for evolution in favor of taking a Biblical approach to how the biological world came to be. The controversy stems from critics who say that creationism is not science, it is faith-based and untestable, while extremists deny the science of evolution. Because of the religious foundation, critics of creationism believe it has no place in education and that it should not replace the teaching of evolution. Yet the controversy continues with fundamentalists pushing their agenda to include the topic in education and curricula. Some districts have taken extreme measures by redacting biology textbooks to eliminate sections on evolution. Such steps reject accepted science in favor of preferences by religious or political factions on school boards or in communities.

The anti-vaxxer movement has become a contentious issue in public health and in education. Even before the COVID pandemic, the movement denied scientific evidence about the importance of vaccinating children from childhood disease as a preventive measure to promote broader safety. The issue becomes a public health nightmare when segments of the population refuse to get their children vaccinated. It is especially problematic in schools where disease can spread among the students. The anti-vaxxer position is that there is no scientific evidence for the positive effects of vaccination, and, in fact, they hold to alternative science that says that vaccinations cause autism and other disease. Their denial of evidence is grounded in religious beliefs, individual rights, government intrusion, as well as unfounded reports of data.

Other medical issues also have been fair game for deniers. Tobacco and smoking have a long history of medical evidence about their deleterious effects. Because of the strong tobacco lobby, scientific evidence often has been questioned. Much of the resistance comes from businesses who stand to gain monetarily. Recently, vaping has emerged as an alternative to more traditional smoking, yet deleterious evidence has emerged, with companies such as Juul launching public campaigns to counter the evidence. These companies have been masterful at manipulating their messaging by ignoring the increasing data about the negative effects of vaping (Blum, 2020) and targeting advertising to young people.

The most consequential public health issue in generations is the Coronavirus. As the reality of the virus came to global awareness, the medical and scientific communities firmly advocated for concrete and valid evidence of cause, testing, and cure. Until proven vaccines became available, individuals were told to wear masks and maintain social distancing. Masks, however, became a political statement more than a personal safety device. Moreover, there was denial that the virus existed as a real public health issue. There was an effort to diminish its potency, saying that it was no worse that the flu. There was suppression and manipulation of the number of cases as an attempt to diminish the broadness of the pandemic through the way the data were presented. Many insisted it was a hoax perpetuated by segments of the population, foreign entities, and conspiracy fanatics. The hoax theory was perpetuated by politicians and the extreme conservative media. Research shows that belief in the virus is related to how the media reported about it (Bursztyn et al., 2020) and could be traced to specific news shows and commentators. Education was caught in the controversy, becoming a hockey puck in decisions about how best to safely reopen schools and universities.

Overview and Denial

Skepticism taken to the extreme can become denial. We live in a time where subsets of the population deny science, evidence, and data in favor of politics, emotions, and personal beliefs. McIntyre (2019) defines denialism as "the refusal to believe in well-warranted scientific theories even when the evidence is overwhelming. The most common reason for this is when a scientific theory conflicts with someone's ideological beliefs" (p. 150). People deny due to insecurity, threat, and lack of knowledge—an era called a time of anti-enlightenment. Deniers try to intentionally subvert the credibility of science. This goes beyond confirmation bias, which has some level of rationality to it, to blatant disregard for information. The denial is about ignorance or a lack of scientific literacy, information literacy, or the ability to use critical thinking skills, particularly in terms of vetting the veracity of information. It is the abandonment of truth and evidentiary rules and about drawing distinctions between falsehoods and lies (McIntyre, 2018). Lies are intentional, purposeful, and deliberate, whereas falsehoods may not be, though falsehoods are inconsistent with evidence. They promote doubt and uncertainty. McIntyre (2018) states, if the "intent is to manipulate someone into believing something *that we know to be untrue*, we have graduated from the mere 'interpretation' of facts into their falsification" (p. 8).

There is a well-known mantra in education to facilitate the understanding of why data are important—without data, you are only an opinion. Unsupported opinions are beliefs. Data are empirical evidence, which can be verified. We need to ensure that decision-makers are armed with data. Decisions must be made with data and empirical evidence that have been properly vetted. To be clear, *evidence* is defined as, "facts, data, or other information supporting a belief, argument, or view" (Kavanaugh & Rich, 2018, p. 8). Decisions must be carefully considered based on valid analytics. This is opposite to decisions based on selective and personally chosen beliefs and preconceived notions.

Misinformation is unintentional whereas disinformation is an intentional distortion of empirical evidence. As Lewandowsky and colleagues (2017) note, misinformation "can no longer be considered solely an isolated failure of individual cognition that can be corrected with appropriate communication tools. Rather, it should also consider the influence of alternative epistemologies that defy conventional standards of evidence" (p. 353). Sinatra and Lombardi (2020) add "malinformation" as a distinction. Malinformation is actual information that is used to cause harm. Such is the basis for denial and skepticism.

We differentiate denial from skepticism. *Denial* is clinging to beliefs despite acknowledgement of incontrovertible evidence and is more extreme than skepticism. Skepticism is more about doubting. Skeptics believe there is too much reliance on data that may dehumanize any situation. Skepticism can be helpful, but it can also be unproductive if taken to the extreme. Both denial and skepticism can lead to what Krugman (2020, p. 26) calls "intellectual degradation." One school of thought says that this degradation could be mitigated by better educating the public, starting with the education system, which can promote critical thinking skills that enable individuals to think deeply about a topic, discern fact from fiction, understand how to appropriately question things that do not make sense, and exhibit data and information literacy (Brazilia & Chinn, 2020). Education can increase awareness about misinformation and how to address arguments that distort facts, but even education cannot counter the irrational denial of facts.

The phrase "Truth Decay" is helpful in understanding denial. Kavanaugh and Rich (2018) study the demise of truth and pose four trends in the erosion of facts. First, they note disagreement about what is considered factual and how facts are interpreted. The authors distinguish that facts can be verified whereas interpretations can vary despite having used sound analytics. Skepticism can arise from interpretations, especially when findings are not modified and updated based on new results. Second, they note the failure to distinguish between fact and opinion, called "blurring" (p. 2). Third, people may believe opinion over fact. We have discussed the disregard for fact, instead using opinions and belief as confirmation bias. Fourth, Kavanaugh and Rich note the decrease in trust of previously trusted sources of factual information.

We may never fully understand why people reject science. Kavanaugh and Rich (2018) pose a possible and broad-reaching explanation:

> Decline in trust in key institutions that provide information might be partially driven by increasing skepticism about and distrust of data and analysis, but it might also be caused by unintentional errors, deception, and malfeasance by many of these institutions themselves. Specifically, at least a portion of the recent decline in trust for institutions, such as government, media, big business, and academic research, might be driven by recent instances of intentional manipulation of information and data by researchers purporting to be unbiased, errors made by government and specific research organizations, political leaders who do not deliver on promises, and deception practiced by large corporations and banks. A lack of transparency might also be to blame. (p. 36)

The rejection of science may be grounded in the desire for something to be false, a drive to denial; an effort to make something fit one's worldview, frame of reference, belief structure, or social circumstances; or about not knowing when to use evidence as opposed to intuition. Decision-making must be based on appropriate practices, grounded in valid, sound, and quality data. Decision-making should avoid the use of emotions and partisanship, and it must consider situational context.

We briefly mention criticisms of educational decision-making that fuel skeptics who criticize data use, research, and theory. There are those who criticize data use because the research literature has not supported positive student achievement outcomes (Hill, 2020). The studies that Hill surveyed had mixed results, and some had flawed methodologies. Their insistence on using student achievement as the sole outcome measure is challenging at best. It speaks to the need to move beyond the "does it work?" question. There is a need to expand what is meant by data (Mandinach & Schildkamp, 2021). International studies have found positive effects of data use in educational improvement (e.g., Lai et al., 2020; van Geel et al.,

2016). The logic model is too simplistic (Gummer, 2021)—train teachers to use data that impacts classroom practice and therefore improves student performance. We need more nuanced models and questions that consider the many confounding variables that may interfere with measurement and interventions. Mandinach and Schildkamp (2021) outline criticisms of the field and provide an evidentiary base for why data-driven decision-making continues to be essential to educational practice, and why it should not be summarily rejected because experiments fail to show effects solely on student achievement.

We pose some thought-provoking questions for consideration. The objective of science is accepted knowledge through the acquisition of rigorous empiricism. How do we reconcile that science can never prove something with total uncertainty? What is evidence? What is sufficient evidence? How do we reconcile when data are not accurate, yet they are used to "prove" something? What about the generalizability of findings? These questions address the distinction between internal and external validity, as well as the uniqueness of circumstances. We cannot just ask, "Does it work?" Can a phenomenon ever be fully proved in contrast to how disproval can occur? Where is the burden of proof? We must more importantly explain whether something works, under what circumstances, for whom, and through what mechanisms. These answers go to the issue of proving versus disproving.

Strategies and Cognition

As we have noted, there are skills, knowledge, and dispositions that underlie responsible data use, and cognitive processes and strategies are engaged as well. We have discussed psychology research that explores cognitive misconceptions and fallacies in thinking and decision-making, that is, cognitive bias. Spillane and Miele (2007) note that decision-making is a process of sensemaking that includes attention and interpretation as well as schemas and mental models. They further differentiate the need to assimilate and accommodate existing information.

In addition to the cognitive components, there are motivational, situational, and knowledge factors to consider. We draw a parallel to other forms of literacy such as media, information, and scientific literacy. Chang and colleagues (2020) developed a game to teach young children to use media literacy skills so that they can identify misinformation and be effective consumers of information. We pose a question: If young children can successfully query the veracity of information, then what are the impediments for adults? Is it unwillingness, purposeful rejection, or cognitive impairment? Gleick and colleagues (2010) note the following:

> All citizens should understand some basic scientific facts. There is always some uncertainty associated with scientific conclusions; science never absolutely

proves anything. . . . But when some conclusions have been thoroughly and deeply tested, questioned, and examined, they gain the status of "well-established theories" and are oft spoken of as "facts." (p. 689)

Some of the strategies are conscious or unconscious efforts to discount evidence. Some are explicit and intentional, whereas others less so, such as the distinction McIntyre (2018) makes about the differences between lies and falsehoods. People can be motivated to deny through willful ignorance or through self-aggrandizement. They may deny through the use of feelings and beliefs that make something "true." They may deny evidence because it does not confirm their beliefs, or they may fabricate data to match their beliefs. Research shows that people arrive at desired conclusions—those they want to believe (Kunde, 1990). There may be conspiracy theories that seek to debunk evidence. There may be peer pressure and a herd mentality to ensure that people agree with others, despite evidence.

Given our work on data literacy, we clearly see the role that knowledge plays in denial. People may not have knowledge of or the ability to properly scrutinize information; determine reliability, validity, and credibility; or evaluate the sources of the information. They may not be able to ask the right questions. They may not know how to check their beliefs against evidence. They may simply accept what they hear or read through willful ignorance or through an actual lack of knowledge.

Skepticism plays out two ways. There is healthy skepticism that is part of being a good consumer of information, using vetting processes, and trying to make sense of something that may not sound right. In contrast, other skeptics may opt for willful ignorance, choosing not to question but to blindly accept, confirming their beliefs; that is, they use confirmation bias. Accordingly, they may dismiss interpretations that do not confirm their beliefs. They may take cognitive shortcuts and use false heuristics that are not grounded in sound cognition. They may cherry-pick or selectively choose what evidence to use and what to reject, what to believe or not believe. They may suppress certain data to gain an advantage. They may simply be unwilling to put the effort into validating information—failing to vet information or fact-check, see error, or even admit error. The overwhelming amount of data may contribute to this unwillingness. Instead of properly examining the wealth of data, they choose what to believe and what not to believe. It may be inconvenient for them to seek out facts and evidence, or they may use inaccurate, incomplete, or outdated data. They may not take into consideration contextual factors. Put simply, people may lack knowledge; knowledge such as scientific information, data, and media literacy, and general problem-solving and critical thinking skills to enable them to understand data, information, and evidence for decision-making. They may not have the skills or knowledge to wade through and synthesize the morass of information with which they have been bombarded, prioritize it, and then evaluate the evidence. The lack of any of these skill sets may contribute to outright rejection of expertise, science, and the use of evidence. Any or all of these factors may provide justification for failure to reject disputable evidence, for the superficial treatment of evidence, for failures of sound reasoning and mental errors, and simply willful ignorance. Denial is intentional, deeply grounded in a belief of what is right. Our fear is that no amount of sound evidence, data, and reasoned argument can mitigate these factors.

The Role of the Media

As noted earlier, Bursztyn and colleagues (2020) find that inaccurate reporting of news has societal consequences. In examining the impact of reporting about the pandemic, they trace how reporters present information on indices such as wearing masks and social distancing. They also review studies on how the media impact other behaviors, such as preparedness for weather-related crises and natural disasters, perceived risks of health issues, and issues about hate crimes, mass killings, domestic violence, voting choice, and fertility choices. According to Bursztyn and colleagues (2020), when the media repeat falsehoods enough times, the public believes them.

The proliferation of technology has exacerbated the potential harm that the news media and social media have had on the dissemination of fake news, causing skepticism about what is real and what is fake. News today is superseded by something else tomorrow and easily forgotten, but the damage has been done. We live in a time of short news cycles and sound bites. Some reporting emphasizes sensationalism. Many people have their preferred news sources, mostly those that confirm their beliefs and perspectives. The issues are compounded by the huge amount of information that is available every moment of the day, much without any filters for veracity, especially with social media. It is not just the national print and visual media that are complicit here, but more so the Internet and social media, which blur news from opinions. Students often go to such sites as sources for projects, so it is important to understand the importance of determining the credibility of the information through a vetting process and the use of critical thinking skills. McIntyre (2018) aptly captures the essence of the issue:

> The rise of social media has of course facilitated this informational free for all. With fact and opinion now presented side by side on the Internet, who knows what to believe anymore? With no filters and no vetting, readers and viewers these days are readily exposed to a steady stream of pure partisanship. With the reputation of the mainstream media at its nadir, those with a stake in distributing propaganda no longer need worry about getting others

to tell *their* side of the story anymore. Now they have their own media outlets. (p. 87)

Internet sites can skew information, which is a major concern given that
the public, including schoolchildren and college students, get much of their
information on the Internet. They no longer seek information from encyclopedias or vetted sources. It is the go-to source for the general public. In
terms of social media, people are unrestricted regarding what they say and
post, and some people post absolute lies. Celebrities, politicians, and other
public figures have their followers who heavily weigh every word and post.
Social media sites are rife with falsehoods. Because of this, they may perpetuate skepticism. Facebook, for example, has been hacked to post fake news,
such as during the 2016 election. Facebook also knows what people post,
and advertising is sent to users based on their histories, which can either be
confirmatory or the reverse. We are surrounded with true and fake news
sources. The key to dispel cynicism and skepticism is to increase the popu-
lace's ability to distinguish real from fake information through healthy critique. People must be discerning consumers of information with the ability
to invoke problem solving, general literacy, and information literacy skills.

Politics

Politics and policies play a major role in skepticism about and acceptance
of evidence. No doubt the contentious political climate has contributed to
this fact, especially in the past 2 decades. The polarization along political
and ideological lines has led to an erosion of trust not only in the politicians
but in the science that must be used to inform policies (Lewandowsky &
Oberauer, 2016). The public either does not believe what politicians say,
even if evidence-based, or consumes lies with total confidence in their veracity. Skepticism pervades every part of the political system from both
sides. Neither believes others' sources and what they say. Politicians say one
thing on the record and on camera, only to later deny ever having said it.
Newspapers regularly use fact-checkers and lie detectors each time certain
political figures speak because of the pervasion of malinformation. Friedman
and Plumer (2020) quote one of the fired COVID scientists, Dr. Rick Bright,
who said that the administration has put "politics and cronyism ahead of
science" (p. 3). The authors further quote that there has been a "systematic
downplaying or ignoring of science" (p. 3).

There is a balance between science and policy. Scientific evidence should
and must be used to inform policy, and actions must be taken on those
findings. Interpretations will differ, and inaccurate interpretations may arise
from the same data due to political differences, religious beliefs, social affiliations, and other contextual factors. Politicians can argue that the evidence
does not tell them what to do. Policy decisions are rarely about the science,

and more often about the politics, which is why data literacy is important. There is a very real reason why hospitals have ethics committees to ensure that decision-making adheres to strict standards.

Yet skepticism and denial about the findings of the Coronavirus have had a major social and economic impact. People reject evidence that conflicts with their worldview and political, religious, and social beliefs (Lewandowsky & Oberauer, 2016). They want their lives free of the control of the government. They reject regulations despite the potential consequences. Some people refused to wear masks or maintain social distancing. Many flaunted the regulations and possibly endangered others by ignoring scientific evidence about best practices.

We consider superintendents as both educators and politicians. These education leaders are often torn between evidence and political pressures. Superintendents are public servants and sometimes yield to community or political pressure, eschewing evidence to the contrary. This occurs at the highest levels of the educational system.

DATA ETHICS IN EDUCATION: AN OVERVIEW OF THE BOOK

We have described and provided examples of how data ethics have played out in other disciplines. Many lessons can be drawn from these examples and can be translated to educational practice. Part I of the book lays out the landscape of data ethics within education. This part begins with an overview chapter written by Mandinach and Gummer that explores what counts as data ethics in education. It extends the prior discussion to education, using examples where ethical issues have arisen around the use of data. The chapter also examines how state codes of ethics address data ethics. The chapter discusses responsible data use, how it ties to data literacy, and the concepts of good data use.

In the second chapter, Vance and Waughn discuss what might be considered an introduction to data privacy or FERPA 101. The chapter provides the history of FERPA and an overview of the regulations and the complexities of the Act. The chapter defines privacy in the context of FERPA and then describes how FERPA plays out in practice. The chapter reviews the PPRA and then concludes by bringing the discussion around to focus on data ethics.

Parton and Hochleitner examine the landscape of what states are doing in terms of their policies and regulations around privacy and confidentiality in the third chapter. The Data Quality Campaign has a unique perspective because the group constantly monitors how states are adapting their laws to address privacy and confidentiality. The chapter highlights key themes that can be found in legislative policies. The authors note that data privacy must extend to be part of data literacy. The chapter concludes by stating the need for education leaders and others to communicate about the importance of data privacy in practice.

In the fourth and final chapter of Part I, Nichols addresses issues around accountability pressures and how they impact responsible data. The chapter reviews the various policies that have guided education over the past decades and their impact on accountability and the data that feed compliance. The chapter describes how high-stakes accountability pressures educators. Data use has long been adversely related to accountability that serves to marginalize certain students (Datnow, 2017; Diamond & Cooper, 2007; Schildkamp et al., 2019). Nichols reviews some of the research and perspectives around accountability and how accountability links directly to data ethics.

Part II of the book focuses on use cases, examples of where and how data ethics emerge and should be addressed. Recommended steps are posed. In the fifth chapter, Mandinach and Jimerson address how data ethics play out in local education agencies. The chapter describes how data ethics are exercised across levels of districts. They explore issues that link to other chapters such as accountability pressures, equity, and technology. The chapter provides salient examples of good and bad practices that touch on data ethics topics.

The sixth chapter examines capacity building in the form of professional development. Mandinach and Nunnaley explore what is happening in professional development by using two models to highlight how responsible data use is addressed. The chapter touches on how technology vendors deal with training. It aligns the data literacy for teachers construct (Mandinach & Gummer, 2016) with the Using Data Solutions professional development model (Love et al., 2008) specifically to show how data ethics can be addressed.

In the seventh chapter, Gummer, Gibbs, and Dorn address the extent to which educator preparation programs teach data ethics. Data ethics and data literacy go hand in hand, so this chapter explores what preparation programs are doing and what they might do in the future to bring awareness to data ethics and better prepare educators to be more responsible data users. The chapter provides a link between data ethics and assessment literacy/data literacy. The chapter addresses both teachers and leaders.

In the eighth chapter, Camara, Croft, and von Davier address what large testing organizations are doing to deal with data ethics. The chapter discusses cheating scandals, inappropriate uses of standardized test results, gaming the system, and testing policies. The authors focus on large-scale summative assessments and address various components of testing such as data collection and access to data. The chapter also addresses equity issues and testing during COVID.

In the ninth chapter, Dieterle, Holland, and Dede discuss issues of data ethics as they pertain to educational technology platforms. The chapter addresses big data and data platforms. They provide a framework that outlines four divides that can deter ethical decision-making. The chapter presents salient case studies and examples to illustrate the impact of data ethics.

In Chapter 10, the final chapter of Part II, Datnow, Lockton, and Weddle address data ethics dealing with special populations. As highlighted in several chapters, special populations tend to be marginalized due to a focus on accountability pressures (Datnow & Park, 2018). Datnow (2017) has long advocated for the use of an equity lens and an asset-based model to mitigate the marginalization. This chapter describes prior research around ethical issues in data-driven decision-making. It draws from examples where ethical issues become apparent, particularly around raising test scores rather than improving student learning.

In the concluding portion of the book, Mandinach and Gummer address what ethical decision-making is from the perspective of positive skepticism, recognizing what it means for professionalism and that no matter how well intentioned and transparent, decisions can have unintended consequences. The authors note that decisions cannot be easily made solely with accountability data but require diverse sources of data. They summarize the chapters to illuminate the data ethics landscape. Finally, recommendations are given regarding how various groups working in the educational data field can better address the issues around data ethics.

A final Dilbert cartoon is relevant to data ethics (Adams, 2020d). In the first panel, the Boss asks, "Which of your two projections do you think is more accurate?" Dilbert responds, "They are both random guesses. I made two of them to create the illusion of a credible range." The Boss responds, "So . . . would it be reasonable to pick the midpoint?" Dilbert then replies, "It's as reasonable as your other decisions." The key in this cartoon and in educational practice is that decisions must not only be reasonable but also informed by data, responsible and based on sound interpretations. This is foundational to data ethics.

It is our hope that this volume provides a comprehensive overview of how ethics apply to educational data use. We recognize that education, although often criticized as not changing easily due to its systemic nature and deeply engrained practices and cultures, has been pressured to respond and evolve in unprecedented ways as global circumstances have impacted the delivery of educational services. The use of virtual education and data have similarly presented new challenges and ethical issues. We hope that most educators take ethical behavior seriously and do not intentionally or purposefully seek to violate the ethics of the profession. As will be seen in the following chapters, there are instances when data ethics are violated due to accountability pressures, political expedience, or simply a lack of understanding of what constitutes the ethical components of data literacy. In exploring the landscape, the chapters provide examples of such ethical violations and seek recommendations for how to ameliorate violations in the future. We hope this book will both increase awareness of the importance of data ethics in educational practice and provide some solutions to avoid potential pitfalls.

NOTE

1. We would like to thank Jori Beck for her feedback and Andrea Lash for directing us to the American Statistical Association's code of ethics and the Cooper volume. We would also like to thank Eli Gruber for providing insights into data use in big business, such as pharmaceuticals.

REFERENCES

Adams, S. (2020a, May 6). *Dilbert.* https://dilbert.com/search_results?month=5& year=2020

Adams, S. (2020b, May 7). *Dilbert.* https://dilbert.com/search_results?month=5& year=2020

Adams, S. (2020c, October 14). *Dilbert.* https://dilbert.com/search_results?month =10&year=2020

Adams, S. (2020d, December 10). *Dilbert.* https://dilbert.com/search_results?month =12&year=2020

Alwine, J., & Goodrum Sterling, F. (2020, May 26). Manipulation of pandemic numbers for politics risks lives. *The Hill.* https://thehill.com/opinion /healthcare/499535-manipulation-of-pandemic-numbers-for-politics-risks-lives

American Educational Research Association. (2011). *Code of ethics.* https://www .aera.net/Portals/38/docs/About_AERA/CodeOfEthics(1).pdf

American Educational Research Association, American Psychological Association, & National Council on Measurement in Education. (2014). *Standards for educational and psychological testing.* https://www.apa.org/science/programs /testing/standards

American Medical Association. (2001). *AMA code of medical ethics.* https:// www.ama-assn.org/sites/ama-assn.org/files/corp/media-browser/principles-of -medical-ethics.pdf

American Psychological Association. (2020). *Ethical principles of psychologists and code of conduct.* https://www.apa.org/ethics/code/

American Statistical Association. (2018). *Ethical guidelines for statistical practice.* Committee on Professional Ethics of the American Statistical Association. https://www.amstat.org/ASA/Your-Career/Ethical-Guidelines-for-Statistical -Practice.aspx

Blum, J. D. (2020). Tobacco product warnings in the mist of vaping: A retrospective on the Public Health Cigarette Smoking Act. *Chapman Law Review,* 23(1), 53.

Brazilia, S., & Chinn, C. A. (2020). A review of educational response to the "post-truth" condition: Four lenses on "post-truth" problems. *Educational Psychologist, 55*(3), 107–119.

Bursztyn, L., Rao, A., Rother, C., & Yanagizawa-Drott, D. (2020). *Misinformation during a pandemic* (Working Paper No. 2020–40). University of Chicago, Becker Friedman Institute. https://bfi.uchicago.edu/wp-content/uploads/BFI _WP_202044.pdf

Casola, L. (2020). *Roundtable on data science postsecondary education: A compilation of meeting highlights*. National Academies Press.

Chang, Y. K., Literat, I., Price, C., Eisman, J. I., Chapman, A., Gardner, J., & Truss, A. (2020). News literacy education in a polarized political climate: How games can teach youth to spot misinformation. *Harvard Kennedy School Misinformation Review, 1*(4), 1–9.

Cooper, A. (2021, February 25). Arizona Speakers Series [Speech transcript]. https:// www.arizonaseries.com/

Cooper, H. (2016). *Ethical choices in research: Managing data, writing reports, and publishing results in the social sciences*. American Psychological Association.

Cronbach, L. J. (1988). Five perspectives on validity argument. In H. Wainer & H. Braun (Eds.), *Test validity* (pp. 3–17). Lawrence Erlbaum.

Datnow, A. (2017). *Opening or closing doors for students? Equity and data-driven decision making*. https://research.acer.edu.au/cgi/viewcontent.cgi?article=1317 &context=research_conference

Datnow, A., & Park, V. (2018). Opening or closing doors for students? Equity and data use in schools. *Journal of Educational Change, 19*(2), 131–152.

Diamond, J. B., & Cooper, K. (2007). The uses of testing data in urban elementary schools: Some lessons from Chicago. In P. A. Moss (Ed.), *Evidence and decision-making* (106th Yearbook of the National Society for the Study of Education; pp. 241–263). Blackwell Publishing.

Dias, A. (2020, May 1). U.S. women's soccer team's equal pay demands are dismissed by judge. *The New York Times*. https://www.nytimes.com/2020/05/01 /sports/soccer/uswnt-equal-pay.html

Diaz, J. (2020, October 8). Florida principal rehired after Holocaust dispute. *The New York Times*. https://www.nytimes.com/2020/10/08/us/spanish-river-principal -holocaust.html?searchResultPosition=5

Dror, I. E. (2020). Cognitive and human factors in expert decision making: Six fallacies and eight sources of bias. *Analytical Chemistry, 92*, 7998–8004.

Evanega, S., Lynas, M., Adams, J., & Smolenyak, K. (2020). *Coronavirus misinformation: Quantifying sources and themes in the COVID-19 "infodemic."* Cornell University, Cornell Alliance for Science. https://allianceforscience .cornell.edu/wp-content/uploads/2020/09/Evanega-et-al-Coronavirus -misinformationFINAL.pdf

Farley-Ripple, E. N., Oliver, K., & Boaz, A. (2020). Mapping the community: Use of research evidence in policy and practice. *Humanities & Social Science Communication, 7*, 1–10. https://www.nature.com/articles/s41599-020-00571-2.pdf

Forde, P. (2020, November 6). Follow the signs: How Clemson football mastered the (totally legal) art of signal stealing. *Sports Illustrated*. https://www.si.com/college/2020/11/06/clemson-signal-stealing-dabo-swinney-daily-cover

Friedman, L., & Plumer, B. (2020, April 28). Trump's response to virus reflects a long disregard for science. *The New York Times*. https://www.nytimes.com/2020/04/28/climate/trump-coronavirus-climate-science.html?searchResultPosition=2

Friedman, R. (2020, August 20). Improper revenue recognition tops SEC fraud cases. CFODive. https://www.cfodive.com/news/improper-revenue-recognition-sec-fraud-cases/583889/

Geckoboard. (n.d.). *Data fallacies*. https://www.geckoboard.com/best-practice/statistical-fallacies/

General Services Administration. (2020, September). *Data ethics framework* [Draft]. https://strategy-staging.data.gov/assets/docs/data-ethics-framework-action-14-draft-2020-sep-2.pdf

Gilovich, T., Vallone, R., & Tversky, A. (1985). The hot hand in basketball: On the misperception of random sequences. *Cognitive Psychology*, 17, 295–314.

Gleick, P. H., Adams, R. M., Amasino, R. M., Anders, E., Anderson, D. J., Anderson, W. W., Anselin, L. E., Arroyo, M. K., Asfaw, B., Ayala, J., Bax, A., Bebbington, A. J., Bell, G., Bennett, M. V. L., Bennetzen, J. L., Berenbaum, M. R., Berlin, O. B., Bjorkman, P. J., Blackburn, E., . . . Zoback, M. L. (2010). Climate change and the integrity of science. *Science*, 328(5979), 689–690.

Gummer, E. S. (2021). Complexity and then some: Theories of action and theories of learning in data-informed decision making. *Studies in Educational Evaluation*, 69, 1–6. https://doi.org/10.1016/j.stueduc.2020.100960

Herman, J. (2018, April 10). Cambridge Analytica and the coming data bust. *The New York Times*. https://www.nytimes.com/2018/04/10/magazine/cambridge-analytica-and-the-coming-data-bust.html?searchResultPosition=3

Hill, H. C. (2020, February 7). Does studying student data really raise test scores? *Education Week*. https://www.edweek.org/ew/articles/2020/02/10/does-studying-student-data-really-raise-test.html

Kahneman, D. (2011). *Thinking fast and slow*. Farrar, Straus, and Giroux.

Kahneman, D., & Tversky, A. (1983). On the psychology of prediction. *Psychological Review*, 80(4), 237–251.

Kahneman, D., & Tversky, A. (1984). Choices, values, and frames. *American Psychologist*, 39(4), 341–350.

Kavanaugh, J., & Rich, M. D. (2018). *Truth decay: An initial exploration of the diminishing role of facts and analysis in American public life*. RAND Corporation.

Korn, M., & Levitz, J. (2020). *Unacceptable privilege, deceit & the making of the college admissions scandal*. Portfolio/Penguin.

Krugman, P. (2020, May 4). Trump and his infallible advisers. *The New York Times*. https://www.nytimes.com/2020/05/04/opinion/trump-coronavirus.html

Kunde, Z. (1990). The case for motivated reasoning. *Psychological Bulletin*, 108(3), 480–498.

Lai, M. K., McNaughton, S., Jesson, R., & Wilson, A. (2020). *Research-practice partnerships for school improvement: The Learning Schools Model.* Emerald Publishing.

Lapowsky, I. (2019, March 17). How Cambridge Analytica sparked the great privacy awakening. *Wired.* https://www.wired.com/story/cambridge-analytica-facebook-privacy-awakening/

Legg, P. A., Chung, D. H. S., Parry, M. L., Jones, M. W., Long, R., Griffiths, I. W., & Chen, M. (2012). MatchPad: Interactive glyph-based visualization for real-time sports performance analysis. *Eurographics Conference on Visualization, 31*(3), 1–10.

Lewandowsky, S., Ecker, U. K. H., & Cook, J. (2017). Beyond misinformation: Understanding and coping with the "post-truth" era. *Journal of Applied Research in Memory and Cognition, 6*(4), 353–369.

Lewandowsky, S., Gignac, G. E., & Oberauer, K. (2013). The role of conspiracist ideation and worldviews in predicting rejection of science. *PLoS ONE, 8,* e75637.

Lewandowsky, S., & Oberauer, K. (2016). Motivated rejection of science. *Current Directions in Psychological Science, 25*(4), 217–222.

Lewis, M. (2004). *Moneyball: The art of winning an unfair game.* W. W. Norton & Company.

Lipstadt, D. E. (2006). *History on trial: My day in court with a Holocaust denier.* Harper Perennial.

Love, N., Stiles, K. E., Mundry, S., & DiRanna, K. (2008). *A data coach's guide to improving learning for all students: Unleashing the power of collaborative inquiry.* Corwin Press.

Mandinach, E. B., & Gummer, E. S. (2016). *Data literacy for educators: Making it count in teacher preparation and practice.* Teachers College Press.

Mandinach, E. B., Honey, M., Light, D., & Brunner, C. (2008). A conceptual framework for data-driven decision making. In E. B. Mandinach & M. Honey (Eds.), *Data-driven school improvement: Linking data and learning* (pp. 13–31). Teachers College Press.

Mandinach, E. B., & Schildkamp, K. (2021). Misconceptions about data-based decision making in education: An exploration of the literature. *Studies in Educational Evaluation, 69,* 1–10. https://doi.org/10.1016/j.stueduc.2020.100842

McCright, A. M., & Dunlap, R. E. (2011). Cool dudes: The denial of climate change among conservative white males in the United States. *Global Environmental Change, 21,* 1163–1172.

McIntyre, L. (2018). *Post-truth.* MIT Press Essential Knowledge Series.

McIntyre, L. (2019). *The scientific attitude: Defending science from denial, fraud, and pseudoscience.* CMIT Press.

Messick, S. J. (1989). Validity. In R. L. Linn (Ed.), *Educational measurement* (3rd ed.; pp. 13–103). Macmillan Publishing Company.

National Education Association. (2020, September 14). *Code of ethics for educators.* http://www.nea.org/home/30442.htm

National Forum on Education Statistics. (2021). *Forum guide to strategies for education data collection and reporting* (NFES 2021013). U.S. Department of Education, National Center for Education Statistics.

Nierenberg, A. (2020, April 24). Please do not eat disinfectant. *The New York Times.* https://www.nytimes.com/article/coronavirus-disinfectant-inject-ingest.html

Pasquale, F. (2015). *The black box: The secret algorithms that control money and information.* Harvard University Press.

Paul, C., & Brookes, B. (2015). The rationalization of unethical research: Revisionist accounts of the Tuskegee Syphilis Study and the New Zealand "Unfortunate Experiment." *American Journal of Public Health*, *105*(10), e12–e19.

Pelosi, N. (2020, July, 21). *Transcript of Pelosi interview on CNN's Situation Room with Wolf Blitzer.* https://www.speaker.gov/newsroom/72120-1

Robson, D. (2015, August 14). Considered a data dinosaur, a sport is trying an analytic approach. *The New York Times*, B8. http://mobile.nytimes.com/2015/08/14/sports/tennis/a-data-dinosaur-tennis-tries-an-analytic-approach.html?emc=edit_th_20150814&nl=todaysheadlines&nlid=1524904&_r=0&referrer=

Rosenthal, E. (2014, September 20). After surgery, surprise $117,000 medical bill from doctor he didn't know. *The New York Times.* https://www.nytimes.com/2014/09/21/us/drive-by-doctoring-surprise-medical-bills.html

Schildkamp, K., & Poortman, C. L. (2015). Factors influencing the functioning of data teams. *Teachers College Record*, *117*, 1–42.

Schildkamp, K., Poortman, C. L., Ebbeler, J., & Pieters, J. M. (2019, July 2). How school leaders can build effective data teams: Five building blocks for a new wave of data-informed decision making. *Journal of Educational Change*, *20*, 1–43. https://doi.org/10.1007/s10833-019-09345-3

Simon, H. A. (1992). What is an "explanation" of behavior? *Psychological Science*, *3*, 150–161.

Sinatra, G. M., & Lombardi, D. (2020). Evaluating sources of scientific evidence and claims in the post-truth era may require reappraising plausibility judgments. *Educational Psychologist*, *55*(3), 120–131.

Spiegelhalter, D. (2019). *The art of statistics: How to learn from data.* Basic Books.

Spillane, J. P., & Miele, D. E. (2007). Evidence in practice: A framing of the terrain. In P. A. Moss (Ed.), *Evidence and decision making* (106th Yearbook of the National Society for the Study of Education, Part I; pp. 46–73). Blackwell Publishing.

Tene, O., & Polonetsky, J. (2018). Taming the Golem: Challenges of ethical algorithmic decision-making. *North Carolina Journal of Law & Technology*, *19*(1), 125–173.

Theel, S., Greenberg, M., & Robbins, D. (2013, October 10). Study: Media sowed doubts in coverage of UN climate change report. *Media Matters.* https://www.mediamatters.org/washington-post/study-media-sowed-doubt-coverage-un-climate-report

Tracy, M. (2019, April 4). College sports 101: A U.N.C. class reviews a scandal at its source. *The New York Times.* https://www.nytimes.com/2019/04/04/sports/unc-scandal.html

Tversky, A., & Gilovich, T. (1989). The cold facts about the "hot hand" in basketball. *Chance, 2*(1), 16–21.

Tversky, A., & Kahneman, D. (1971). Belief in the law of small numbers. *Psychological Bulletin, 76*(1), 105–100.

Tversky, A., & Kahneman, D. (1974). Judgment under uncertainty: Heuristics and biases. *Science, 185,* 1124–1131.

Tversky, A., & Kahneman, D. (1983). Extensional vs. intuitive reasoning: The conjunction fallacy in probability judgment. *Psychological Review, 77,* 65–72.

Van Geel, M., Keuning, T., Visscher, A. J., & Fox, J-P. (2016). Assessing the effects of a school-wide data-based decision-making intervention on student achievement growth in primary schools. *American Educational Research Journal, 53*(2), 360–394.

Vanlommel, K., Van Gasse, R., Vanhoof, J., & Van Petegem, P. (2021). Sorting pupils into their next educational track: How strongly do teachers rely on data-based or intuitive processes when they make the transition decision? *Studies in Educational Evaluation, 69,* 1–10. https://doi.org/10.1016/j.stueduc.2020.100865

Vigdor, N. (2020, July 16). The Houston Astros' cheating scandal: Sign-stealing, buzzer intrigue and tainted pennants. *The New York Times.* https://www.nytimes.com/article/astros-cheating.html

Wang, Y. (2021). When artificial intelligence meets educational leaders' data-informed decision-making: A cautionary tale. *Studies in Educational Evaluation, 69,* 1–9. https://doi.org/10.1016/j.stueduc.2020.100872

Part I

LANDSCAPE

CHAPTER 1

The Landscape of Data Ethics in Education

What Counts as Responsible Data Use

Ellen B. Mandinach and Edith S. Gummer

This chapter describes data ethics throughout education. It considers what counts as data and the appropriate use of data, linking responsible data use to data literacy (Mandinach & Gummer, 2016a, 2016b). The chapter also examines state standards and codes of ethics in terms of how they address data ethics. It sets the stage for subsequent chapters.

We used Dilbert cartoons in the prior chapter to emphasize that data use is about evidence, not guessing. The cartoons capture the arguments for data quality, accuracy, and adequacy. Educational data-driven decision-making requires the use of empirical evidence, without which educators will improvise, solely using intuitions, anecdotes, emotions, opinions, and beliefs. As is often said, without data, one's statements are only opinions. As one education service provider notes, educators often use "cardiac assessments" to make decisions; that is, they believe in their hearts that something is true (J. Reyes, personal communication, July 30, 2020).

EXAMPLES FROM EDUCATION

We illustrate data ethics through examples in which topics are interrelated but can be categorized into cheating and accountability pressures, politics and policy, infrastructure, and data use and data literacy. Some of the examples relate directly to protection and confidentiality, whereas most relate to responsible data use.

COVID and School Openings

One of the most public intersections of data ethics and education is how data are being used to decide whether or not to open schools during the

2020 COVID pandemic. Incomplete and contradictory evidence coupled with conflicting political pressures became problematic. Different data models were used that evolved rapidly. Federal and state mandates required in-person instruction, while local officials encountered resistance from faculty, staff, and parents (Harticollis, 2020). Districts adopted models that were aligned with the local situation (Faden et al., 2020). Faculty unions were vocal about the risks, and some faculty refused to teach in person or quit for fear of health risks. Decisions needed to be made based on the best data available, weighing health risks and educational, social–emotional and contextual considerations for students and teachers. Updated data formed the basis for decision-making, allowing for necessary short-term modifications. It was imperative to use sound data processes on which to ground decisions.

Cheating and Accountability Pressures

Earl and Katz (2006) note that "Accountability without improvement is empty rhetoric, and improvement without accountability is whimsical action without direction" (p. 12). Accountability can force educators to engage in activities that are questionable at best and unethical at worst. Scandals in education have gained national attention. In 2009, it was discovered that educators in the Atlanta Public Schools altered answers on the state standardized test (Perry, 2009). Educators were prosecuted and found guilty (Blinder, 2015). More recently, affluent parents bribed educators at universities to gain admission for their children (Halleck, 2019). Parents falsified student records, and some parents paid adept test takers to actually take college admissions tests on behalf of their children.

Students have been documented stealing past tests (Mele, 2017). Teachers may teach solely to the test specifications without consideration to long-term learning (Jennings & Bearak, 2014; Popham, 2001). Parents may threaten schools and administrators about what and how to teach so that their children will be advantaged. Parents may bribe and threaten teachers to ensure their children get the needed grades and recommendations for the admission to higher education institutions of choice (Betweli, 2013). Administrators may game the system to enhance their districts' public standing (Hibel & Penn, 2020).

Accountability pressures do not always result in cheating. The pressures can result in discriminatory practices that foster systemic inequities. Garner and colleagues (2017) note that accountability pressures work against educators considering relevant factors, such as student agency and experiences, that may influence the most challenged students:

Using biased assessments as the markers of success or underachievement of marginalized populations continues the tradition the institutional injustices and disenfranchisement that these communities have historically faced and presently endure more broadly in society. (p. 419)

They further describe how educators feel undue pressure from standardized assessments due to their use in high-stakes decisions, including tenure, school funding, and student promotion. Such pressures result in a focus on the tests to raise scores to meet accountability standards.

School and District Politics and Policies

Decision-making occurs at all educational levels, influenced by politics (Cooper et al., 2009). Perhaps the least studied aspect of data-driven decision-making may be high-level central office administrators (Honig & Venkateswaran, 2012), where politics and other factors most likely come into play. Begley (2009) notes that ethical decision-making by administrators requires a "normative and cultural context" (p. 20). Begley further notes that decisions are influenced by values, motivation, attitudes, valuation, and self-interest, both conscious and unconscious. Pressures come from all directions: parents, school boards, and the community. Increasingly though, administrators make decisions based on data, emphasize data for presentations, and expect their educators to use data to create data-driven cultures where data use is embedded.

Building leadership is one of the most essential components and enablers of data-driven decision-making (Hamilton et al., 2009; Jimerson et al., 2019). Administrators create an environment where data use is either excepted or avoided. They may shame, blame, and take punitive actions against teachers and students (Lasater et al., 2021) rather than creating open and trusting environments for teachers without fear of retribution. Administrators can create policies that unfairly evaluate teachers by using limited and invalid data. They make hiring, promotion and tenure, and contractual renewal decisions based on measures not developed for that use (Potter & Stefkovich, 2009). This is a fundamental violation of validity (Cronbach, 1988; Messick, 1989).

Data Infrastructure

Infrastructure issues influence data ethics, including data access, data disposal, lack of security, and data quality. Data access includes giving educators access to data to which they are not entitled. Specific procedures are required for disposing data with personally identifiable information (PII) (Privacy Technical Assistance Center [PTAC], n.d.). Documents with PII, test papers, and other artifacts need to be properly secured to avoid improper access. Computers and mobile devices where data are stored must be password protected. Frequently, teachers use computers or applications where students, family members, or others can see what they are doing. Teachers may walk away from the computer, and students may access a grade book or a site where student information is saved. Teachers may work from home, and family members may open a file on the computer or mobile device.

Vendors that provide data systems can precipitate data ethics violations. Having the proper protections in place and ensuring that educators know the procedures to protect data is important (Tsukayama, 2015). Unbeknownst to educators, downloaded apps may violate protections and collect student data that can then be sold by vendors.

Data breaches occur at all levels. Student data were accessed from the Arizona Department of Education by a vendor who offered free dental services to low-income students (Freedberg, 2012). A spreadsheet containing data for low-income families receiving special services was inadvertently released (Arizona Department of Education, 2020). Both breaches caused problems for the Department of Education. A nonprofit research organization was working with a large district to provide services for special education students (St. George, 2016) and experienced a break-in at one of their offices. Computers were stolen, one of which contained a nonencrypted data file from the district about the special education students. Not having computers locked down and not having data encrypted were clear violations of Institutional Review Board processes and data management security.

The final infrastructure issue is data quality. Data must be complete, accurate, relevant, and timely. Data also must be valid and reliable. An easy way to talk about data quality is "garbage in and garbage out." There are many examples of bad practice in education. Validity is both a characteristic of a measure and of the interpretations made on the resulting data (Cronbach, 1988; Messick, 1989). We use the definition provided by Kavanaugh and Rich (2018) that interpretation is "an explanation or understanding of a topic or issue that is based on facts, past experience, and analysis" (p. 10).

It is not unusual for educators to use measures or data for purposes other than for which they were intended. Test results are used for teacher evaluation or as a proxy for school rankings and real estate values (Baker et al., 2010). State summative test scores are often required of teachers to inform instructional practices (Lasater et al., 2021), which is an example of nonrelevant data use. The data must be aligned to the purposes for which they are being used and the kinds of decisions informed.

More typical data quality issues are completeness, accuracy, and timeliness. Heritage and Yeagley (2005) also add levels of detail such as the right grain size and comprehensiveness, and sensitivity to differences. Decisions should be understood within the framing of "sense and reasonableness" (p. 333). An example includes state summative test scores that are often called dead on arrival data because of the lag time from administration to score reporting and use. Data are delayed by months, endangering the validity of the results. Incomplete data or inaccurate data can easily be used inappropriately.

Educational data move through many hands, and data entry issues, errors, and missing data occur (Bowen et al., 2005). For example, districts may require teachers to take attendance by period or by day. Students come late or leave in the middle of class. The National Forum on Education Statistics (2018) provides a guide on how to code various kinds of attendance indices. It is a complex process with several different attendance metrics. Teachers forget to enter the data immediately and then do it much later, with the potential for memory error.

Data Use and Data Literacy

Another cartoon highlights the need for data literacy (Adams, 2020b). Dilbert explains to Dogbert that in the past, decisions were made based on superstitions and biases and that decision-making evolved into the scientific use of data. The next two panels indicate that this did not work out so well. Dilbert discusses how the data were unreliable and conflicting, indicating that people do not have the mental capacity to use reason. Dogbert asserts that this is still better than guessing. The cartoon concludes, "How do you know that?" and Dogbert asserts "You are hard to talk to." This dialogue illustrates the need to understand how to use data competently and responsibly. Individuals must have the right data, know how to use the data, and make decisions from the data rather than making guesses, using anecdotes, and activating biases.

We have defined data literacy for teachers as follows:

> Data literacy for teaching is the ability to transform information into actionable instructional knowledge and practices by collecting, analyzing, and interpreting all types of data (assessment, school climate, behavioral, snapshot, longitudinal, moment-to-moment, etc.) to help determine instructional steps. It combines an understanding of data with standards, disciplinary knowledge and practices, curricular knowledge, pedagogical content knowledge, and an understanding of how children learn. (Gummer & Mandinach, 2015, p. 2)

Taking a statistical view, Spiegelhalter (2019) defines data literacy as "the ability to understand the principles behind learning from data, carry out basic data analyses, and critique the quality of claims on the basis of data" (p. 387). These definitions are foundational.

Responsible data use is essential to data ethics. A panel of experts on big data posed a call for action around the development of global data literacy (Oceans of Data Institute, 2016). This panel argued that the world economy depends on data literacy, that effective decision-making must rely on the use of evidence and data, and that the proliferation of data requires attention to data privacy and security.

Just because educators have data literacy does not ensure that they will use data responsibly (Greene, 2018). There are questions about the extent to which educators understand the regulations that surround the protection of the confidentiality and privacy of student data. It is unclear who has responsibility for ensuring that educators obtain Family Educational Rights and Privacy Act (FERPA) training. State education agencies do not feel responsible and fear legal ramifications. Local education agencies may not have individuals sufficiently knowledgeable to do such training and may look to educator preparation programs, professional development, or federal guidance. Resources that relate to student data privacy, data security, and data in the pandemic can also be found on the Future of Privacy Forum's Student Privacy Compass (n.d.) website (https://studentprivacycompass.org /resources/educatortraining/#reducingrisk).

Beyond FERPA, educators need to understand responsible data use. With appropriate training, educators will know the basics of what not to do: talk about a student by name in public, share student work products with their names on them or provide PII, use devices on which student data are stored but not encrypted or password protected, release information about students in special programs or services, and post pictures of students on class trips or in class without parental permission.

Part of using data responsibly is knowing what data should be used for particular kinds of decisions, understanding the context for the decision, and considering the whole child, instead of just looking at student performance data (Mandinach & Mundry, 2021; Mandinach et al., 2019; Mandinach et al., 2020). Educators must exhibit culturally responsive data literacy and understand contextual validity.

Responsible data use is about making valid interpretations from the data and understanding the intended and unintended consequences of the decision, that is, the consequential validity. People can see what they want to see in data without considering all possible relevant data sources. Confirmation bias—the interpretation of data based on existing beliefs (Nickerson, 1998)—might be the belief that student athletes are dumb jocks, that all Asian students are good at math, or that African American girls are not good at math (known as stereotype threat). Misinterpretation of data is based on preconceived notions, implicit biases, and unconscious beliefs, occurring when educators take information they do not understand and draw inaccurate conclusions. This can be done consciously or unconsciously. Most misinterpretation occurs innocently due to poor knowledge, lack of information, lack of data literacy, or simply not knowing what to look for. Educators may examine student performance data and not understand what the data say but still make decisions or fail to take into consideration the context of the decision, making assumptions about students (Fjortoft & Lai, 2021). Educators make decisions without considering root causes.

Another example of misinterpretation is described by Atwood and colleagues (2019) where a student is caught stealing food from students and the teachers' lounge. An initial interpretation is that the student has a behavioral issue. A deeper look at the mitigating factors uncover that the student is hungry, has a food insecurity, and the student and family need assistance. The first interpretation is a rush to judgment. Only with the deeper examination of the situation and the consideration of other data does the truth emerge. This kind of misinterpretation happens when educators fail to consider all relevant data and mitigating circumstances.

The failure to triangulate data sources is another issue. A foundational concept of both data and assessment literacy is the need to use multiple data sources and analytic methods (Means et al., 2009). Educators may take the most expeditious route to a decision by using one measure. That measure may be inaccurate, may fail to provide the level of detail needed, may be misaligned for the decision, or may fail to explain the context.

Teachers may give end-of-section assessments and use them as the sole determinant for quarterly grades, taking into consideration no other data. Administrators may penalize teachers for not attaining certain levels of student performance based on inappropriate or premature measures. Teachers may grade students solely on failing one performance task. Teachers may insist that struggling students be absent on testing day so class performance looks better. Administrators may dumb down results in ways that remove the nuances of information (Sadeghi & Callahan, 2013). Educators may distort findings to ignore outliers to qualify for funding and special services. Such manipulating or withholding of relevant information is irresponsible data use. Deleting or burying data to skew results, such as excluding struggling students from averages, is unacceptable (Koretz, 2017).

Fundamental to data literacy is knowing how to read data displays and discuss them, give presentations with data, and craft reports based on accurate information. This means knowing about data disclosure and how to communicate with data to different audiences. Educators can falsify data, distort reports, and report with partial data. Educators can misrepresent data through inaccurate and misleading displays and presentations, such as redlining.

Another Dilbert example illustrates the ethics of sound reporting and communicating with data (Adams, 2020c). The Boss says, "When you write the project summary, make it seem as if we didn't make any mistakes." Alice, an employee asks, "You want me to lie? That would be a massive ethical violation." The Boss responds, "No. No. I only want you to omit important context." Alice responds, "Why does my stomach hurt?" The accurate presentation, representation, and communication of data is foundational to data ethics.

Data use requires having the ability to engage in the full range of skills that comprise data literacy for teachers (Mandinach & Gummer, 2016a, 2016b). It also includes more generic dispositions such as the ability to collaborate and communicate.

GUIDANCE FROM THE LITERATURE

The National Forum on Education Statistics (NFES) examines aspects of data use and provides resources and guides to education agencies. The guides provide recommendations for good practice and include materials that can help educators on specific topics. The NFES (2010, 2016) produced two guides that are relevant: *The Forum Guide to Data Ethics* and *The Forum Guide to Education Data Privacy*.

One of the main messages is that data ethics are much broader than the laws that govern privacy and confidentiality. This premise aligns with our view of a broad definition of data ethics to responsible data use. A second key message is that data ethics must be enculturated into education agencies. This is not unlike the finding from the Institute of Education Sciences practice guide on data use (Hamilton et al., 2009) that recommends building a data culture with strong and supportive leadership and the expectations for responsible data use. The *Forum Guide* (NFES, 2010) recommends a culture in which data ethics are expected; leaders who support data ethics; the creation of organizational norms, policies, and standard procedures; explicit expectations for using data responsibly; and proper training on data ethics.

The guide distinguishes five types of information that all require different forms of protection:

- **PII:** PII can identify a specific individual and is traceable, so it must be protected.
- **Private information:** This information is private and cannot be released unless there is a need to know.
- **Confidential information:** This information will not be released.
- **Sensitive information:** This information includes student schedules and class assignments.
- **General information:** This information is not confidential; instead, it is helpful to the functioning of the education agency.

The *Forum Guide* (NFES, 2010) presents what is entitled, "The Forum Code of Data Ethics" (p. 7), which focuses on three themes: integrity, data quality, and security.

Integrity

1. Demonstrate honesty, integrity, and professionalism at all times.
2. Appreciate that while data may represent attributes of real people, they do not describe the whole person.
3. Be aware of applicable statutes, regulations, practices, and ethical standards governing data collection and reporting.
4. Report information accurately and without bias.
5. Be accountable, and hold others accountable, for ethical use of data.

Data Quality

6. Promote data quality by adhering to best practices and operating standards.
7. Provide all relevant data, definitions, and documentation to promote comprehensive understanding and accurate analysis when releasing information.

Security

8. Treat data systems as valuable organizational assets.
9. Safeguard sensitive data to guarantee privacy and confidentiality. (p. 7)

The guide aligns with data literacy, such as using data for their intended purposes, understanding the need for data integrity by not taking data out of context, the need to use multiple sources of data, and the awareness of how assumptions can create biased and prejudiced interpretations. One must understand the limits of data; that is, data cannot describe a complete entity or phenomenon. Educators must understand the appropriate release of data and the principles of data quality. Educators also must be able to understand data displays and how to appropriately represent data. They must adhere to appropriate data access procedures. The guide recognizes different levels of expertise as have Mandinach and Gummer (2016a) and Beck and Nunnaley (2021). The guide (NFES, 2010) notes the role-based nature of data use: "Everyone who collects, handles, or reports data on individuals has legal and ethical responsibilities for this information. Organizations should provide training on these responsibilities to teachers, data clerks, and volunteers, among others" (p. 13). Mandinach (2012) differentiates between being data literate and being a good consumer of information. Everyone in an educational agency who has their hands on data must understand the basics of data literacy. Others may only need to consume information that comes from data analytics.

Another relevant resource is the Statewide Longitudinal Data Systems Grant Program (2015) *SLDS Data Use Standards* from the State Support Team. The document lays out various components of data literacy and even has been used as a means of validating the data literacy for teachers construct (Gummer & Mandinach, 2015; Mandinach & Gummer, 2016a, 2016b). The standards contain a category entitled, "Professional Behaviors," which is similar to our habits of mind or dispositions. Ethics fall under this category. The *SLDS Data Use Standards* document lists data quality, transparency, representation, ethics, culture, and use under the category of "Ethical Use." The processes of data collection, analysis, and sharing must be clear. *Representation* means that any data presentation must strive to be accurate, to be unambiguous, and to use straightforward information. The document addresses rules and laws, protection, and advocacy for protections, focusing on the legal aspects of data ethics. *Collaboration* includes collaborative use, climate, outreach, and prioritization. *Climate* refers to creating a culture that is accepting, receptive, trusting, safe, and nonpunitive with respect to collaborative data inquiry. *Outreach* entails the use of data to communicate beyond educational agencies. *Prioritization* is a data culture and infrastructure issue focusing on the need for time and support to engage in data use. A final section is *Continuous Improvement* in which problem solving, improving outcomes, and engaging in professional development are recommended to enculturate data use. This section also addresses data limitations, such as interpretations and utility, data assumptions, and data context and formats.

WHAT ARE DATA AND DATA ETHICS

A looming problem has plagued data-driven decision-making in education, namely the issue of what information is considered to be data. When one asks educators what data refer to, they immediately respond, "test scores." Data are more than quantitative indices of student performance or phenomena that can be measured by numbers. Data can be qualitative, observational, in-the-moment, snapshot or longitudinal, and formative or summative. Data in education come from diverse sources (Mandinach & Gummer, 2016a). Just because data cannot be entered into a data system does not mean they are not data. Data are operationalized in nuanced ways, such as the complex definitions of attendance, absence, and graduation rate mentioned earlier. Data-driven decision-making can be intuitive or deliberate (Kahneman, 2011). We must be mindful about what we accept and reject regarding data.

We provide another caveat that the same data may look different for different people and from different perspectives and at different levels of granularity. We use the Seurat painting, *A Sunday Afternoon on the Island La Grande Jatte*, to illustrate (Mandinach, 2017). The pointillist painting has small dots that create the form of the painting. Taking the broadest view, the entire painting is clear. Yet, moving closer, the dots of paint blur the image. We use this as a metaphor for the examination of data. Different views can yield different perspectives, optics, and interpretations. While we strive for the broadest possible definition of data, the closest possible examination is required. As noted in the *Forum Guide* (NFES, 2010), different data must be treated differently for their own protections.

We use data ethics interchangeably with responsible data use. The mention of data ethics brings to mind data privacy and confidentiality, basically the adherence to FERPA. But data ethics are much broader, and we take an even broader view of data ethics than is typically used. It is our belief that the ethical use of data is about responsible data use. Well after we began to develop what would become the data literacy for teachers construct (Mandinach & Gummer, 2016a, 2016b), Mandinach advised the Data Quality Campaign (DQC, 2014) on their effort to define data literacy for more public consumption. This resulted in a policy brief entitled *Teacher Data Literacy: It's About Time*. The biggest debate was whether ethics and responsible data use should be included in the definition along with other parts of the skill set. The definition begins, "Data-literate educators continuously, effectively, and ethically" (p. 1). The brief further defines ethically as "using information with professionalism and integrity for intended uses only and with consciousness of the need to protect student privacy" (p. 6). Even here, one can see the interplay between a broad and limited view of ethics.

We speak more about responsible data use than data ethics and link responsible data use to data literacy for teachers (Mandinach & Gummer, 2016a, 2016b); however, in the construct, we refer to data ethics, which includes the protection of privacy and confidentiality. Looking at data ethics from the view of responsibility enables us to differentiate levels of various skills and knowledge. Good and effective data use implies responsible data use.

RESPONSIBLE DATA USE: DATA LITERACY

We spent several years operationalizing the data literacy for teachers construct (Gummer & Mandinach, 2015; Mandinach & Gummer, 2012, 2013, 2016a, 2016b). The expectation is that educators use data both effectively and responsibly. As we identified each aspect of data literacy, we questioned what evidence of that aspect would look like at various levels of expertise. We had suppositions about how each aspect would be manifested at the novice and expert levels, but little specificity about intermediate points along the continuum. Recently, Beck and Nunnaley (2021) provided a preliminary continuum. They recognized that it may be difficult to look at each aspect in isolation because, in practice, educators use data literacy as a composite. That said, the invocation of the data literacy knowledge and skills with increasing expertise could be considered both effective and responsible data use.

It is not our intention here to wade through all of the more than 50 skills, knowledge, and dispositions in the construct. We look across the construct's five components: (1) identify a problem of practice; (2) use data; (3) transform data into information; (4) transform information into a decision; and (5) evaluate the outcomes of the decision, and select a subset of knowledge skills to illustrate the expert-novice continuum of responsible data use.

Understand the context of the student in terms of a problem of practice. Educators must understand the context of each student in terms of performance, behavior, motivation, home context, and other relevant information that can impact a decision. Without such contextual data, a decision might be flawed by having ignored valuable information that can provide insights. Shulman (1986, 1987) recognized knowledge of the learner and knowledge of context as essential, and Mandinach and colleagues (2020) use these as part of culturally responsive data literacy. Experts recognize the importance of contexts, whereas novices might not.

Understand student privacy. Educators must be aware of the basic regulations that protect student data. Without such knowledge, educators can inadvertently violate privacy and confidentiality. Novices might have a passing understanding, but that knowledge grows with experience. Even experts have more to learn as regulations and laws are modified over time.

Identify possible sources of data, understand the purposes of different data sources, understand what data are appropriate, understand the specificity of the data to the question, and understand data properties. These aspects relate to the knowledge that data must be aligned to the purposes for which a decision is being made and that data have different underlying properties that make them more or less relevant to the particular decision. Using the wrong data or level of data is problematic and may invalidate decisions. These are acquired practices that come from experience and proper training.

Use multiple measures or sources of data. This is a foundational concept of validity and reliability. Sound decisions require triangulated data sources and multiple data points. Using only one data point is fraught with error. Inexperience may mean that novices may rely on single sources as an easy way out, whereas experts know better.

Understand data quality and understand elements of data accuracy, appropriateness, and completeness. Such knowledge is fundamental to the issue of data quality and reflects what is outlined about data ethics (NFES, 2010). The use of data that are not relevant, lack timeliness, or are incomplete or inaccurate can result in poor decision-making. Recognition of bad data results from experience.

Use technologies to support data use, understand and use data displays and representations, and assess patterns and trends. Technology helps to enable data use but also poses threats to data ethics due to potential misrepresentation of data and reporting and violations of privacy and confidentiality. Penuel and Shepard (as cited in Mandinach et al., 2018) criticize vendors for simplifying data displays in ways that misrepresent data. Such misrepresentation and distortion can impact interpretations and the ensuing decisions. Vendors must extend their training beyond technical aspects to ensure proper data use. Novices may not be adept at reading data displays and identifying patterns and trends. They may not understand multiple risks posed by the applications. Experts have acquired these skills, but still must be aware of potential pitfalls when it comes to the underlying algorithms of apps that capture data.

Understand how to analyze, organize, prioritize, examine, integrate, and manipulate data, and understand how to drill down into data. These skills are essential and, if done poorly, have the potential to create inaccuracies and result in violations of responsible data practice.

Test assumptions, probe for causality, articulate inferences, interpret, summarize, and explain data. These skills are key to responsible data use. Testing assumptions helps to mitigate confirmation bias by using evidence to dispel inaccurate beliefs and theories. Probing for causality enables educators to better understand the root causes of performance, behavior, or other issues that may look very different at the surface level. Inferences and interpretations go to the heart of ethical data use and can be inaccurate based on poor data or poor analytics. They can be skewed, biased, and simply wrong. Similarly, the summarization or explanation about the data can be problematic for the same reasons.

Diagnose what students need, and make instructional adjustments. Taking action on the data relies not just on the understanding of the data but also on other sources of knowledge that are laid out in the data literacy for teachers construct. Pedagogical content knowledge is especially relevant here. Teachers may understand the data within a trajectory of student learning, but they also need to transform that information into actions. Such actions must be made based on the context of the situation, the soundness of the data, their understanding of the data, and the interpretations. These skills, part of the component called *Transform Information into a Decision,* is the pedagogical part of the construct. It pertains to the ability to take action on the information. There is a symbiotic relationship across data skills, content knowledge, and pedagogical content knowledge (Mandinach & Gummer, 2016a, 2016b). We have often asked the following question: How much content and pedagogical content knowledge do teachers need to be able to use data effectively? Experienced educators are likely to have deeper content knowledge and more pedagogical strategies in their repertoires from which to make instructional decisions.

Reexamine the original question, monitor changes, and compare pre- and post-decision. Educators need to recognize that decisions are not finite but part of an iterative and cyclical process. To truncate this decision-making process prematurely in a rush to end it is bad practice. Novices may assume that the decision-making process is linear and that it is done after they have reached a decision. In contrast, experts know that the process is iterative and cyclical.

Finally, the dispositions (or habits of mind) of the construct include the *belief in the inquiry process, the belief in ethics, the belief that all students can learn,* the value of *collaboration,* and the need to take care in *communication.* We have discussed the first two. The belief that all students can learn addresses an equity issue. Inequities can occur through confirmation bias, stereotype threat, and other unconscious and conscious beliefs. Responsible data use requires collaboration and communication as educators share, reason about, and communicate with data. Educators must know the parameters about what data can be discussed and shared with whom and under what conditions. And when educators present with data, the information they use must be accurate and presented in ways that do not distort the findings. Novices may not understand the nuances of these dispositions. These issues will be illustrated in later chapters.

DATA ETHICS IN STATE CODES

Codes of Ethics

Mandinach and Wayman (2020) reviewed if and how states address data ethics and whether states have a code of ethics. The review also examined how state standards for teacher licensure handle data ethics. They found that 34 states have some form of code of ethics that mentions data, and 10 states have a code with no mention of data. Some of the states use the *Model Code of Ethics for Educators* (MCEE) developed by the National Association of State Directors of Teacher Education and Certification (NASDTEC, n. d.). For most of the states with their own code, coverage of data and data ethics was cursory at best. In terms of relevant topics, 19 states mentioned confidentiality; 9 disclosure; 4 falsification or fraudulent data use; 3 accuracy and proper presentation; 2 communication with data, FERPA, use of evidence, and disposal of data; and 1 maintaining data and equitable data use. Only two states mentioned FERPA. The MCEE has a better focus on data ethics with four of its five principles addressing aspects of data ethics. The MCCE addresses (1) the use of evidence, instructional data, research, and professional knowledge to inform practice; (2) the creation, mainte- nance, dissemination, storage, retention, and disposal of records and data; and (3) the use of data, data sources, or findings in an accurate and reliable manner. Clearly, state codes of ethics do not adequately address data ethics, even though they could be valuable sources of guidance for education agen- cies and how to prepare educators to use data responsibly.

State and National Standards

Standards also reveal how states think about data literacy. Many states have adopted the Interstate New Teacher Assessment and Support Consortium (InTASC) standards as part of the work from the Council of Chief State School Officers (CCSSO, 2013). InTASC produced the "model core teach- ing standards" to guide the performances, essential knowledge, and critical dispositions that teachers must have. Mandinach and colleagues (2015) first surveyed the states with an update by Mandinach and colleagues (2017) and more recently by Mandinach and Wayman (2020). An increasing number of states have adopted or incorporated the InTASC standards into their own standards (31 of 50 in 2020 versus 6 in 2014). Almost all states address data in some way. Some states have little to say about data or data ethics. Some address data but fail to address data ethics. Some address various topics around data ethics, such as confidentiality and privacy, test security, proper analysis or accurate representation of evidence without distortion or misrepresentation, ethical digital citizenship, disclosure, data disposal, use of data with honesty and integrity, data access, the use of data rather than opinions or beliefs, avoidance of false statements, use of quality and com- plete data, and communicating results accurately and ethically. Four states mention FERPA. The states with the most explicit links to data ethics are Kansas and Rhode Island.

Mandinach and Wayman (2020) provide recommendations about how data ethics should be addressed. First, there must be an operationaliza- tion of what data ethics are that can be used to inform the standards and codes. Second, there is a need to reach out to state education agencies and NASDTEC to help them begin to incorporate data ethics into their documen- tation, making clear statements about what it means to use data responsibly.

COVID and Virtual Learning

We would be remiss to not address how COVID has affected data eth- ics. The pandemic presented challenges to education in many ways, one of which is the protection of student data. Privacy considerations abound. Schwartz (2020) describes privacy issues that may arise in virtual learning environments. There are concerns about how to protect the access to, transmission of, and collection of student data in a secure manner. Educators are concerned about not just virtual instruction but also virtual assessment. Virtual instruction presents many challenges around data security and the use of cameras. Privacy issues extend beyond student data to disclosure of family and home environmental issues that can reveal problematic circumstances. Virtual delivery impacts the collection of instructionally relevant assessments and standardized tests.

To address some of the concerns, CCSSO (2020) released a report geared to state education agencies to provide potential guidance. CCSSO reminds agencies that legal compliance remains necessary but promotes the idea that collected data should be targeted to their intended use through a principle called *data minimization*. The report raises concerns about restrictions on data access, secure data collection, and secure data transfer. These issues pertain to traditional education venues but become all the more challenging and relevant in the move to virtual and hybrid environments.

FINAL THOUGHTS

We have covered a lot of ground, some of which is negative. That said, there are important lessons to be drawn. We want to stress that much data use is responsible. The examples are intended to be educative. First, people, not just educators, need to have knowledge that can be applied to make more informed and objective decisions. The skill set is necessary. Educators perhaps more than the general public are invoking these skills in their practice. If educators pass on that knowledge and model appropriate data use to students and stakeholders, perhaps the broader use of data and evidence will be the outcome. Second, we acknowledge the complexity of the world in which we live. Decisions are not made in isolation. We therefore must take into consideration the context of any decision. Not all individuals will have their hands on the data, and therefore they must be good consumers of information, rather than data literate. Good and objective consumerism of information and what counts as fact and evidence will have great social value.

We close with a final Dilbert cartoon (Adams, 2020a). Dilbert states, "We don't have any data yet, but we are hearing good reports." Then the Sciencesplainer, brought in to explain how science works, interjects, "Those reports are anecdotal. You need a controlled study to be certain." Dilbert responds, "Literally *everyone* already knows that." The Sciencesplainer has the final word, "Sure. But did you know accurate data are better than bad data?" This is the essence of data ethics.

REFERENCES

Adams, S. (2020a, May 13). *Dilbert*. https://dilbert.com/search_results?month=5&year=2020

Adams, S. (2020b, August 16). *Dilbert*. https://dilbert.com/search_results?month=8&year=2020

Adams, S. (2020c, September 22). *Dilbert*. https://dilbert.com/search_results?month=9&year=2020

Arizona Department of Education. (2020, January 28). *Arizona Department of Education statement regarding data breach*. https://www.azed.gov/communications/2020/01/28/arizona-department-of-education-statement-regarding-data-breach

Atwood, E. D., Jimerson, J. B., & Holt, B. (2019). Equity-oriented data use: Identifying and addressing food insecurity at Cooper Springs Middle School. *Journal of Cases in Educational Leadership*, 1–16. https://doi.org/10.1177/1555458919859932

Baker, E. L., Barton, P. E., Darling-Hammond, L., Haertel, E., Ladd, H. F., Linn, R. L., Ravitch, D., Rothstein, R., Shavelson, R. J., & Shepard, L. A. (2010). *Problems with the use of student test scores to evaluate teachers* (EPI Briefing Paper No. 278). Economic Policy Institute. https://files.epi.org/page/-/pdf/bp278.pdf

Beck, J. S., & Nunnaley, D. (2021). A continuum of data literacy for teaching. *Studies in Educational Evaluation*, 69, 1–8. https://doi.org/10.1016/j.stueduc.2020.100871

Begley, P. T. (2009). Ethics based decision making by educational leaders. In T. K. Kowalski & T. J. Lasley II (Eds.), *Handbook of data-based decision making in education* (pp. 20–37). Routledge.

Betweli, O. (2013). The nature of teacher professional misconduct in Tanzanian public primary schools: The case of Sumbawanga municipal and rural districts. *International Journal of Education*, 5(1), 81.

Blinder, A. (2015, April 1). Atlanta educators convicted in school cheating scandal. *The New York Times*. https://www.nytimes.com/2015/04/02/us/verdict-reached-in-atlanta-school-testing-trial.html

Bowen, E., Price, T., Lloyd, S., & Thomas, S. (2005). Improving the quantity and quality of attendance data to enhance student retention. *Journal of Further and Higher Education*, 29(4), 375–385.

Cooper, B. S., Sureau, J., & Coffin, S. (2009). Data: The DNA of politically based decision making in education. In T. K. Kowalski & T. J. Lasley II (Eds.), *Handbook of data-based decision making in education* (pp. 382–396). Routledge.

Council of Chief State School Officers. (2013). *InTASC model core teaching standards and learning progressions for teachers 1.0*. Interstate Teacher Assessment and Support Consortium. https://ccsso.org/sites/default/files/2017-12/2013_INTASC_Learning_Progressions_for_Teachers.pdf

Council of Chief State School Officers. (2020, July). *Home digital access data collection: Blueprint for state education leaders*. https://ccsso.org/sites/default

/files/2020-07/7.22.20_CCSSO%20Home%20Digital%20Access%20Data
%20Collection%20Blueprint%20for%20State%20Leaders.pdf

Cronbach, L. J. (1988). Five perspectives on validity argument. In H. Wainer &
H. Braun (Eds.), *Test validity* (pp. 3–17). Lawrence Erlbaum.

Data Quality Campaign. (2014). *Teacher data literacy: It's about time*. https://
dataqualitycampaign.org/resource/teacher-data-literacy-time/

Earl., L. M., & Katz, S. (2006). *Leading schools in a data-rich world: Harnessing
data for school improvement*. Corwin Press.

Faden, R., Collins, M., & Anderson, A. (2020, June 1). Ethical issues to consider when
reopening schools: Commentary. *Baltimore Sun*. https://www.baltimoresun
.com/opinion/op-ed/bs-ed-op-0601-ethics-reopen-schools-20200601
-n26yyqm6xrbzfk5fwhxtqky27m-story.html

Fjortoft, H., & Lai, M. K. (2020). Affordances of narrative and numerical data: A
social-semiotic approach to data use. *Studies in Educational Evaluation, 69*,
1–8. https://doi.org/10.1016/j.stueduc.2020.100846

Freedberg, S. (2012). Dental abuse seen driven by private equity investments. *Bloomberg*. https://www.bloomberg.com/news/articles/2012-05-17
/dental-abuse-seen-driven-by-private-equity-investments

Future of Privacy Forum, Student Privacy Compass. (n.d.). *Student privacy training
for educators*. https://studentprivacycompass.org/resources/educatortraining
/#reducingrisk

Garner, B., Thorne, J. K., & Horn, I. S. (2017). Teachers interpreting data for instructional decisions: Where does equity come in? *Journal of Educational Administration, 55*(4), 407–426.

Greene, P. (2018, October 15). Teachers and privacy and telling tales out of
school. *Forbes*. https://www.forbes.com/sites/petergreene/2018/10/15/teachers
-and-privacy-and-telling-tales-out-of-school/?sh=6bfea8703aef

Gummer, E. S., & Mandinach, E. B. (2015). Building a conceptual framework for
data literacy. *Teachers College Record, 117*(4), 1–22. http://www.tcrecord.org
/PrintContent.asp?ContentID=17856

Halleck, R. (2019, March 12). Who's been charged in the college admissions
cheating scandal? Here's the full list. *The New York Times*. https://www
.nytimes.com/2019/03/12/us/felicity-huffman-lori-loughlin-massimo-giannulli
.html?searchResultPosition=4

Hamilton, L., Halverson, R., Jackson, S., Mandinach, E., Supovitz, J., & Wayman,
J. (2009). *Using student achievement data to support instructional decision
making* (NCEE 2009–4067). National Center for Education Evaluation and
Regional Assistance, Institute of Education Sciences, U.S. Department of Education. https://ies.ed.gov/ncee/wwc/PracticeGuide/12

Hartocollis, A. (2020, July 3). Colleges face rising revolt by professors. *The New York
Times*. https://www.nytimes.com/2020/07/03/us/coronavirus-college-professors
.html

Heritage, M., & Yeagley, R. (2005). Data use and school improvement: Challenges
and prospects. In J. L. Herman & E. H. Haertel (Eds.), *Uses and misuses of*

data for educational accountability and improvement (104th Yearbook of the National Society for the Study of Education, Part II; pp. 320–339). Blackwell Publishing.

Hibel, J., & Penn, D. M. (2020). Bad apples or bad orchards? An organizational analysis of educator cheating on standardized accountability tests. *Sociology of Education, 93*(4), 331–352.

Honig, M. I., & Venkateswaran, N. (2012). School-central office relationships in evidence use: Understanding evidence use as a systems problem. *American Journal of Education, 118*(2), 119–222.

Jennings, J. L., & Bearak, J. M. (2014). "Teaching to the test" in the NCLB era: How test predictability affects our understanding of student performance. *Educational Researcher, 43*(8), 381–389.

Jimerson, J. B., Garry, V., Poortman, C. L., & Schildkamp, K. (2019, April). *Implementing a data use intervention in a United States context: Enabling and constraining factors* [Conference presentation]. Annual conference of the American Educational Research Association, Toronto, Canada.

Kahneman, D. (2011). *Thinking fast and slow*. Farrar, Straus, and Giroux.

Kavanaugh, J., & Rich, M. D. (2018). *Truth decay: An initial exploration of the diminishing role of facts and analysis in American public life*. RAND Corporation.

Koretz, D. (2017). *The testing charade: Pretending to make schools better*. University of Chicago Press.

Lasater, K., Bengtson, E., & Albiladi, W. S. (2021). Data use for equity?: How data practices incite deficit thinking in schools. *Studies in Educational Evaluation, 69*, 1–10. https://doi.org/10.1016/j.stueduc.2020.100845

Love N., Stiles, K. E., Mundry, S., & DiRanna, K. (2008). *A data coach's guide to improving learning for all students: Unleashing the power of collaborative inquiry*. Corwin Press.

Mandinach, E. B. (2012). A perfect time for data use: Using data-driven decision making to inform practice. *Educational Psychologist, 47*(2), 71–85.

Mandinach, E. B. (2017, January). *Data literacy for teachers: A new construct and why it is important* [Conference presentation]. Annual conference of the International Congress for School Effectiveness and Improvement, Ottawa, Ontario, Canada.

Mandinach, E. B., Bocala, C., & Perrson, H. (2017). *Findings from the new review of state licensure documents*. WestEd.

Mandinach, E. B., Friedman, J. M., & Gummer, E. S. (2015). How can schools of education help to build educators' capacity to use data: A systemic view of the issue. *Teachers College Record, 117*(4), 1–50. http://www.tcrecord.org/PrintContent.asp?ContentID=17850

Mandinach, E. B., & Gummer, E. S. (2012). *Navigating the landscape of data literacy: It IS complex*. WestEd; Education Northwest.

Mandinach, E. B., & Gummer, E. S. (2013). A systemic view of implementing data literacy into educator preparation. *Educational Researcher, 42*(1), 30–37.

Mandinach, E. B., & Gummer, E. S. (2016a). *Data literacy for educators: Making it count in teacher preparation and practice.* Teachers College Press.

Mandinach, E. B., & Gummer, E. S. (2016b). What does it mean for teachers to be data literate: Laying out the skills, knowledge, and dispositions. *Teaching and Teacher Education, 60*, 366–376.

Mandinach, E. B., & Mundry, S. E. (2021). Data-driven decision making and its alignment with educational psychology: Why data are more than student performance results. In S. L. Nichols & D. Varier (Eds.), *Teaching on Assessment* (pp. 269–291). Information Age Publishing.

Mandinach, E. B., Penuel, W. R., Shepard, L. A., Hamilton, L. S., Miller, S. R., & Gummer, E. S. (2018, April). *Data-driven decision making: Does it lack a theory of learning to inform research and practice?* [Facilitated discussion]. Annual meeting of the American Educational Research Association, New York, NY.

Mandinach, E. B., Warner, S., & Lacireno-Paquet, N. (2020, September). *Culturally responsive data literacy: Integration into practice in schools and districts* [Webinar]. Regional Educational Laboratory Mid-Atlantic. https://ies.ed.gov/ncee/edlabs/regions/midatlantic/app/Docs/Events/RELMA_culturally_responsive_data_literacy_webinar_slides_508.pdf

Mandinach, E. B., Warner, S., & Mundry, S. E. (2019, November). *Using data to promote culturally responsive teaching* [Webinar]. Regional Educational Laboratory Northeast & Islands. https://ies.ed.gov/ncee/edlabs/regions/northeast/Docs/Events/CRDL_Workshop_Sep_30_2019_508c.pdf

Mandinach, E. B., & Wayman, J. C. (2020). *Survey of curriculum: First deliverable in privacy training resources project.* WestEd.

Means, B., Padilla, C., DeBarger, A., & Bakia, M. (2009). *Implementing data-informed decision making in schools: Teacher access, supports and use.* U.S. Department of Education.

Mele, C. (2017, May 4). Student arrested after crawling into a duct to steal an exam. *The New York Times.* https://www.nytimes.com/2017/05/04/us/university-of-kentucky-stolen-test.html?searchResultPosition=4

Messick, S. J. (1989). Validity. In R. L. Linn (Ed.), *Educational measurement* (3rd ed.; pp. 13–103). Macmillan Publishing Company.

National Association of State Directors of Teacher Education and Certification. (n.d.). *Model code of ethics for educators (MCEE).* https://www.nasdtec.net/page/MCEE_Doc

National Forum on Education Statistics. (2010). *Forum guide to data ethics* (NFES 2010–801). U.S. Department of Education, National Center for Education Statistics. https://nces.ed.gov/pubs2010/2010801.pdf

National Forum on Education Statistics. (2016). *Forum guide to education data privacy* (NFES 2016–096). U.S. Department of Education, National Center for Education Statistics. https://nces.ed.gov/pubs2016/NFES2016096.pdf

National Forum on Education Statistics. (2018). *Forum guide collecting and using attendance data* (NFES 2018–007). U.S. Department of Education, National Center for Education Statistics. https://nces.ed.gov/pubs2017/NFES2017007.pdf

Nickerson, R. S. (1998). Confirmation bias: A ubiquitous phenomenon in many guises. *Review of General Psychology*, 2(2), 175–220.

Oceans of Data Institute. (2016). *Building global interest in data literacy: A dialogue* [Workshop report]. Education Development Center Oceans of Data Institute.

Perry, J. (2009). Are drastic swings in CRCT scores valid? *Atlanta Journal-Constitution*. https://www.ajc.com/news/local/are-drastic-swings-crct-scores-valid/1uNxbbiLUZjvYQx6gMkyyN

Popham, W. J. (2001). Teaching to the test? *Educational leadership*, 58(6), 16–21.

Potter, R. L., & Stefkovich, J. A. (2009). Legal dimensions of using employee and student data to make decisions. In T. K. Kowalski & T. J. Lasley II (Eds.), *Handbook of data-based decision making in education* (pp. 38–53). Routledge.

Privacy Technical Assistance Center. (n.d.). *Best practices for data destruction.* U.S. Department of Education, Privacy Technical Assistance Center. https://studentprivacy.ed.gov/sites/default/files/resource_document/file/Best%20Practices%20for%20Data%20Destruction%20%282019-3-26%29.pdf

Sadeghi, L., & Callahan, K. (2013). Shifting educational accountability from compliance to outcomes. *Public Manager*, 42(3), 62.

Schwartz, S. (2020, September 9). As teachers livestream classes, privacy issues arise. *Ed Week*, 12–13. https://www.edweek.org/ew/articles/2020/08/20/as-teachers-livestream-classes-privacy-issues-arise.html

Shulman, L. S. (1986). Those who understand: Knowledge growth in teaching. *Educational Researcher*, 15(2), 4–14.

Shulman, L. S. (1987). Knowledge and teaching: Foundations of the new reform. *Harvard Educational Review*, 57(1), 1–22.

Spiegelhalter, D. (2019). *The art of statistics: How to learn from data*. Basic Books.

Statewide Longitudinal Data Systems Grant Program. (2015). *SLDS data use standards: Knowledge, skills, and professional behaviors for effective data use (Version 2)*. U.S. Department of Education, National Center for Education Statistics.

St. George, D. (2016, February 29). Stolen computer had special-education student data on hard drive. *The Washington Post*. https://www.washingtonpost.com/local/education/stolen-computer-had-special-education-student-data-on-hard-drive/2016/02/29/040a040c-daf7-11e5-891a-4ed04f4213e8_story.html

Tsukayama, H. (2015). More than 70 companies just signed a pledge to protect student data privacy—with some notable exceptions. *The Washington Post*. https://www.washingtonpost.com/news/the-switch/wp/2015/01/12/more-than-70-companies-just-signed-a-pledge-to-protect-student-data-privacy-with-some-notable-exceptions/?arc404=true

CHAPTER 2

Turning to Data Ethics to Resolve FERPA's Modern Questions

Amelia Vance and Casey Waughn

The Family Educational Rights and Privacy Act of 1974 (FERPA) is the primary federal law that regulates student privacy. The law still governs the vast technological landscape and data collection practices that currently are commonplace in today's classrooms. When FERPA was enacted, lawmakers' primary concern was correcting the power imbalance between the data collector and the data subject. The goal of FERPA today remains the same—ensuring that student data are collected and processed fairly and ethically.

Over time, data misuses have demonstrated that although a practice may be legal, that does not mean it is ethical. For example, schools creating lists of "problem students" that are shared with all teachers, or education technology (edtech) companies using an algorithm with biased or incomplete data that recommends certain students should not take advanced courses are both legal, but not ethical.

Despite technological advancements that were unimaginable when FERPA was passed, the original foundation of information privacy and ethical principles imbued the law with flexibility, allowing it to respond to the widespread adoption of educational technology and cloud computing, and giving practitioners an ethical framework within which to deploy these technologies. By focusing on understanding FERPA's privacy and ethical principles, educators can accurately answer what the law requires, despite the challenges of fitting modern technology within its framework. This chapter gives an overview of the FERPA requirements and the related law, the Protection of Pupil Rights Amendment (PPRA), as well as an overview of FERPA's underlying principles, rooted in data ethics, which allow practitioners to understand how to ethically apply FERPA to modern questions.

A SHORT HISTORY OF FERPA

FERPA was introduced by Senator James Buckley in 1974 as arguably the first privacy law in the United States. It was enacted in the wake of Watergate during a climate of general mistrust of the government (Igo, 2018; Vance & Waughn, 2020). In 1968, the Russell Sage Foundation conducted a study surveying 68 districts about the extent to which schools maintained, used, and shared student records. One of the study's key findings was that only eight out of 54 school district superintendents indicated that their district provided parents (in this chapter, the term "parents" is inclusive of parents, guardians, and other caregivers) with access to their child's education record, while more than half of the districts surveyed indicated that law enforcement could access these records (Wheeler et al., 1976). This study sparked a public outcry on inappropriate sharing and access limitations surrounding student records.

Senator Buckley referenced several accounts of abuses when introducing FERPA, including one student who was prohibited from walking across the stage during graduation due to a record of being a "bad citizen" that neither she nor her parents knew about, with the school refusing to provide access to that record (120 Cong. Rec. 14580 at 189, reprinted from Divoky 1974). Buckley stated that "such inaccurate materials can have devastatingly negative effects on the academic future and job prospects of an innocent, unaware student" (120 Cong. Rec. 14580 at 189) and that FERPA was meant "to restore parental rights and to protect privacy" (120 Cong. Rec. 14581 at 190).

DEFINING PRIVACY IN THE CONTEXT OF FERPA

Establishing a single, concrete definition of "privacy" has eluded scholars for years, as privacy is an amorphous and evolving concept (Solove, 2008). Kaltheuner (2018) argues that "privacy was once misconstrued as being about hiding and secrecy. Now, it's understood to be something much more pressing: power dynamics between the individual, the state, and the market" (para. 4). Kaltheuner further notes that data protection "must seek to mitigate the inherent power imbalances between people—and those that collect, process and profit off their data" (para. 16).

By using this framework of privacy, it is easier to see what FERPA was trying to address: power. FERPA sought to rectify the power imbalance between schools and students by giving some of the power back to parents and students through FERPA's twin aims of *access* and *privacy*. When discussing the National Education Association's opposition to FERPA during the floor debate, Buckley noted the following:

> It is their position that as between the parent and the school official, the latter has the more fundamental right to determine whether the child should be subject to programs of behavior alteration and value modification. Beneath such a position is a very serious threat to the traditional notion long respected by this

Nation that it is the parents who are ultimately responsible for the welfare of their children. It borders on shocking that one of the national organizations representing educators would move to have the Senate oppose a reaffirmation of this important and real parental right. (120 Cong. Rec. at 14581 at 190)

Buckley recognized the importance of access to student records. Giving students or parents access to student records would serve not only as a transparency mechanism but also as a way to reduce errors, especially as many districts and at least one state had computerized their record-keeping systems (Wheeler et al., 1976). The same study that helped spur the introduction of FERPA found that without any parental access rights or consistent intra-school examination of student records in computerized record-keeping systems, any errors made would be less likely to be discovered (Wheeler et al., 1976). Buckley argued that increased access to student records would also increase parental involvement in their children's education while offsetting adverse effects students might incur by not having access, including consequences to their academic future and possible job prospects (120 Cong. Rec. 14582 at 191). To address these benefits and negate these perils, FERPA codifies several important access rights. Parents and eligible students (defined as a student who has reached 18 years of age or is attending an institution of postsecondary education) (FERPA, 34 CFR § 99) have the right to inspect and review their education records. Schools have 45 days to respond to requests to inspect and review, may not delete or destroy the relevant records while access is pending, and cannot charge an unreasonable amount of money for a parent or student to obtain these records (34 CFR § 99.10).

FERPA also aimed to give students *privacy rights*. While data were increasingly collected, stored, and shared by schools over the years leading up to FERPA's passage, schools and districts had not developed policies around responsible, privacy-preserving data practices (120 Cong. Rec. 36529). In the 1970s, the Department of Health, Education, and Welfare (1973) realized the lack of uniform policy in this area, and released a report titled, *Records, Computers, and the Rights of Citizens*, which focused largely on student data. This report resulted in a list of *Fair Information Practices* (FIPs) to guide data stewards, setting a baseline for what is fair (and ethical) regarding collecting, storing, sharing, and using data.

Today, the FIPs are still fundamental privacy principles that form the baseline for almost every information privacy law in the world (Hartzog, 2018; Igo, 2018). The FIPs provide the following:

1. There must be no personal data record-keeping systems whose very existence is secret.
2. There must be a way for a person to find out what information about the person is in a record and how it is used.

3. There must be a way for a person to prevent information about the person that was obtained for one purpose from being used or made available for other purposes without the person's consent.

4. There must be a way for a person to correct or amend a record of identifiable information about the person.

5. Any organization creating, maintaining, using, or disseminating records of identifiable personal data must ensure the reliability of the data for their intended use and must take precautions to prevent misuses of the data. (U.S. Department of Health, Education, and Welfare, 1973, pp. XX–XXI)

The FIPs ideally ensure that data stewards employ and are accountable for using ethical data practices: transparency, choice, consent, data security, data integrity, and access. With the FIPs as its foundation, FERPA aims to ensure that education data stakeholders are subject to these same ethical data practices and that students and parents are empowered with privacy rights and can hold stakeholders accountable for violations of those rights.

FERPA IN PRACTICE

Because FERPA was written with the FIPs in mind, it similarly provides a baseline ethical framework that allows flexibility in practice. This flexibility provides educational institutions latitude with which to interpret and apply the law within a common ethical framework. Many education policy decisions are made locally in the United States, and the data practices of educational institutions vary widely, so FERPA's adaptability can be useful. However, this also means that most questions about FERPA's application can be answered with the phrase, "it depends," and that understanding the law—and the interpretation of how to comply with it—can vary significantly across and within educational institutions.

FERPA allows parents (and eligible students) to exercise some amount of control over the records that an educational agency or institution keeps on their children. FERPA applies to all educational levels and the U.S. Department of Education. The law protects *personally identifiable information* (PII) maintained by institutions (or someone acting for that institution) in *education records* from unauthorized disclosure by requiring schools to gain a parent's or eligible student's consent before sharing PII, unless an exception to the consent requirement applies (34 CFR § 99). When PII in education records is shared, FERPA requires third parties that receive this information to agree not to re-disclose this information (34 CFR § 99.33).

FERPA broadly defines PII as information that is linked *or linkable* to a specific student that would allow a reasonable person in the school community to identify the student with reasonable certainty (34 CFR § 99.33).

Essentially, if the information could be linked back to an individual, it falls under FERPA's PII definition. Ostensibly, as long as student information does not meet the "linked or linkable" standard, which can mean student data in the aggregate form or when student data are sufficiently de-identified, schools may share that information without first obtaining parental consent, subject to other legal protections (such as a state student privacy law).

However, only student PII that is in an education record is protected by FERPA. *Education records* are (1) directly related to a student, and (2) maintained by an educational agency or institution, or by a party acting for the agency or institution (20 U.S.C. § 1232g; 34 CFR § 99). Educators, school volunteers, and others who work in schools are also subject to FERPA's consent requirements, meaning that they cannot share student PII from an education record unless an exception to the consent requirement applies.

FERPA's consent requirements are relatively detailed: consent forms must describe what information will be disclosed, to whom, and for what purpose (34 CFR § 99.3). However, there are a number of exceptions to FERPA's consent requirement (34 CFR § 99.4). Four of the most commonly invoked exceptions are the directory information exception, the school official exception, the studies exception, and the audit and evaluation exception.

The *directory information exception* allows schools to share certain limited information that the school designates as "directory information" each year (34 CFR § 99.3 and § 99.37). That information must "generally not be considered harmful" if disclosed to third parties, and often includes a student's name, address, email address, grade, height and weight for sports, and similar demographic information. The purpose of this exception is to allow schools to engage in routine data-sharing activities; for example, the directory information exception enables schools to share contact information with Parent-Teacher Associations, publish student-athlete performance statistics, publish the "Dean's List" in the school newspaper, or print student-actor names in playbills. Every year, schools must provide parents with the categories of information the school has chosen to designate as directory information. Schools must give parents and eligible students the opportunity to opt out of having their child's or their own directory information shared. Because parents and eligible students can opt out, and the types of directory information that can be shared are limited, this exception is generally not used to enable data use or sharing that is core to the curriculum, such as a learning management system or a reading application. An educational agency or institution may specify that disclosure of directory information will be limited to specific parties, for specific purposes, or both.

When schools share student data with internal staff, such as teachers, or external third parties, such as edtech companies, the data are usually shared through FERPA's *school official exception* (34 CFR § 99.1(a)(1) and

§ 99.33(a)), allowing student data to be shared with an edtech company *without consent* if the following are true:

- The edtech company is doing something that the school would use internal staff for.
- The company has a "legitimate educational interest," which can be loosely defined as the company needing that specific student PII from the school to provide the educational service. The school should only give companies access to the information the company needs to do whatever the school has contracted with them to do.
- The data can only be collected, used, and shared by the company for the original purpose it was collected for.
- The company has to be under the "direct control" of the school when it comes to the use and maintenance of student information.

"Direct control" is not defined under FERPA, but U.S. Department of Education (2016) guidance provides several indicators of when direct control might not exist, such as a privacy policy where the company retains the right to share information with partners or may use student data to market or advertise to students. When disclosing PII from education records to external third parties under the school official exception, schools should be mindful of FERPA's provisions governing parents' (and eligible students') right to inspect and review their education records. This exception is one of the places where the FIPs and data ethics principles are most evident in FERPA: The requirement that data must only be collected, used, and shared for the original purpose mirrors the "secondary use" principle in FIPs, and the requirement that the company has a "legitimate educational interest" when data are shared with the company is in line with the FIPs principle that precautions are taken to prevent misuses of data.

Under FERPA's *audit and evaluation exception* (34 CFR § 99.1(a)(3) and § 99.35), federal, state, and local officials, or their authorized representatives, can access education records in connection with an audit or evaluation of federal- or state-supported education programs or for the enforcement of, or compliance with, federal requirements related to those programs. The exception requires a written agreement that clearly describes the purpose of the data sharing, prevents further disclosure and unauthorized use, and provides a level of accountability.

The *studies exception* (34 CFR § 99.1(a)(6)) allows student PII from education records to be disclosed for certain studies conducted for or on behalf of schools, school districts, or postsecondary institutions. The studies must be for the purpose of developing, validating, or administering predictive tests, administering student aid programs, or improving instruction. The studies exception also requires a written agreement that specifies the purpose, scope, and duration of the study and the information to be disclosed, and it requires the third party to limit access to those with legitimate interests and to destroy PII upon completion of the study.

It is important to note that most of these exceptions are *may*, not *must* exceptions, meaning that an education agency *may* share PII from an education record without consent if an exception applies but is not *required* to. There are several other less frequently used exceptions under FERPA where student PII can be shared without consent, such as disclosure to deal with health and safety emergencies (34 CFR § 99.1(a)(10)). To learn more about FERPA's exceptions, see the Department of Education's student privacy website at https://studentprivacy.ed.gov.

PROTECTION OF PUPIL RIGHTS AMENDMENT

Another related federal student privacy law, mentioned earlier, the Protection of Pupil Rights Amendment (PPRA) (20 U.S.C. § 1232h; 34 CFR § 98), was initially introduced as a part of FERPA, though it was later excluded (120 Cong. Rec. 14579–80). PPRA was revisited and passed 4 years after FERPA's initial introduction when Senator Orrin Hatch introduced it as part of the Education Amendments of 1978. Its legislative history indicates that parents were concerned about their children's privacy and worried their children were being brainwashed by invasive surveys and psychological tests being administered in schools (Greene & Pasch, 1985). Similar to FERPA, giving parents control and power over the types of sensitive information collected from students was at the heart of the rationale for PPRA (120 Cong. Rec. at 14580 and 14586). Therefore, PPRA works in tandem with FERPA to provide substantive protection for student privacy by giving parents specific rights regarding data collected through surveys, evaluations, and similar assessments. However, unlike FERPA, PPRA only applies to elementary and secondary schools.

PPRA requires that schools obtain written consent from parents before K–12 students are required to participate in any U.S. Department of Education funded survey, analysis, or evaluation that reveals information concerning the following areas:

1. Political affiliations;
2. Mental and psychological problems potentially embarrassing to the student and his/her family;
3. Sex behavior and attitudes;
4. Illegal, anti-social, self-incriminating, and demeaning behavior;
5. Critical appraisals of other individuals with whom respondents have close family relationships;
6. Legally recognized privileged or analogous relationships, such as those of lawyers, physicians, and ministers;

7. Religious practices, affiliations, or beliefs of the student or student's parent; or
8. Income (other than that required by law to determine eligibility for participation in a program or for receiving financial assistance under such program). (20 U.S. Code § 1232h)

Local education agencies are required to develop and adopt policies related to PPRA in consultation with parents (20 U.S.C. § 1232h(c)(1)). They must also provide notice to parents and eligible students of their PPRA rights and obtain consent or offer the right to opt out in certain circumstances (20 U.S.C. § 1232h(b)). Table 2.1 explicates the conditions when parental opportunity to opt in or opt out is required under PPRA.

PPRA also places limits on how personal information collected from surveys is used, including a requirement that schools develop policies to protect student privacy when sharing data for marketing purposes. However, PPRA does contain a broad exception to this requirement when the information is collected, disclosed, or used for the "exclusive purpose" of developing or providing educational products or services (20 U.S.C. § 1232h(c)(4)(A)). This exception raises ethical concerns about the monetization of student survey information and is arguably at odds with the FIPs principle discouraging secondary use that a person does not directly consent to. Schools should consider the PPRA's requirement to develop and adopt local policies, in consultation with parents, as an opportunity to manage this risk and integrate ethical data practices into its PPRA compliance. Although not required by PPRA, schools may choose to regularly review their existing PPRA-mandated policies based on changing technologies, norms, and

Table 2.1. When is parental opt in or opt out required under PPRA?

Student Participation Required	Covers Eight Protected Categories	Opt In/Opt Out
Yes	Yes	Provide notice and parents must opt in for the student to take the survey.
Yes	No	Provide notice and parents have the right to opt out.
No	Yes	Provide notice and parents have the right to opt out (but check your specific state law first).
No	No	Provide notice only if the survey was created by a third party. In that case, parents have the right to opt out.

Source: Sallay and Vance, 2020.

parent input. This is consistent with the FIPs, which include that data stewards should be transparent; provide notice and choice; and ensure that data is accurate, reliable, and not misused.

BEYOND THE LAW: STUDENT PRIVACY AND DATA ETHICS

The U.S. Department of Education (2014) released best practices outlining considerations for schools when using online educational services. Although these best practices succeed the FIPs by more than 50 years, many of the FIPs key principles regarding data ethics are embodied in these best practices, underscoring the important role that data ethics continues to play in federal guidance (U.S. Department of Education, 2014). The best practices include the following:

1. Maintain awareness of other relevant federal, state, tribal, or local laws.
2. Be aware of which online educational services are currently being used in your district.
3. Have policies and procedures to evaluate and approve proposed online educational services.
4. When possible, use a written contract or legal agreement, and be aware that extra steps are necessary when accepting click-wrap licenses for consumer apps.
5. Be transparent with parents and students.
6. Consider when parental consent may be appropriate.

When schools consistently apply these practices, they support notice and choice, as well as transparency and limits on data use, collection, sharing, and misuse.

It is essential for practitioners to zoom out and understand the historical context and intent behind FERPA and PPRA. In doing so, they will be better equipped to collect, use, and share student data ethically. A myopic view of these laws can lead to fear or paralysis, which may result in either forgoing beneficial data use, sharing because of low-risk privacy concerns, or, on the other hand, sharing data unnecessarily in a way that could be harmful. An understanding of the foundational principles behind the laws can empower education stakeholders to assess each situation through the lens of data ethics and provide new protections or safeguards beyond the law to ensure that student privacy is protected as technology evolves.

FERPA is far from perfect; it could use reorganization to bring clarity, and new or expanded definitions, to better address 21st-century questions, such as when class video recordings become part of an education record. But average education practitioners do not need to wait for that update or become an expert in FERPA or PPRA, and how to collect, use, and share student data ethically. Instead, data ethics best practices, such as FIPs and its many updated iterations, may be easier to understand and apply to daily work (Gellman, 2019).

REFERENCES

120 Cong. Rec., 36529. (1974). Reprinted from Divoky, D. (1974). Cumulative Records: Assault on Privacy. *Learning*, 2(1), 18–23.

120 Cong. Rec., 14579–14595. (1974, May 14). https://www.govinfo.gov/content/pkg/GPO-CRECB-1974-pt11/pdf/GPO-CRECB-1974-pt11-3.pdf

120 Cong. Rec., 14580. (1974, May 14). Reprinted from Divoky, D. (1974, March). How secret records can hurt your child. *Parade Magazine*, 4–5. https://www.govinfo.gov/content/pkg/GPO-CRECB-1974-pt11/pdf/GPO-CRECB-1974-pt11-3.pdf

20 U.S.C. § 1232g; 34 CFR §§ 99.1–99.67. Family Education Rights and Privacy. https://www.law.cornell.edu/cfr/text/34/part-99

20 U.S.C. § 1232h; 34 CFR § 98. Protection of Pupil Rights. Student rights in research, experimental programs, and testing. https://www.law.cornell.edu/cfr/text/34/part-98

Gellman, R. (2019). *Fair information practices: A basic history* (version 2.19). https://bobgellman.com/rg-docs/rg-FIPshistory.pdf

Greene, B. I., & Pasch, M. (1985). *Observing the birth of the Hatch Amendment regulations: Lessons for the education profession*. Association for Supervision and Curriculum Development. http://www.ascd.org/ASCD/pdf/journals/ed_lead/el_198512_greene.pdf

Hartzog, W. (2018). *Privacy's blueprint: The battle to control the design of new technologies*. Harvard University Press.

Igo, E. S. (2018). *The known citizen: A history of privacy in modern America*. Harvard University Press.

Kaltheuner, F. (2018, May 27). Privacy is power. *Politico* [Editorial]. https://www.politico.eu/article/privacy-is-power-opinion-data-gdpr

Sallay, D., & Vance, A. (2020, March 27). *FAQs: The Protection of Pupil Rights Amendment*. Student Privacy Compass. https://studentprivacycompass.org/faqs-ppra

Solove, D. (2008). *Understanding privacy*. Harvard University Press.

U.S. Department of Education. (2014, February). *Protecting student privacy while using online educational services: Requirements and best practices*. Privacy Technical Assistance Center. https://studentprivacy.ed.gov/sites/default/files/resource_document/file/Student%20Privacy%20and%20Online%20Educational%20Services%20%28February%202014%29_0.pdf

U.S. Department of Education. (2016, May). *Protecting student privacy while using online educational services: Model terms of service*. Privacy Technical Assistance

Center.   https://studentprivacy.ed.gov/sites/default/files/resource_document/file
/TOS_Guidance_Mar2016.pdf

U.S. Department of Health, Education, and Welfare. (1973). *Records, computers, and the rights of citizens.* https://www.justice.gov/opcl/docs/rec-com-rights.pdf

Vance, A., & Waughn, C. (2020). Student privacy's history of unintended consequences. *Seton Hall Legislative Journal, 44*(3). https://scholarship.shu.edu/shlj/vol44/iss3/4

Wheeler, S., Goslin, D. A., & Bordier, N. (1976). Record-keeping in elementary and secondary schools. In S. Wheeler (Ed.), *On record: Files and dossiers in American life* (pp. 29–65). Transaction Books.

CHAPTER 3

Policies That Promote Student Data Privacy and Teacher Data Literacy Are Essential for Ethical Data Use

Brennan McMahon Parton and Taryn A. Hochleitner

INTRODUCTION

Ethical data use in education is "using information with professionalism and integrity, for intended uses only, and with consciousness of the need to protect students' privacy" (Data Quality Campaign [DQC], 2014, p. 6). As data use in education spreads, it is imperative that educators understand their responsibility and know how to use their students' data ethically. This will require policies, practices, training, leadership, and will.

As educators seek to use data to improve student outcomes, there is an ongoing national conversation about the privacy and security of all types of data, from social media to elections. Education efforts to collect and use data are not insulated from public and policymaker awareness regarding how much individual data are collected and the need to maintain privacy and security. Keeping data private is just part of effective and ethical use, but it is related to how people inside and outside of education perceive the use and value of data.

Increased education data use requires crafting new policies and practices as well as updating existing ones designed to ensure that student information is kept private and secure. Even the most well-written policy cannot ensure that information will be used *ethically*. Policy guardrails for how data should be kept private and secure are a starting point and must be put into place. But efforts to protect student data cannot stop there and must extend into standards for ethical data use and the training to be good stewards of data.

Ethical data use stands alone as a set of skills and mindsets all educators need. Teachers should not be left to guess which are appropriate uses of data; they need preservice and career-long training and support regarding effective and ethical data use (National Association of State Directors of Teacher Education and Certification, n.d.). State policy should provide mandates and incentivize training. Increased public and policymaker scrutiny on how student data are used has thrust teacher data use into the center of the conversation. A 2014 Louisiana bill[1] included civil financial penalties and even jail time for anyone, including teachers, inappropriately disclosing students' information. Actions like this make ethical data use not only good practice, but essential practice.

We discuss the ways in which nearly every state in the nation has sought to use legislation to keep students' information private and secure within an evolving ecosystem of data use in schools. We describe other policies and practices, including educator data literacy and meaningful communication, that are needed to build trust and contribute to a culture of ethical data use.

DATA PRIVACY CONCERNS AND PUBLIC UNDERSTANDING OF DATA IN EDUCATION

Data and Technology Are Part of Daily Classroom Life

Data use has become widespread in K–12 public education. As data use has grown, so too has public awareness of the use and the vulnerability of data. Parents try to do their best for their children in an era when it is not uncommon for national headlines to publicize data breaches of sensitive information. Schools have not been spared. Schools have occasionally been the target of "ransom" scams (Bogel-Burroughs, 2019), contributing to concerns over the ways in which students' information may do harm.

Further, technology is more prevalent in classrooms and schools. Millions of children and their parents have had to go virtual during the pandemic. While many schools were already employing apps and online learning tools, teachers, students, and families have become dependent on videoconferences and online learning applications. Using technology in education has expanded the amount and types of data that are collected; the actors who may have access to student information; and the potential for and perception of unethical use. Acknowledging this, the Consortium of School Networking (CoSN, 2019) released *Trusted Learning from the Ground Up: Fundamental Data Policies and Procedures*, to help districts take stock of their data governance, privacy, and security policies. Though geared toward helping districts create trusted online learning environments, the checklist goes further than just districts' relationships with technology vendors. CoSN details *data governance* practices and those related to students' social media. This demonstrates how intertwined data use and technology have become and the need for good, baseline practices that help educators better understand their roles and responsibilities with student data. As technology has changed, new risks and legitimate concerns are on the minds of parents, educators, and the public.

Data use is not new, having always been part of education. At the state level, investments in the statewide longitudinal data systems (SLDS) infrastructure are more than a decade old, with many states innovating on those systems and providing new and evolving services to educators and the public. Georgia teachers have access to students' longitudinal records and daily information generated at the classroom level (DQC, 2013). Teachers have data that make it possible for them to identify students' academic strengths and areas for improvement. They can access teacher-rated instructional resources to help meet their students' needs. High school teachers can see where their students went after graduation. Rich, contextual detail that supports teachers in their practice is available in just a few clicks from one dashboard.

This type of innovation has promise for helping teachers use data. But even as the use of classroom technology has grown, parents often do not have access to tools that give them easy access to students' data. And while state leaders have spent years investing in building data systems, the public has been unaware of these investments and about how the role of data is changing in education.

State Data Collection Enters the Spotlight

The creation of the inBloom educational technology initiative to provide open-source software for data collection highlighted education data issues. InBloom was capable of collecting and analyzing data to provide information on student progress. The promise of inBloom was evident to those aware of the value of data and who had been working on improving data use.

As families and advocates became aware of the amount of information that was being collected about students in schools, the announcement of inBloom quickly sparked a public backlash. Meanwhile, state agencies had not done the work to ensure that the public could easily find basic facts about student data collection, use, and protection. This lack of transparency was a glaring oversight that raised concerns that privacy had been at best an afterthought in the desire to use data and technology in education.

The rise and fall of inBloom exposed the lack of attention to ensuring that the public understood the role of educational data. It stimulated a nationwide conversation about how data should be used and protected. Most state and district leaders could only point to the Family Educational Rights and Privacy Act (FERPA), governing students' data privacy. Many saw FERPA as outdated and insufficient for a modern world (DQC, 2015).

Two clear lessons emerged: People outside of state agencies need more transparency and clarity about how student information is used for their education; and policy change is needed to account for evolving data practices in modern classrooms.

Policymakers Act

The growing concern about data use influenced state legislatures. In 2014, 36 states introduced 110 bills resulting in 27 new laws addressing data privacy. By comparison, just one state acted on student data privacy in 2013. In their initial efforts to address fears and demands for action, legislators focused on limiting the scope of data collection and use. Some bills attempted to respond to acute concerns that were bubbling up from advocates, such as the collection of biometric data. Others were unsuccessful, as in Mississippi, which attempted to defund and eradicate the state education data system. Most states took a measured approach, with the strongest bills setting up clear data governance policies and establishing a state chief privacy officer.

In addition to creating guardrails for data collected by state agencies, another focus was how vendors could access and use student data. At the end of 2014, California enacted the first and most significant state law governing the activities of service providers' use of student data. The *Student Online Personal Information Protection Act* prohibited education service providers from using student data for targeted advertising or marketing, and from selling data. This law signaled a shift in the state policy toward addressing when and how information is shared with third parties. Other states soon followed, introducing laws that drew identical language from California. In 2015, 47 states introduced 188 bills resulting in 28 new laws addressing data privacy.

By 2016, the number of new laws passed decreased (112 bills resulted in 19 new laws in 15 states) as states implemented the privacy protections passed in recent years and began to grapple with implementing the Every Student Succeeds Act (ESSA). Even as the number of bills introduced decreased, 36 states had passed a data privacy law. As discussed in the next section, efforts to pass a bipartisan bill at the federal level that would provide similar protections on a national scale were ultimately unsuccessful, leaving states to create and implement their own patchwork of laws to govern service providers (Harold, 2015).

How State Legislators Sought to Tackle Student Data Privacy

Privacy conversations driving state policy change have evolved, but the themes have been consistent since 2014. Because the approach to privacy and security policies were so nascent, states emulated their peers. Policymakers were concerned with who should make decisions about how data are used, collected, and shared, as well as how to increase transparency about these processes. Mainly, legislators have aimed to govern the way states and districts collect, use, and communicate data, and to limit the activities of third-party vendors.

Key Themes in State Student Data Privacy Policies

Data Governance. The strongest approach to managing student data privacy is to establish a body and processes for decision-making about data. Some bills required the establishment of a chief privacy officer to lead data privacy efforts in state departments of education. New York was the first to do this. Legislation can be effective for ensuring that data governance has resources to be effective (DQC, 2018b).

Role of Service Providers. Governing the role of vendors became the thorniest challenge for policymakers. In 2014, California passed the first state law governing such activities. The key elements prohibit vendors from using student data for targeted advertising and from marketing or selling student data. Since 2014, 100 states have considered bills that have these provisions, and 25 states have enacted laws.

Parental Consent. Parents were the most important stakeholders omitted from conversations about the collection and use of students' data, and therefore their role became a key theme in legislation. Some states introduced bills to give parents "opt out" power to keep their students' information from being included in data collection. Others asked for parental notification and consent for data collection, particularly for data collected by vendors.

Transparency. Another tack that state legislators took to address privacy concerns was to make more information available about how data are used and protected. Bills offered provisions such as the publishing of education data dictionaries online and annual reports to the legislature about implementation of privacy policies.

Federal Policymakers Respond

Members of Congress responded to privacy concerns by holding hearings and introducing several new bills in 2015. The most significant attempts to legislate were bipartisan and far reaching in scope. Senators Edward Markey (D-MA) and Orrin Hatch (R-UT) were first to offer a bill to amend FERPA, followed quickly by Representatives Luke Messer (R-IN) and Jared Polis (D-CO) introducing the Student Digital Privacy and Parental Rights Act (SDPPRA). The bill was supported by a coalition of organizations but ultimately did not move past introduction. In public statements, supporters applauded legislative provisions that would protect students' privacy while ensuring that educators and families could still use data and education technology to improve outcomes. Representative Polis stated during a conference panel discussion, "Our bipartisan bill is a much needed first step in providing a framework that can address these concerns of parents and educators while at the same time allowing for the promise of education technology to transform our schools" (Messer & Polis, 2016). At the same time, Senators Richard Blumenthal (D-CT) and Steve Daines (R-MT) introduced the SAFE KIDS Act with similar provisions to the Polis/Messer bill. Representatives Marcia Fudge (D-OH) and Todd Rokita (R-IN) introduced an amendment to FERPA to essentially rewrite the law to reflect the data realities of the 21st century.

To date, none of these attempts have resulted in changes to federal law. There were attempts to include privacy provisions in ESSA when it was passed with bipartisan support in 2015; however, all but one failed in conference.

Taking Stock of Legislative Efforts to Protect Student Privacy

A New Legal Landscape. Between 2014 and 2019, every state considered data privacy legislation, with 45 states enacting 130 new laws (see Table 3.1 and Figures 3.1 and 3.2). While there was significant momentum in 2014 and 2015, with almost half of those 130 bills being signed into law in those 2 years, protecting students' information has remained a legislative priority. While in the initial years, the focus of student data privacy legislation was almost uniform, in recent years, the conversation has diverged as state legislators have focused on making amendments to existing laws; ensuring policies are adapted to local contexts; and, in those states that still have not passed modern student data privacy laws, working to get them enacted for

Figure 3.1. Number of State Student Data Privacy Laws Enacted

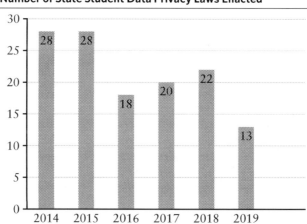

Figure 3.2. State Student Data Privacy Legislation, 2014–2020

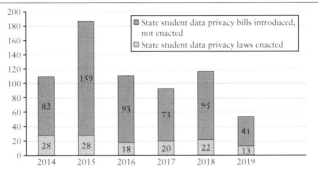

the first time. While the sheer volume of student data privacy bills introduced has decreased, this issue is evergreen for legislators who have continued to introduce student data privacy legislation during the 2020 sessions[2] (DQC, 2020).

The impact of these laws is largely unknown as states and districts work on the realities of implementation. Some laws served to codify existing practices in state education agencies, ensuring that data governance and privacy practices would endure beyond leadership changes and creating a precedent. The most important impact was demonstrating that a state acted in response to public conversation about the role of education data.

Why Data Governance? The strongest approach to managing data privacy is to establish processes for decision-making called *data governance*. Data governance policies create the "rules of the road" for those who collect, access, and use data and should be inclusive of the rules for privacy and security. The best legislation ensures that agencies have the resources to effectively protect and improve the state's data systems. Rather than one-offs that may result in ad hoc approaches to data collection and create a cobweb of compliance exercises, codifying data governance creates a clear mandate for agency leaders to prioritize the "hygiene" of their data systems. According to the National Center for Education Statistics (2020):

Data governance is crucial to the effective and safe management, use, analysis, and communication of education data. It includes:

- establishing responsibility for individual data elements, datasets, and databases;
- continuously improving data systems through the development and enforcement of policies, roles, responsibilities, and procedures;
- clarifying procedures and best practices for both internal and external access to data: that is, how data will be communicated between individuals within

the agency, but also how data may be shared with researchers, other governmental agencies, policymakers, or outside stakeholders; and

• *Specifying rules and expectations related to data privacy and security* [emphasis added]. (p. 1)

Building and sustaining intra-agency data governance policies for state education agencies is essential—those agencies are charged to be the stewards of student information. Leading states, such as Kentucky, Maryland, and Washington, mandated cross-agency governance to collectively determine use cases, practices, and procedures for the state's cross-agency data system (DQC, 2018a).

While these bodies rarely interact with educators, their work is important for building a foundation of quality, well-managed data that can be trusted and used. Data governance provides state agencies with a structure in which to define the roles and responsibilities needed to ensure clear processes for collecting and reporting data and to ensure accountability for data quality and security. Recent data privacy laws required greater transparency about the types of data that are collected and how they are kept secure with well-defined data governance bodies, practices, and procedures. State leaders can think broadly about data governance as a base on which to build the relationships and trust needed to securely share data within and across agencies.

Ethical Data Use Goes Beyond Student Data Privacy Guardrails

Educator Data Literacy Is Critical. For the education data to be used to support student learning and to advance equity, teachers must be equipped with the needed skills. Data literacy includes knowing how to distinguish between data sources and their purposes, being able to analyze and interpret data, and being able to use information *ethically* (DQC, 2014). Data literate educators use data with integrity, only for intended uses, and with an understanding of the need to protect privacy.

Often, concerns over data use extend beyond the legally inappropriate uses to those that give one the feeling that something is *not quite right*. Beyond understanding their responsibility to uphold FERPA and other state policies, teachers must navigate the delicate balance of using data to understand students' strengths, limitations, and opportunities without doing them academic harm. Such knowledge includes how and when to discuss students' performance, behavior, attitudes, and so on with other teachers, administrators, and parents. It also includes knowing how to remove identifying information from a student record and how to maintain proper student records. It includes knowing who has access to student records and when, how, and by what process to release data or results. Responsible data use also includes knowing when and when not to discuss a student's performance in public or online. Table 3.1 is adapted from Mandinach and colleagues (2015).

Table 3.1. Examples of Ethical Educator Data Use: Good Practice and Things to Avoid

Good Data Use Practices	Data Use Practices to Avoid
• Using data to differentiate instruction and group students to support learning and drive equitable outcomes	• Using a student's information to predetermine their ability to succeed, and in particularly labeling them as unable to achieve
• Using physical and electronic data tools, such as data walls, applications, or spreadsheets, to organize and clearly understand student data • Using data tools to talk to other teachers about what data show and problems of practice • Leaving physical and electronic tools that contain student identifiers along with their performance and other data where only teachers and school leaders can access them • Removing student identifiers from physical tools	• Placing physical and electronic data tools with student names and other clear identifiers in classrooms or common spaces where anyone who comes into the room can see them
• Discussing student data at school in collaboration with other colleagues to set goals and identify problems of practice	• Talking about an individual student's success or challenges in public
• Using student artifacts (i.e., classroom assignments, homework, assessments of all types) with other educators for collaboration in order to improve practice and instruction	• Sharing student artifacts outside of an education setting, such as on a social media site (e.g., Pinterest, Facebook, or Twitter)
• Communicating about an individual student's data with the child's parent or guardian	• Dismissing or ignoring parents' requests for student data, or ignoring concerns about how a student's information is being used
• Using only secure technological systems to upload and manipulate students' personally identifiable information, such as those approved and provided by the state or district	• Storing or manipulating student data through online applications that are not secure

State policies and practices, including teacher preparation, licensure, and evaluation, should be used to signal to preparation programs and districts that teachers must be equipped with the data literacy skills needed to use data effectively. Although ensuring that teachers have these skills is critical, few are getting the needed training. According to analysis conducted by Mandinach and colleagues (2017) for DQC, 41 states include at least some requirements for data use skills in teacher licensure policies. But in the DQC's (2019) national teacher poll, 45% of teachers report teaching themselves to use data on the job, and only 17% report learning how to use data in preservice training. This ad hoc, teacher-driven training represents a critical gap in ensuring ethical data use.

While teachers cannot be expected to be experts in data system security, they do need a clear understanding of their role in protecting students' privacy. Teachers report[3] to the Data Quality Campaign in annual focus groups that their schools or districts provide FERPA training. Teachers often discuss small practices that are meant to keep them in compliance with FERPA, such as never using students' full names in an email. These focus groups do not provide a comprehensive picture of the types of training that teachers receive. But they provide an anecdotal sense that districts are, at least, providing an overview of FERPA and how to comply. These practices are important, but likely do not go far enough in helping teachers understand all the nuances and requirements of keeping information private and secure while also using it for instruction, nor do they provide an understanding of how to act as ethical data users.

To date, state policies have not addressed the needs of teachers to understand the interconnectedness between how to use data to inform instruction and how to be ethical stewards of information. System leaders have yet to carve out a clear set of policies or practices to ensure that teachers receive career-long training on data literacy, including keeping information private and using it ethically and effectively. Not only does policy and practice need to change but also culture within preparation programs and districts to examine the complex role teachers have in using and protecting education data.

State Leaders Should Communicate With and About Data. The public cannot be expected to support policies and practices that they do not understand or, worse, fear will cause children harm. Those who raised the alarm about student data use often "won" the conversation, sometimes with misinformation. Vocal advocates kept students—and the potential harm misuse of data could cause them—at the center of their messages, while state agency leaders often cited FERPA and data dictionaries in their efforts to respond to and assuage concerns.

Now that almost every state has had a public conversation about protecting students' data via the legislative process, leaders must be proactive in communicating about how information is collected, secured, and used. State leaders must go further to build trust not only in the processes for administering student data but also in the information and what it says about student outcomes. Too often, state leaders and staff within agencies are hesitant to talk about what the data are showing or how they may be using data without careful consideration of the narrative that the information conveys. Several things may play into this: risk aversion, lack of incentive to release information beyond compliance with what is required, or lack of capacity to analyze and communicate data beyond what is required. But having a more honest conversation about the ways state leaders within the K–12 state education agencies, as well as in higher education agencies and even governors' offices, use data to create narratives of student and school success is also essential to creating a culture of ethical data use. Leaders can and should use their bully pulpit to highlight the value of data to inform improvement and advance equity.

State leaders must consider three realities as they seek to be more transparent about how data are used in education[4] (DQC, 2021).

Data reflect a series of decisions made by people.

- Data are often considered cold facts, but in practice, the numbers that are presented about students and schools reflect a series of decisions made by someone at the school, district, or state level. At each step in the process, a group or individual makes decisions about how to collect information, and what "counts" for the purposes of the collection. State leaders must examine these decisions and what implications they may have on the way data are used.

Data do not create meaning; people create meaning.

- Data can be used to confirm existing narratives instead of used to objectively inform. Leaders have a responsibility to examine the narratives they are constructing using data, particularly if that information is being used to mask a critical opportunity or weakness that could improve outcomes for students.

Data use promotes quality.

- Often, state leaders who are tasked with data collection and quality can be overly cautious about releasing information because of concerns over how the broader public will understand the information. But when data are shared with the public, stakeholders such as school leaders, advocates, and even the media have a vital role to play in the auditing process—identifying errors and missed opportunities—and, ultimately, in promoting and demanding data quality. Leaders must pursue policies and practices that foster data quality, protect student privacy, *and* improve and increase transparency.

CONCLUSION

Everyone who has a stake in education—especially families and educators—needs the right[5] data in the right format at the right time to serve students along their unique journeys. A tremendous amount of time, process, compliance, and financial and human capital resources go into making that possible. And even as states have invested resources in improving and increasing data collection and use, its promise has not been fully met. Parents and students themselves rarely, if ever, are able to see their own students' day-to-day information along with longitudinal trends. As states and districts seek to change this landscape, they should build the infrastructure side by side with the culture—trust in data goes hand in hand with trust in the user.

How can that be achieved? Privacy policies, teachers who use data ethically and effectively, and clear and constant communication. This straightforward combination for embedding ethical data use into education to support student success is not easy to achieve. Leaders must *continuously* use the policy and practice levers to contribute to changing the culture of data in education from one in which data are widely available but underused, into one where data are considered a trusted tool to improve student outcomes and advance equity. Legislators and state education agency leaders are among the actors who have a critical role to play in making that possible.

Policy cannot do everything needed to ensure ethical data use at the classroom level, but it can and *must* be used to create essential guardrails for promoting data quality, privacy, and security, as well as to send signals to the field about the knowledge, skills, and habits of mind educators need to use data effectively and ethically. State leaders must do the following:

- *Sustain quality intra- and cross-agency data governance policies.* Legislation can provide the mandate and the financial and human capital resources that make data governance possible. Data governance promotes data quality, provides for student privacy, and serves as a means to greater transparency about data collection and use.
- *Use available policy levers to promote data literacy.* Data literate educators know how to use data ethically and effectively. State

policymakers can use legislation, regulation, accountability, and incentive to promote career-long data literacy training.

- *Communicate.* Leaders should learn the lessons of the debate about student data privacy. Keeping information about data collection, protection, access, and use does not still the waters, but rather delays the storm. Leaders should communicate with and about data.

NOTES

1. Louisiana Revised Statute, 2014, https://law.justia.com/codes/louisiana/2019/revised-statutes/title-17/rs-3914/.

2. Legislatures were still in session as we drafted this chapter. For details of student data privacy bills introduced and passed into law during the 2020 legislative sessions, see https://dataqualitycampaign.org/resource/education-data-legislation-review-2020-state-activity/.

3. Since 2014, DQC has conducted annual focus groups of 10–12 teachers in three cities across the country. We do not publicly release the direct findings from these focus groups, but this is reflective of the trends we have seen across groups.

4. DQC developed this framework, which will be included in a forthcoming release titled *The Consumer's Guide to Data* in response to increasing mistrust in evidence in data following the 2016 election cycle.

5. We could certainly write another chapter on what "right" means. For these purposes, we define "right" as information that is timely, useful, and tailored to the stakeholder's need.

REFERENCES

Bogel-Burroughs, N. (2019, July 28). Hackers' latest target: School districts. *The New York Times.* https://www.nytimes.com/2019/07/28/us/hacker-school-cybersecurity.html%20%3chttps:/www.nytimes.com/2019/07/28/us/hacker-school-cybersecurity.html

Consortium of School Networking. (2019). *Trusted learning from the ground up: Fundamental data governance policies and procedures.* Author. https://www.cosn.org/sites/default/files/TLE%20Data%20Governance%20Policies%20and%20Procedures%20Checklist.pdf

Data Quality Campaign. (2013). *Georgia information tunnel linking district ingenuity with state resources to make data matter.* https://dataqualitycampaign.org/resource/georgia-information-tunnel-linking-district-ingenuity-state-resources-make-data-matter/

Data Quality Campaign. (2014). *Data literacy: It's about time.* https://dataqualitycampaign.org/resource/teacher-data-literacy-time/

Data Quality Campaign. (2015). *The federal role in safeguarding student data.* https://dataqualitycampaign.org/resource/federal-role-safeguarding-student-data/

Data Quality Campaign. (2018a). *The art of the possible. Data governance lessons learned from Kentucky, Maryland, and Washington.* https://dataqualitycampaign.org/resource/art-of-the-possible-data-governance-lessons-learned/

Data Quality Campaign. (2018b). *Roadmap from cross-agency data governance.* https://dataqualitycampaign.org/resource/roadmap-cross-agency-data-governance/

Data Quality Campaign. (2019). *Parent and teacher opinions of education data.* https://dataqualitycampaign.org/resource/parent-and-teacher-opinions-of-education-data/

Data Quality Campaign. (2020). *Education data legislation review: 2020 state activity.* https://dataqualitycampaign.org/resource/education-data-legislation-review-2020-state-activity/

Data Quality Campaign. (2021, June). *The consumer's guide to data.* https://dataqualitycampaign.org/wp-content/uploads/2021/06/DQC-Consumers-Guide-to-Data.pdf

Harold, B. (2015, April 29). Messer-Polis data privacy bill endorsed by educator groups: Industry wary. *Education Week.* http://blogs.edweek.org/edweek/DigitalEducation/2015/04/messer-polis_data_privacy_bill_reaction.html

Mandinach, E. B., Bocala, C., & Perrson, H. (2017). *Findings from the new review of state licensure documents.* WestEd.

Mandinach, E. B., Parton, B. M., Gummer, E. S., & Anderson, R. B. (2015, February). Ethical and appropriate data use requires data literacy. *Phi Delta Kappan,* 96(5), 25–28.

Messer, L., & Polis, J. (2016, April). *Build a supportive federal framework for student success.* Data Quality Campaign's Time to Act: Making Data Work for Students conference [Panel discussion]. Washington, DC.

National Association of State Directors of Teacher Education and Certification. (n.d.). *Model code of ethics for educators.* https://www.nasdtec.net/page/MCEE_Doc#Principle%203

National Center for Education Statistics. (2020). *Forum guide to data governance* (NFES 2020–083). U.S. Department of Education, National Center for Education Statistics. https://nces.ed.gov/pubs2020/NFES2020083.pdf

CHAPTER 4

Educational Policy Contexts and the (Un)ethical Use of Data

Sharon L. Nichols

Being awash in data is nothing new to educators. As long as we have had classroom instruction and teachers who care about what students learn, how fast they learn it, and how deeply, we have had mechanisms for measuring those outcomes. Over the past century, technological advances have paved the way for the proliferation of increasingly sophisticated and diverse measurement tools (Banta et al., 2002), leaving 21st-century educators and administrators steeped in data in a variety of forms and for different purposes.

We have data for quantifying students' behavior (absenteeism, truancy), social conditions (poverty, family characteristics), personal characteristics (race, gender, age, disposition/attitude surveys), and achievement. In the achievement category, numerous forms of data are available. In classrooms, teachers grade students' work (e.g., homework, tests, classroom projects) that yields information to help teachers evaluate students' progress and assign end-of-course grades. Although classroom-level graded work might not fit the typical idea of data, it is still information that is used to make decisions about students (e.g., Mandinach & Gummer, 2016; Nichols & Varier, 2021). There are also district-level standardized exams (benchmark assessments) that provide data to teachers to help them understand how well a student may be grasping the curriculum (or how well the teachers are covering the curriculum) as well as how their students' learning compares to their peers in other classes and schools. And, since at least 2002 (and for some states even earlier), all states also collect annual standardized achievement test data used to gauge (and compare) how students are progressing on curriculum standards in every grade and subject across the state. We also have national and international assessments available to educators and policymakers for making education admissions decisions (e.g., SAT since 1926 and Advanced Placement [AP] since 1954) and for gauging American students' progress against international peers (e.g., Programme for International Student Assessment [PISA] since 2000; Progress in International Reading Literacy Study [PIRLS] since 2001; and Trends in International Mathematics and Science Study [TIMSS] since 1995).

This chapter traces American education policies of the past several decades to show how a *specific mandate* for how achievement data should be used has had deleterious effects on teacher practices and student outcomes. Although most forms of data from educational settings are quite useful to practitioners who are trained in how they might be used (Mandinach et al., 2015), the more important the data are to certain types of decision-making, the greater the likelihood that it changes the conditions under which those decisions are made in the first place (Nichols & Berliner, 2007a; Ryan, 2004).

EDUCATION POLICIES AND AN EMPHASIS ON DATA

Our evolving national education policies, and the more recent mandates regarding how data would be used, originate from at least the 1950s (and perhaps even earlier) when politicians, supported by the media, promulgated a narrative that our public education system was failing or in "crisis" (Glass, 2008) and that teachers and their students were woefully underperforming (Good, 1996; National Commission for Excellence in Education, 1983). Importantly, data were often used in the service of these arguments, with the media playing a significant role in repeating them (Bracey, 1997). Over and over, stories emerged pointing to American students' performance on international standardized tests showing that, on average, our students were often in the middle of the international pack. This purported mediocre performance fueled an alarmist reaction that public schools were failing. Scholars at the time vigorously debated the merits of this narrative, pointing out that the use of aggregated data (average U.S. student achievement performance) failed to tell the real story of student achievement in American schools. Specifically, when disaggregated, we discover that students from higher socioeconomic groups performed better than most other countries, whereas students from lower socioeconomic groups tended to perform worse. Turns out, poverty is a stronger predictor of student success than good or bad teachers (Berliner, 2006; Biddle, 2014; Books, 2004).

In spite of well-documented evidence countering the narrative that all American students and teachers were performing poorly (e.g., Berliner, 2006; Berliner & Biddle, 1995; Biddle, 2014; Bracey, 2009), the misleading and overly simplistic narrative had many decrying the problem with education to be lazy and ineffective teachers. The "blame the school and the teacher" approach inevitably led to a series of federal reforms that put educational "accountability" at the center. In essence, the whole evolution of our current education policy system rests largely with arguments centered on the inappropriate interpretation of data.

Educational accountability emerged in the late 20th century as a possible solution to the perceived inadequacies of public education teachers and students. As reformers would argue, the blame for lackluster standardized test performance should be placed squarely at the feet of our teachers, and because they cannot be trusted to improve student outcomes, the federal government must come in and take over. This position was fueled by the *Nation at Risk* report (National Commission for Excellence in Education, 1983) that proclaimed our very economic and national security systems were at serious risk if we did not do something to change education. Subsequent to the release of this report were a series of federal initiatives (e.g., Clinton's 1994 reauthorization of the 1965 Elementary and Secondary School Act, subsequent education "policy summits," and George H. W. Bush's Goals 2000) aimed at ameliorating these "problems." Collectively, these initiatives laid the groundwork for what was to come next—the No Child Left Behind (NCLB) act. NCLB became an unprecedented federal and monolithic mandate (Sunderman & Kim, 2004a, 2004b) that directed all states toward a single goal (i.e., 100% of students reaching "proficiency") via a single system of implementation (i.e., standards-based assessment and accountability).

No Child Left Behind

NCLB was a massive 1,000-page piece of federal legislation mandating a series of requirements with which states had to comply to receive federal funding. The centerpiece of this law was high-stakes standardized testing—the practice of using standardized test scores to hold teachers and students "accountable." To be in compliance, states had to (1) define and describe a set of curriculum standards across all subjects and grade levels, (2) create a standardized test that would gauge students' progress on those standards, (3) set performance levels that would determine whether students did or did not meet a level of proficiency, (4) outline a set of annual targets for student passing rates over the course of 15 years in which 100% of students would be "proficient" by year 15, and (5) employ and implement a set of consequences for schools that failed to make progress over time.

High-stakes testing is the cornerstone of this entire effort. The theory of action is that by attaching significant rewards or serious threats to changes in student test scores, teachers and their students will inevitably work harder, better, and learn more (as measured by tests; Ryan, 2004). Because standardized test scores were the sole indicator of teacher and student success, the entire focus of education "reform" centered on the test data for making important decisions about teachers and students.

Race to the Top

Race to the Top (RttT) of 2011 was a $4 billion competitive grants program awarded to states that aligned their policies to comply with federal government education priorities at the time (U.S. Department of Education, 2015a). To receive RttT money, states had to write into their state laws the promise that they would (1) adopt performance-based evaluation systems of teachers (using growth models or value-added measures [VAM] to evaluate teacher effectiveness), (2) adopt common core standards, and (3) create policies that would allow for the expansion of charter schools throughout the state (U.S. Department of Education, 2015a). Eighteen states and the District of Columbia received RttT funds and thus had changed their laws to comply with the three mandates. Relevant to the discussion here is the expansion and promotion of teacher evaluation systems that put greater focus on the use of data for evaluating teachers' work. Specifically, states receiving RttT monies employed VAM evaluation techniques as the strategy for evaluating teachers.

VAM is a way of predicting a teacher's "added value" to students' standardized test scores from year to year. By using students' standardized test scores from year to year, statistical models are then used to make a "guess" as to how much of students' improvement (or decline) could be attributed to the teacher. In spite of a wealth of research demonstrating this approach to be quite unreliable and therefore meaningless (Amrein-Beardsley, 2008; Kane, 2017; Koedel et al., 2015), the use of VAMs proliferated for a few years. By about 2014, 40 states and the District of Columbia were "using, piloting or developing some type of growth model or VAM" for measuring teacher effectiveness (Close et al., 2018, p. 8). Encouragingly, the problems of VAM in combination with several lawsuits has since led to the declining use of VAM for evaluating teachers (Close et al., 2018). Still, for a period of time, teachers in many states experienced extreme pressures to make sure students passed tests in order to ensure positive VAM outcomes.

Every Student Succeeds Act

In 2015, Congress passed the Every Student Succeeds Act (ESSA) that reauthorized NCLB and shifted the control of education reform and accountability back to the states (U.S. Department of Education, 2015b). Although state testing was still a mandate, the federal government's role in its form, function, and value was lessened, turning greater responsibility for oversight and control over to the states (Berg-Jacobson, 2016; Loewus, 2017). As a result, and for the past few years, states have begun to minimize the importance of tests in evaluations of schools, teachers, and students (e.g., using multiple indicators, or reducing the importance of test scores). Importantly, although the role, purpose, and importance of tests vary widely from state to state, standardized testing continues to play a central role in teachers' and students' lives (Close et al., 2018).

HIGH-STAKES TESTING AND PRESSURE

The focus of this discussion centers on the time period under NCLB and when the national practice of high-stakes testing was at its peak (2002–2015). Under high-stakes testing accountability systems as mandated by NCLB, test scores became the central data point that functioned both as a *detector* and *effector* of educational change. Test scores were used to *detect* change because scores would be used to determine whether students were learning and therefore if teachers were effective; that is, how students performed on the state standardized test was the primary data point used for judging school/teacher effectiveness. However, test scores were also used to *effect* change through a system of threats and incentives that would be attached to students' test scores. If students performed well (at or above some predefined cutoff point), then teachers, students, and schools could be rewarded. However, if students performed poorly, teachers, students, and schools could be punished. In spite of experts' warnings against these practices (American Educational Research Association, 2000; Haladyna & Downing, 2005; National Research Council, 1999; Nichols & Berliner, 2007a), high-stakes testing continued for decades.

One reason high-stakes testing was bound to fail has to do with the motivational theory of action on which it relies. The theory of action of high-stakes testing is that the external *pressures* foisted on teachers to ensure students pass standardized tests will compel them to become better and more effective teachers (i.e., by becoming more effective teachers, students will learn more). By threatening teachers with sanctions and promising rewards, teachers and students will improve. The psychological experience of this extrinsically applied "pressure" is theorized to be the source of improved teacher motivation. However, we know from a wealth of research that extrinsic motivators are often detrimental to motivation, especially in high-stakes testing contexts (Amrein & Berliner, 2003; Deci & Ryan, 2016; Markowitz, 2018; Wentzel & Wigfield, 2009), and yet over a decade of education policy relied on this type of motivational system to improve outcomes of education.

Another reason high-stakes testing is exceedingly problematic comes from what we know about appropriately evaluating complex social systems. Donald Campbell (1975) warned us decades ago against the use of a single indicator to gauge the effectiveness of complex systems: "The more any quantitative social indicator is used for social decision-making, the more subject it will be to corruption pressures and the more apt it will be to distort and corrupt the social processes it is intended to monitor" (p. 49). Campbell warned us of the inevitable problems associated with undue weight and emphasis on a single indicator or data point for monitoring complex social-cultural phenomena. And, unfortunately, we know Campbell was right.

Evidence has since emerged to underscore the corrupting effects of relying on a single data point for evaluating our schools, teachers, and students.

Intended Consequences of Using Test Data to Evaluate Education

Decades of high-stakes testing policy have yielded a large amount of evidence to suggest that high-stakes testing does not increase student learning as intended (Amrein & Berliner, 2002a, 2002b; Bishop et al., 2001; Braun, 2004; Braun et al., 2010; Grodsky et al., 2009; Nichols et al., 2006, 2012; Rosenshine, 2003). When disaggregated by grade and subject area, we learn that high-stakes testing does not increase learning in 8th-grade math, might decrease learning in 4th- and 8th-grade reading, and might have a moderately positive influence on 4th-grade math (Braun, 2004; Dee & Jacob, 2011; Nichols et al., 2006, 2012). Importantly, there is also little to no evidence that high-stakes testing has decreased the achievement gap (Braun et al., 2006; Reardon, 2011; Timar & Maxwell-Jolly, 2012), and it has negatively impacted student graduation rates (Holme et al., 2010; Marchant & Paulson, 2005; Reardon et al., 2008; Reardon et al., 2009), especially for minority populations (Heubert & Hauser, 1999; Orfield et al., 2004; Valenzuela, 2005; Vasquez Heilig, 2011; Vasquez Heilig & Darling-Hammond, 2008). Although general academic trends were positive before NCLB and continue to increase over time in general, studies that look at the connection specifically between high-stakes testing policies and student outcomes reveal there is no direct connection. In fact, some evidence shows that in some contexts and with some students, greater pressures of high-stakes testing are actually related to decreases in student achievement (Amrein & Berliner, 2002a; Nichols et al., 2006; 2012). High-stakes testing accountability reform has not improved student learning or helped to create conditions that lead to positive conditions for student learning or motivation.

Unintended Consequences of Using Test Data to Evaluate Education

The achievement patterns just discussed suggest something systematic may be happening in classrooms. Specifically, the wealth of data that shows relationships between high-stakes testing and student achievement that are modest but positive for 4th-grade math achievement, but not for 8th-grade math or for 4th-grade or 8th-grade reading invite hypotheses that something might be happening with instruction as a result of the pressure attached to the test scores. Fourth-grade math curriculum is more "rote" and therefore makes it possible to consider how approaches to instruction in that grade and subject area might be systematically different from that in 8th-grade math or 4th- or 8th-grade reading. The pressures to pass tests have corrupted the process of education as Campbell (1975) warned decades ago. Specifically, the pressures have changed how teachers teach and how they relate to students, incentivized a range of unethical behavior or questionable teaching practices, and raised questions regarding how we prepare teachers.

How and What Teachers Teach. In our book, *Collateral Damage: How High-Stakes Testing Corrupts America's Schools*, David Berliner and I accumulated a range of examples of the ways in which the pressures to get students to pass tests changed how and what teachers teach (Nichols & Berliner, 2007a). For example, there are numerous accounts of teachers focusing all their efforts on the test at the expense of focusing on other curriculum areas that aren't tested, of teachers teaching to the test, and of teachers watering down their approach to instruction and presenting material in a more rote, disconnected fashion (Au, 2007; Nichols & Berliner, 2007a). For example, surveys with teachers early in the NCLB era reveal that the pressures to prepare students to take tests change what they do:

> We don't take as many field trips. We don't do community outreach like we used to, like visiting the nursing home or cleaning up the park because we had adopted a park and that was our job, to keep it clean. Well, we don't have time for that anymore. We only teach to the test, even at second grade, and have stopped teaching science and social studies. . . . Our second-graders have no recess except for 20 minutes at lunch. (Taylor et al., 2003, pp. 30–31)

These teaching patterns are more prevalent in contexts where the pressures are greater (i.e., when teaching marginalized populations who have more difficulty passing these tests; Nichols & Castro-Villarreal, 2017; Valenzuela, 2005). There have emerged a seemingly limitless supply of teacher anecdotes revealing this trend (Nichols & Berliner, 2007a; Perlstein, 2007; Ravitch, 2011).

How Teachers Relate to Students. There are also a host of examples underscoring how test pressures change how teachers relate to students. In our book, my coauthor Berliner shared a story of his grandson going to school on test day despite having had a severe asthma attack that morning. In spite of pleas from his parents to the teacher to call them should another attack occur, when it actually did during test-taking time, the teacher instead asked him if he could still complete his test before they contacted his parents. His grandson was a good test taker, and if he were to stop, his test score would not be included in her classroom average. Her preoccupation with how his absent test score would reduce her class average altered how she engaged with him. Sadly, all he learned that day was that he could not trust his teacher (Nichols & Berliner, 2007a).

Examples abound of these kinds of interactions where teachers, under the gun to get students to pass their test, engage with them in undesirable ways that otherwise wouldn't occur if the test-score pressure was absent (Jones et al., 2003; Perlstein, 2007; Ravitch, 2011; Vasquez Heilig & Darling-Hammond, 2008). In another more egregious example, Booher-Jennings (2005) found that the professional development practices for Texas teachers, under extraordinary pressure to get their students to pass the test, encouraged teachers to blatantly ignore high (good test takers) and low achievers (bad test takers) and focus their energies solely on middle achievers (or those students who were just at the cusp of passing the test).

Gaming, Cheating, and Other Forms of Bad Behavior. We know from ground-breaking studies by Hartshorne and May (1928, 1929, 1930) that students who cheat do so because of the situation they find themselves in and not because of some personality flaw. We also learned that even when students valued honesty and integrity, they still could be found to be cheating (peeking at answers, changing answers) depending on the situation in which they found themselves. Indeed, cheating, it was concluded, was a function of a person in a situation. NCLB and the high-stakes testing policies it endorsed created a particular set of conditions in which we find otherwise honest individuals (e.g., teachers and administrators) engaged in what would be considered "cheating" behavior. Examples unfortunately abound from this time period. In our analysis of "cheating" or inappropriate behaviors under high-stakes testing conditions, we found a range of examples of questionable teaching practices based on intentionality (whether the act was "blatant" cheating or whether it would be considered a "gray" area) and based on what type of data indicators were at play (Nichols & Berliner, 2007b; see Table 4.1).

Examples from Cell A include actions taken by administrators or teachers in which the cheating or unethical behavior was "obvious" but that were indirectly related to test scores. For example, in Birmingham, Alabama, educators had 522 students "administratively withdrawn" from school just before the administration of their test. These students were otherwise very low-scoring students, so their withdrawal meant higher overall school test averages and therefore avoidance of potentially negative consequences (Lent & Pipkin, 2003). A similar situation occurred in New York City where there was evidence students had been pushed out of school for years. In Houston, student dropout rates were manipulated to make the Houston School District look better than it actually was. Dropout rate data was part of the accountability matrix, and, therefore, there were incentives to make that data look better than it was (Haney, 2000).

Table 4.1. Matrix of Cheating Categories

	Blatant examples of cheating	Gray areas of cheating
Non-test indicators	CELL A	CELL B
Tests as indicators	CELL C	CELL D

Cell B includes examples where there are indirect attempts to manipulate test outcomes through mechanisms in which non-test indicators are changed in the service of trying to enhance test outcomes. Examples here include teaching to the test, and efforts to narrow the curriculum so that only tested subjects are included in instruction and non-tested subjects are excluded. As described earlier, evidence abounds from the early years of NCLB, showing teachers' increasing discontent over how the pressures to get positive test scores were affecting their classroom instruction. For example, from Florida, we heard teachers talk about the narrowing curriculum as a result of test-based pressures: "Our total curriculum is focused on reading, writing, and math. There is no extra time for students to study the arts, have physical education, science, or social studies. Our curriculum is very unbalanced." (Jones & Egley, 2004, p. 15). Another teacher talked about the pressure to teach to the test:

> I have seen that schools are teaching to the test (how can you not?) and that is not a true reflection of student abilities. This is only a reflection of the abilities of each school to teach effective test-taking strategies, not academics. (Jones & Egley, 2004, p. 17)

These types of sentiments proliferated across America's classrooms (e.g., Perlstein, 2007; Ravitch, 2011; Valenzuela, 2005).

Cell C includes examples where there are blatant efforts to directly manipulate test indicators. In our work, we identified several examples where teachers engaged in direct efforts to help students do well on the test. We found anecdotes where teachers would point out correct answers to students as they were taking the test, or incidents where teachers or administrators would leave Post-it Notes or helpful hints to students as they took the test (Nichols & Berliner, 2007b). From these accounts, we see evidence that educators would violate standardized test administration protocols in an effort to help students do well.

Other more egregious examples of this form of cheating include a wide array of instances where teachers or administrators actively would change wrong test answers to right ones. For example, in the early years after NCLB was enacted, there emerged a cottage industry of entrepreneurs specializing in erasure technology used to detect instances where standardized tests showed a pattern of systematic erasures of wrong answers being changed to correct ones (Jacob & Levitt, 2001, 2002). At the time, we identified several examples where suspicious erasure patterns were used to detect potential cheating on high-stakes tests (Nichols & Berliner, 2007b). These examples continued over time with one of the most highly publicized cheating events occurring in 2009 in Atlanta, Georgia. During that time period, dozens of educators were implicated in changing hundreds of test answers, ultimately resulting in several educators fined and/or jailed for their actions.

This scandal represents one of the most widespread examples of cheating that occurred during the high-stakes testing era of NCLB (e.g., Aronson et al., 2016).

Lastly, examples of questionable unethical behavior characterize Cell D. For example, by law, teachers and parents are supposed to have students take the annual tests; however, we found instances where teachers and parents would refuse or resist. Although technically "inappropriate," we found these actions to be more noble than questionable. For example, in North Carolina, we found one principal who refused to test her special education kids because of her concern they would be humiliated by a test that was "far beyond their abilities" (Winerip, 2003, p. 9). And, the ongoing parent opt-out movement might be characterized in this cell as increasing numbers of parents refuse to let their children sit for state tests (e.g., Evans & Saultz, 2015).

Preservice Teachers. As high-stakes testing proliferated, the effects on preservice teachers (those training to become teachers) emerged. In one study, Brown and Goldstein (2013) performed semi-structured interviews with preservice teachers at the beginning and conclusion of the professional development sequence of their teacher education program in which they found that preservice teachers struggle with how to think about the notion of academic achievement in a standards-based era. Preservice teachers report confusion (and dismay) from conflicting information received by their training that encourages critical thinking and deep learning with the reality of classrooms steeped in pressures to get students to pass tests. Brown (2010) found a similar pattern from interviews with eight female preservice teachers aged 21–26 who had previously taken high-stakes tests in high school in Texas. He found that these teacher candidates expressed deep concern and conflict between their beliefs about what constitutes good teaching and the expectation that they prepare students to pass tests.

Elsewhere, my colleague and I gauged Texas preservice teachers' beliefs about what high-stakes testing experiences were like for them as students in K–12 settings to understand how those views might relate to beliefs about accountability, high-stakes testing in general, and the type of school in which they want to work (Nichols & Brewington, 2020). Among our findings was the fact that preservice teachers who graduated before NCLB and who had fewer (and less intense) experiences with high-stakes tests viewed them as less useful and meaningful than those who graduated under NCLB and who had greater and more regular exposure to high-stakes testing experiences. We theorized that students who "grew up" under a system of high-stakes testing were socialized to hold more accepting views of high-stakes testing and its effects than those who were more likely to learn about high-stakes testing later in life (and who had fewer direct experiences with them). We don't fully know the effects NCLB and the pressures of high-stakes testing have on new or veteran teachers; however, these data raise important questions that merit further consideration.

ESSA: WHAT IS THE CURRENT STATUS OF HIGH-STAKES TESTING?

Since 2015 and the passage of ESSA, the federal government has relegated a wide range of school reform decision-making to the states. Although states are required to have an accountability system, the federal government provides broad discretion to a state to designate what the accountability looks like:

> A State's system includes indicators that measure academic achievement, another academic measure, graduation rates, the progress of English learners in achieving English language proficiency, and school quality or student success. While the ESEA lays out some specifics for State accountability systems, each State has discretion to determine how certain measures are calculated and how many measures to include in order to evaluate school performance. Specifically, each State has discretion to determine a valid and reliable other academic indicator (e.g., student growth) as well as discretion to determine how many indicators of school quality or student success (e.g., educator engagement) it will include in its system and what those indicators will be. A State's accountability system must be used to identify schools for comprehensive, targeted, and additional targeted support and improvement, but a State has discretion to determine precisely how it will design its system, including how it will combine all of the indicators, to identify schools. (ESEA sections 1111(c)(4)(C), (D); 1111(d)(2))[1]

Not surprisingly, states vary in how they have approached this state of affairs. Close and colleagues (2018) did a qualitative analysis of all states' education plans throughout 2017 to describe this variation. Their analysis of surveys with state-level education department personnel or from the U.S. Department of Education website revealed that ESSA has incentivized only marginal changes in how standardized tests are used, as described by three broad trends. First, states continue to rely heavily on standardized achievement tests in grades 3–8 and in high school. Although ESSA allows for broader measures of students' performance (e.g., noncognitive measures), states still heavily rely on what was in place during NCLB (achievement tests). Second, most states (44 plus the District of Columbia) still use standardized achievement information for high-stakes decision-making—specifically in the form of how schools are evaluated and what information is made public (although systems vary). For example, 14 states give their schools A–F grades, 12 give summative scores, and a few other states provide evaluations in different ways (e.g., Massachusetts has six tiers of school performance, and Alaska rates schools on a 100-point scale). Only six states do not give assigned performance categories to schools. In general, most schools continue to rate schools according to some metric that is largely based on how students perform on tests. A third trend has to do with how states define what is meant by academic "proficiency." States vary widely in terms of the proficiency targets they set for how well students must perform on their state tests. For example, "Kansas set a goal of 75% proficiency for all students by 2029–2030. Georgia set a goal of improving proficiency rates by 3% per year for an extended period of time" (Close et al., 2018, p. 11). Thus, states' targets and relative progress vary widely, ensuring that teachers' experiences from state to state and the relative amount of pressure they experience persists but varies widely.

We also know that teachers continue to be evaluated using test scores; however, states again vary widely in the mechanisms they implement for evaluating teachers (some use VAM systems, and some use more locally defined systems). Perhaps more importantly, however, is the fact that state plans include more language about supporting teachers and emphasizing formative teacher feedback and deemphasizing summative evaluations tied to high-stakes consequences. This is a promising trend.

CONCLUSION

In education, the use of data plays an important part. We need data to understand behavior, academic achievement, and other information to be able to assess how schools are functioning. However, we must also be very clear in how these data are used. As illustrated throughout this chapter, the more important a single data point becomes for decision-making, the more likely we will see corruption and distortion. Education policies must guard against this situation or we will continue to see problems in how we educate our students.

This leaves us with a dilemma: How do we improve how our schools function? Inevitably, data will be at least one source of information that will be used in any education reform approach. One potential guard against inappropriate data use is to rely on multiple types of data for making decisions. A more holistic approach on how schools function would help to dilute the intensity of effects seen here when only a single data point is the focus. From the analysis by Close and colleagues (2018), we learn that six states already embrace such an approach. In these six states (California, Idaho, Oregon, North Dakota, Pennsylvania, and Virginia), the public is provided a menu of information meant to reflect a holistic picture of how schools are performing (e.g., absenteeism, student growth, and access to advanced courses). This is an encouraging trend that hopefully more states will adopt. It is only through the embrace of a responsible use of data that we will see any meaningful progress in the overall performance of our schools.

NOTE

1. See pp. 6–7: https://www2.ed.gov/policy/elsec/leg/essa/essa-flexibilities -document-for-publication.pdf.

REFERENCES

American Educational Research Association. (2000). *Position statement on high-stakes testing.* http://www.aera.net/About-AERA/AERA-Rules-Policies /Association-Policies/Position-Statement-on-High-Stakes-Testing

Amrein, A. L., & Berliner, D. C. (2002a). *The impact of high-stakes tests on student academic performance: An analysis of NAEP results in states with high-stakes tests and ACT, SAT, and AP Test results in states with high school graduation exams.* Education Policy Studies Laboratory, Arizona State University. http:// www.asu.edu/educ/epsl/EPRU/documents/EPSL-0211-126-EPRU.pdf

Amrein, A. L., & Berliner, D. C. (2002b). High-stakes testing, uncertainty, and student learning. *Education Policy Analysis Archives, 10*(18). http://epaa.asu.edu /epaa/v10n18/

Amrein, A. L., & Berliner, D. C. (2003). The effects of high-stakes testing on student motivation and learning. *Educational Leadership, 60*(5), 32–38.

Amrein-Beardsley, A. (2008). Methodological concerns about the Education Value-Added Assessment System (EVAAS). *Educational Researcher, 37*(2), 65–75. https://doi.org/10.3102/0013189X08316420

Aronson, B., Murphy, K. M., & Saultz, A. (2016). Under pressure in Atlanta: School accountability and special education practices during the cheating scandal. *Teachers College Record, 118*(14), 1–26.

Au, W. (2007). High-stakes testing and curricular control: A qualitative metasynthesis. *Educational Researcher, 36*(5), 258–267.

Banta, T. W., & Associates. (2002). *Building a scholarship of assessment.* Jossey-Bass.

Berg-Jacobson, A. (2016). *Teacher effectiveness in the Every Student Succeeds Act: A discussion guide.* Center on Great Teachers & Leaders. American Institutes for Research. https://gtlcenter.org/sites/default/files/TeacherEffectiveness_ESSA.pdf

Berliner, D. C. (2006). Our impoverished view of educational reform. *Teachers College Record, 108*(6), 949–995. http://www.tcrecord.org

Berliner, D. C., & Biddle, B. J. (1995). *The manufactured crisis: Myths, fraud, and the attack on America's public schools.* Addison-Wesley.

Biddle, B. J. (2014). *The unacknowledged disaster: Youth poverty and educational failure in America.* Sense Publishers.

Bishop, J. H., Mane, F., Bishop, M., & Moriarty, J. (2001). The role of end-of-course exams and minimum competency exams in standards-based reforms. *Brookings Papers on Educational Policy, 4*, 267–345.

Booher-Jennings, J. (2005). Below the bubble: "Educational triage" and the Texas accountability system. *American Educational Research Journal, 42*(2), 231–268.

Books, S. (2004). *Poverty and schooling in the U.S.: Contexts and consequences.* Lawrence Erlbaum Associates.

Bracey, G. W. (1997). *The truth about America's schools: The Bracey Reports, 1991–1997.* Phi Dela Kappa Educational Foundation.

Bracey, G. W. (2009). *The Bracey report: On the condition of public education, 2009.* Education and the Public Interest Center & Education Policy Research Unit. http://epicpolicy.org/publication/Bracey-Report

Braun, H. (2004). Reconsidering the impact of high-stakes testing. *Educational Policy Analysis Archives, 12*(1), 1–40. http://epaa.asu.edu/epaa/v12n1/

Braun, H., Chapman, L., & Vezzu, S. (2010). The Black-White achievement gap revisited. *Education Policy Analysis Archives, 18*(21), 1–95. http://epaa.asu.edu/ojs/article/view/772

Braun, H. I., Wang, A., Jenkins, F., & Weinbaum, E. (2006) The Black-White achievement gap: Do state policies matter? *Education Policy Analysis Archives, 14*(8), 1–107. http://epaa.asu.edu/epaa/v14n8/

Brown, C. P. (2010). Children of reform: The impact of high-stakes education reform on preservice teachers. *Journal of Teacher Education, 61*(5), 477–491. https://doi.org/10.1177/0022487109352905

Brown, K. D., & Goldstein, L. S. (2013). Preservice elementary teachers' understandings of competing notions of academic achievement coexisting in post-NCLB public schools. *Teachers College Record, 115*(1), 1–37.

Campbell, D. (1975). Assessing the impact of planned social change. In G. Lyons (Ed.), *Social research and public policies: The Dartmouth/OECD Conference.* Public Affairs Center, Dartmouth College, Hanover, NH.

Close, K., Amrein-Beardsley, A., & Collins, C. (2018). *State-level assessments and teacher evaluation systems after the passage of the Every Student Succeeds Act: Some steps in the right direction.* National Education Policy Center. http://nepc.colorado.edu/publication/state-assessment

Deci, E. L., & Ryan, R. M. (2016). Optimizing students' motivation in the era of testing and pressure: A self-determination theory perspective. In W. Liu, J. Wang, & R. Ryan (Eds.), *Building autonomous learners* (pp. 9–29). Springer.

Dee, T., & Jacob, B. (2011). The impact of No Child Left Behind on student achievement. *Journal of Policy Analysis and Management, 30*(3), 418–446.

Evans, M. P., & Saultz, A. (2015, June 9). The opt-out movement is gaining momentum. *Education Week, 34*(34), 20. https://www.edweek.org/teaching-learning/opinion-the-opt-out-movement-is-gaining-momentum/2015/06

Glass, G. V. (2008). *Fertilizers, pills, and magnetic strips: The fate of public education in America.* Information Age Publishing.

Good, T. L. (Guest ed.). (1996, November). *Educational Researcher, 25*(8).

Grodsky, E. S., Warren, J. R., & Kalogrides, D. (2009). State high school exit examinations and NAEP long-term trends in reading and mathematics, 1971–2004. *Educational Policy, 23*, 589–614. https://doi.org/10.1177%2F0895904808320678

Haladyna, T. M., & Downing, S. M. (2005). Construct-irrelevant variance in high-stakes testing. *Educational Measurement, 23*(1), 17–27.

Haney, W. (2000). The myth of the Texas miracle in education. *Education Policy Analysis Archives*, *8*(41).

Hartshorne, H., & May, M. A. (1928). *Studies in the Nature of Character* (Vol. 1). Macmillan/Maxwell Macmillan.

Hartshorne, H., & May, M. A. (1929). *Studies in the Nature of Character* (Vol. 2). Macmillan/Maxwell Macmillan.

Hartshorne, H., & May, M. A. (1930). *Studies in the Nature of Character* (Vol. 3). Macmillan/Maxwell Macmillan.

Heubert, J. P., & Hauser, R. M. (Eds.). (1999). *High stakes: Testing for tracking, promotion, and graduation*. National Academy Press.

Holme, J. J., Richards, M. P., Jimerson, J. B., & Cohen, R. W. (2010). Assessing the effects of high school exit examinations. *Review of Educational Research*, *80*(4), 476–526. https://doi.org/10.3102%2F0034654310383147

Jacob, B., & Levitt, S. D. (2001). *Rotten apples: An estimation of the prevalence and predictors of teacher cheating* (Working Paper No. 9414). National Bureau of Economic Research.

Jacob, B., & Levitt, S. D. (2002). *Catching cheating teachers: The results of an unusual experiment in implementing theory* (Working Paper No. 9414). National Bureau of Economic Research.

Jones, B. C., & Egley, R. J. (2004). Voices from the frontlines: Teachers' perceptions of high-stakes testing. *Education Policy Analysis Archives*, *12*(39), 1–34. http://epaa.asu.edu/epaa/v12n39/

Jones, M. G., Jones, B., & Hargrove, T. (2003). *The unintended consequences of high-stakes testing*. Rowman & Littlefield.

Kane, M. T. (2017). *Measurement error and bias in value-added models*. Educational Testing Service (ETS) Research Report Series. https://doi.org/10.1002/ets2.12153

Koedel, C., Mihaly, K., & Rockoff, J. E. (2015). Value-added modeling: A review. *Economics Education Review*, *47*, 180–195. https://doi.org/10.1016/j.econedurev.2015.01.006

Lent, R. C., & Pipkin, G. (Eds.). (2003). *Silent no more: Voices of courage in American schools*. Heinemann.

Loewus, L. (2017). Are states changing course on teacher evaluation? Test-score growth plays lesser role in six states. *Education Week*, *37*(13), 1–7.

Mandinach, E. B., Friedman, J. M., & Gummer, E. S. (2015). How can schools of education help to build educators' capacity to use data: A systemic view of the issue. *Teachers College Record*, *117*(4), 1–50. http://www.tcrecord.org/PrintContent.asp?ContentID=17850

Mandinach, E. B., & Gummer, E. S. (2016). What does it mean for teachers to be data literate: Laying out the skills, knowledge, and dispositions. *Teaching and Teacher Education*, *60*, 366–376.

Marchant, G., & Paulson, S. (2005). The relationships of high school graduation exams to graduation rate and SAT scores. *Education Policy Analysis Archives*, *13*(6), 1–15. https://epaa.asu.edu/ojs/article/view/111

Markowitz, A. J. (2018). Changes in school engagement as a function of No Child Left Behind: A comparative interrupted time series analysis. *American Educational Research Journal*, *55*(4), 721–760.

National Commission for Excellence in Education. (1983, April). A nation at risk: The imperatives for educational reform. U.S. Department of Education, National Commission for Excellence in Education.

National Research Council. (1999). *High stakes: Testing for tracking, promotion, and graduation*. The National Academies Press. https://doi.org/10.17226/6336

Nichols, S. L., & Berliner, D. C. (2007a). *Collateral damage: How high-stakes testing corrupts America's schools*. Harvard Education Press.

Nichols, S. L., & Berliner, D. C. (2007b). The pressure to cheat in a high-stakes testing environment. In E. M. Anderman & T. Murdock (Eds.), *Psychological perspectives on academic cheating* (pp. 289–312). Elsevier.

Nichols, S. L., & Brewington, S. (2020). Perceptions of accountability: Preservice teachers' beliefs about high-stakes testing and their working environments. *Education Policy Analysis Archives*, *28*(30), 1–38. https://doi.org/10.14507/epaa.28.4877

Nichols, S. L., & Castro-Villarreal, F. (2017). Introduction to the special issue: The social (in)justice of labeling in a high-stakes testing era: Implications for teachers and school psychologists. *Teachers College Record*, *119*(9), 1–8. http://www.tcrecord.org ID Number: 22007

Nichols, S. L., Glass, G. V., & Berliner, D. C. (2006). High-stakes testing and student achievement: Does accountability pressure increase student learning? *Education Policy Analysis Archives*, *14*(1), 1–172. http://epaa.asu.edu/epaa/v14n1/

Nichols, S. L., Glass, G. V., & Berliner, D. C. (2012). High-stakes testing and student achievement: Updated analyses with NAEP data. *Education Policy Analysis Archives*, *20*(20), 1–35. http://epaa.asu.edu/ojs/article/view/1048

Nichols, S. L., & Varier, D. (Eds.). (2021). *Teaching on assessment*. Information Age.

No Child Left Behind (NCLB) Act of 2001, 20 U.S.C.A. § 6301 *et seq* (2001).

Orfield, G., Losen, D., Wald, J., & Swanson, C. B. (2004). *Losing our future: How minority youth are being left behind by the graduation rate crisis*. The Civil Rights Project at Harvard University.

Perlstein, L. (2007). *Tested: One American school struggles to make the grade*. Henry Holt & Co.

Ravitch, D. (2011). *The death and life of the great American school system: How testing and choice are undermining education*. Basic Books.

Reardon, S. F. (2011). The widening academic achievement gap between the rich and the poor: New evidence and possible explanations. In R. Murnane & G. Duncan (Eds.), *Whither opportunity? Rising inequality and the uncertain life chances of low-income children* (pp. 91–116). Russell Sage Foundation.

Reardon, S. F., Arshan, N., Atteberry, A., & Kurlaender, M. (2008). *High stakes, no effects: Effects of failing the California High School Exit Exam* (Working

Paper No. 2008–10). Stanford University, Institute for Research on Education Policy & Practice.

Reardon, S. F., Atteberry, A., Arshan, N., & Kurlaender, M. (2009, April 21). *Effects of the California High School Exit Exam on student persistence, achievement and graduation* (Working Paper No. 2009–12). Stanford University, Institute for Research on Education Policy & Practice.

Rosenshine, B. (2003). High-stakes testing: Another analysis. *Education Policy Analysis Archives, 11*(24). http://epaa.asu.edu/epaa/v11n24/

Ryan, J. (2004). The perverse incentives of the No Child Left Behind Act. *New York University Law Review, 79*, 932–989.

Sunderman, G. L., & Kim, J. (2004a, February). *Inspiring vision, disappointing results: Four studies on implementing the No Child Left Behind Act*. The Civil Rights Project at Harvard University.

Sunderman, G. L., & Kim, J. (2004b, February). *Expansion of federal power in American education: Federal-state relationships under No Child Left Behind Act, Year One*. The Civil Rights Project at Harvard University.

Taylor, G., Shepard, J., Kinner, F., & Rosenthal, J. (2003). *A survey of teachers' perspectives on high-stakes testing in Colorado: What gets taught, what gets lost* (CSE Technical Report No. 588). University of California, National Center for Research on Evaluation, Standards, and Student Testing.

Timar, T. B., & Maxwell-Jolly, J. (Eds.). (2012). *Narrowing the achievement gap: Perspectives and strategies for challenging times*. Harvard Education Press.

U.S. Department of Education. (2015a). *Fundamental change: Innovation in America's schools under Race to the Top*. https://www2.ed.gov/programs/racetothetop/rttfinalrptfull.pdf

U.S. Department of Education. (2015b). Every Student Succeeds Act of 2015, Pub. L. No. 114-95 § 114 Stat. 1177 (2015–2016).

Valenzuela, A. (Ed.). (2005). *Leaving children behind: How "Texas-style" accountability fails Latino youth*. State University of New York Press.

Vasquez Heilig, J. (2011). Understanding the interaction between high-stakes graduation tests and English language learners. *Teachers College Record, 113*(12), 2633–2669.

Vasquez Heilig, J., & Darling-Hammond, L. (2008). Accountability Texas-style: The progress and learning of urban minority students in a high-stakes testing context. *Educational Evaluation and Policy Analysis, 30*(2), 75–110.

Wentzel, K. R., & Wigfield, A. (Eds.). (2009). *Handbook of motivation at school*. Routledge.

Winerip, M. (2003, October 8). How a good school can fail on paper. *The New York Times*. https://www.nytimes.com/2003/10/08/nyregion/on-education-how-a-good-school-can-fail-on-paper.html

Part II

USE CASES

The Role of the Classroom, School, and District to Ensure the Ethical Use of Data

It's More Than Just FERPA

Ellen B. Mandinach and Jo Beth Jimerson

Ethics in education is a topic of increasing importance. Educators are faced daily with ethical dilemmas, some of which squarely fall under data ethics and extend far beyond the execution of the Family Educational Rights and Privacy Act (FERPA) to protect student privacy and confidentiality. FERPA is most certainly essential, complex, and continues to evolve. However, in this chapter, we take the approach that data ethics, as applied to the reality of educational settings, are nuanced and inextricably intertwined with data literacy. Data ethics pertain to the appropriate use of data.

Data ethics also pertain to the use of the appropriate data for a particular decision; that is, data need to be aligned to the specific decision. Rather than simply using *available* data to inform a particular decision, educators must work to ensure that *appropriate* data are used (and collected, where that has not been done) in decision-making efforts. Interpretations of data and subsequent actions are influenced by the lens educators use to ascertain appropriate uses and end objectives of data use. Data ethics also entail awareness of *why* an educator chooses one course of action over another.

This chapter examines ethical data use in the hierarchical structure of school systems, from classroom, to the school, to the district. Each level of the system uses different data for different decisions and may also use the same data at different levels of aggregation for different kinds of decisions.

We briefly consider the kinds of data and decisions that each level of the system typically addresses before discussing what we see happening in terms of data use throughout districts. We then leverage a set of hypothetical examples (drawn from composite professional experiences of the authors as well as conversations with teachers and school leaders across the authors' careers) to highlight some common data ethics issues. Finally, we lay out some foundational actions that can positively facilitate responsible data use.

DATA USE ACROSS LEVELS OF LOCAL EDUCATION AGENCIES

Data in the Classroom

Many decisions teachers face focus on how to improve teaching and learning. That typically translates to improving student learning by using many forms of performance indices. Such data may include quantifiable test results (e.g., summative, interim, benchmark assessments), quizzes, assignments, and projects. Clues to improved teaching and learning may include observations and the moment-to-moment data yielded by ongoing formative assessment processes (Wiliam, 2011). To add to the complexity, there are many other sources of data, both quantitative and qualitative, that provide invaluable contextual information about students. These data are diverse indeed. As Mandinach and Gummer (2016) note, data may include attendance, demographics, motivation, interests, home circumstance (e.g., homelessness, shelter, foster care), behavior and justice (e.g., incidents, probations, arrests), medical, and special status (e.g., English language learner [ELL], special education, immigrant documentation, military, migrant, protective custody). But when people speak of educational data, they most immediately think of numerical test results that can be entered into a data system or grade book.

Data in the School

Data use at the school level sometimes consists of the same data sources as in the classroom, but often for different kinds of decisions that focus on determining curricula and programmatic effectiveness, teacher assignments, and personnel staffing and hiring. Decisions can focus on resource allocation, transportation, finance, and building management (Hess, 2009). Thus, data for such decisions will differ, whereas some data may be the same but examined at different levels of aggregation (Schildkamp & Kuiper, 2010). For example, assessment data may be used for classroom assignments, determination of changes in curricular materials, and identification of students in need of special programs. Assessment data may also be used to inform teacher supervision, coaching, and evaluation.

Data Throughout the District

Data for district use take on an entirely different level of examination and are used in many instances for accountability (Honig & Coburn, 2008; Schildkamp & Kuiper, 2009). Federal and state mandates require specific data to be collected and reported for compliance. These data are reported at an aggregated level to provide snapshots of district performance and characteristics. They may include demographic reporting (e.g., percent of students who qualify for free or reduced-price meals; student population by race, ethnicity, and gender; performance on state assessments; percent of teachers who are certified or otherwise considered "highly qualified"; average class size; per pupil expenditure) as well as reports of outcomes (e.g., assessments, graduation and dropout rates) disaggregated by one or more demographic categories. Decisions focus not only on required data reporting but also on data for district functioning and improvement.

WHAT IS HAPPENING

We approach data ethics broadly in terms of responsible data use. In this section, we discuss our concept of ethical positionality and then outline differences between data use for accountability and continuous improvement. We explore responsible data use in terms of human capacity, that is; data literacy and related skills. We then address the issue of what counts as data (i.e., data being more than test results), data quality, and the issue of validity of interpretation, including the need to align data to decisions.

Ethical Positionality

Beyond being aware of legal aspects of using, sharing, and collaborating around data in the context of education, educators must practice intentional thinking around their rationales for making particular decisions. Starratt (2012) notes the following:

> Being ethical refers to behaving in ways consistent with internal, self-appropriated principles that one can articulate and that, at least sometimes, lead persons to go beyond self-interest. . . . moral persons behave in certain ways because that's what others demand and expect. Ethical persons behave in certain ways because they are convinced that it is the right thing to do, because doing the right thing is tied up with their identity. (p. ii)

Using data ethically requires educators to not only engage with data in ways that are *legal* (e.g., FERPA) and *smart* (e.g., literacy), but also to do what is legal and smart in ways that are *right*. In wrestling with what may be *right* in a given situation, we argue that educators should develop a sense of *ethical positionality*, which we define as an intentional awareness of how one's own goals, aspirations, and expected benefits fit within the context of and subsequently affect any decision made by the educator. School and district leaders who practice awareness of ethical positionality and use data ethically aim to decenter themselves as primary beneficiaries of data-driven decisions; instead, they work to center students as the benefactors of their data-informed decisions.

On any given day, educators face situations that require action; to maintain ethical positionality, they must ask themselves if a decision and the resulting actions are primarily aimed at achieving benefit for the individual educator or for students. (Of course, we acknowledge that some decisions can ethically benefit more than one party.) It is incumbent on leaders to center the good of students in the data-decision-making process (and perhaps, then, to wrestle with what constitutes the highest good for the students, in the context of short-, medium- and long-term schooling goals).

Interrogating one's ethical positionality means that leaders identify and consider their core values/principles, and then align data use acts with those values/principles, even in moments of professional discomfort. For example, a leader in fear for his job may consider it a rational decision to have particular students opt out of an exam, if the result is that school scores look better to his supervisors. He may even rationalize this decision as being "in the best interest of the school" in some way (e.g., school reputation, maintaining student enrollment/parent confidence, or affording the leader another year to work on turnaround efforts). But a leader working to interrogate ethical positionality would wrestle with the rightness or wrongness of choosing to focus on short-term results by sacrificing longer-term gains (or vice versa). A leader interrogating ethical positionality would work to determine whether an intended decision is driven by an effort to center benefit to students, to center benefit to the *individual leader* rather than the students, or to center benefit to the leader *at the expense* of students. The leader would also have to consider the impact of that decision on the development and learning of *all* students affected. Being an ethical leader requires triangulating multiple and appropriate data sources to best understand the context and potential outcomes of decisions.

Interrogating ethical positionality means confronting dilemmas where there may be no easy or "good" answer: any choice may benefit some students and harm others, however unintentionally. Yet a critical component of ethical data use goes beyond using data in legal and accurate ways to a deep examination of why a leader makes the choices she does, at the times she does, and leaves other options on the table. Ethical data use means asking "cui bono?" and working to ensure the answer never abandons students who already may be marginalized. We return to the concept of ethical positionality later in the section on examples.

Data for Accountability and Data for Continuous Improvement

Data use is not a panacea. Effective data use depends on many factors, including the intent of use. Critics have been vocal about their concerns (Penuel &

Shepard, 2016). Much criticism is related to the differences between data use for accountability versus continuous improvement (Firestone & Gonzalez, 2007; Ingram et al., 2004). As Datnow and Park (2018) note, data use is inextricably linked to accountability. Accountability systems that turn on high-stakes test scores exert pressures that can narrow the curriculum; restrict teacher creativity, response, and dialogue; and provide a limited view of data (Au, 2007; Berliner, 2011; Datnow et al., 2018; Nichols & Berliner, 2007). Accountability can demoralize teachers and pressure them to use inappropriate kinds of data (Diamond & Spillane, 2004; Hubbard et al., 2014; Schildkamp & Tedlie, 2008). Data can be (mis)used to confirm existing beliefs and reinforce low expectations for students (Bertrand & Marsh, 2015; Datnow, 2017), which reifies deficit thinking that does a disservice to students and stunts equity efforts (Datnow & Park, 2018). Test scores can be used to game the system and may be used to (further) marginalize groups of students (Booher-Jennings, 2005; Schildkamp et al., 2019).

Accountability pressure is conflated with data use because of the limited focus on test scores rather than a broader view of diverse data sources that inform the whole child and provide an asset-based perspective (Atwood et al., 2019; Garner et al., 2017; Jimerson, 2014; Mandinach & Gummer, 2016). Perhaps a bigger issue here is the limitation of the types of data that are used in accountability measures and the discourse around data-driven decision-making. Because of a narrow accountability framing, some teachers use data superficially, supporting a deficit mindset (Datnow & Park, 2018), and they fail to make meaningful instructional change (Garner et al., 2017). The pressure to frame data use in strict accountability terms can also manifest itself in cultures where teachers feel the potential for retribution and punitive actions (i.e., shaming and blaming), feeding mistrust in data use and data-using leaders (Datnow et al., 2013; Ingram et al., 2004). As Bocala and Boudett (2015) note, it is important for teachers to feel trust and safety in their data use, while using evidence rather than anecdotes. This is similar to the findings of Vanlommel and colleagues (2020) about the use of data-based processes versus intuitive processes for decision-making. Poor data lead to unfounded conclusions and interpretations that lead to fallacies (Kahneman & Klein, 2009; Schneider & Ingram, 1993). Further, the lack of capacity can cause poor decisions and the misuse of data (Daly, 2012; Kahneman & Klein, 2009; Mandinach & Gummer, 2016). Despite these real concerns, when data use is more broadly focused on multiple measures and an improvement perspective with the goal of addressing the whole child to improve instruction, inform educational decisions, and reflect on practice, data use can be a powerful tool for continuous improvement.

Data have been used to evaluate teachers (sometime wrongly) and have been used punitively. Data have been used to promote confirmation bias and affirm inappropriate assumptions (Datnow & Park, 2018). Inappropriate data use has promoted bias and a deficit model instead of facilitating an asset model to address the whole child (Mandinach, Warner, & Lacireno-Paquet, 2020; Mandinach, Warner, & Mundry, 2019). Data have been used to game the system, including focusing intense efforts on students at or near the passing threshold of required exams to the exclusion of other students (and in the process creating a new language of deficit labels including "bubble kids") (Booher-Jennings, 2005).

In response to such pressures, some educators have resorted to blatant cheating on accountability measures (e.g., the Atlanta cheating scandal; Strauss, 2015). In the presence of accountability systems that incentivize numerical wins over substantive (but incidental) improvement, and in the absence of leaders with the moral and ethical fortitude both to resist such pressures and to create avenues for teachers to resist the temptation to take shortcuts, destructive data practices seem to flourish. Unfortunately, much data use to date has had a primary focus on test results to the exclusion of other important metrics (Mandinach & Gummer, 2016). Teachers even use the wrong data for specific decisions (Farrell & Marsh, 2016). Data use has been criticized for misleading and oversimplifying through poor data displays (Penuel & Shepard in Mandinach et al., 2018). Mandinach and Schildkamp (2020) address several of these concerns, criticisms, and misconceptions raised about data use in the literature, making the point that accountability pressures tempt educators to take certain actions that may be unethical. There are many ways that data can be (and are) used inappropriately, yet if used responsibly, the intention should be to transform the teaching and learning process through a focused and informed inquiry process.

At the heart of the issue is the limited (or at least predominant) reliance on data for accountability and compliance rather than data for continuous improvement. These distinctions emanate from the highest level of policymakers through explicit messaging. Take, for example, the juxtaposition between two former Secretaries of Education. Margaret Spellings (2005) came down firmly on the side of data use for accountability and compliance. Arnie Duncan (2009) was a proponent of data use for continuous improvement. Duncan promoted data use as a means to guide instruction to help all students learn.

Educators take their cues from such statements as they convey what policymakers deem important. The policymakers say use data, but the only data that are available or used are assessment data. There is a gap between what the policy indicates and what the educators are provided to make decisions. If the quest of schooling, then, is to improve student performance as measured only by state summative test scores, educators may be pressured to game the system, use inappropriate data, and make inaccurate decisions from inadequate data on how to best help their students.

What should be happening, in contrast, is the use of the right data, aligned to specific kinds of decisions that can lead to the improvement of the educational system at all levels. In some ways, Duncan's position was very different from Spellings; however, under former Secretary of Education Betsy DeVos (2017–2021), data did not rise to a level of importance. These shifting political emphases are troublesome at best. Former Secretary Duncan firmly espoused the use of data to improve education and to inform educators. There is no question that accountability data serve a compliance purpose, but data for continuous improvement are what educators need to inform much of their practice.

The U.S. Department of Education has spent a great deal of money building the technology infrastructure at the state level to support accountability data. Technologies used at the local level support both accountability and improvement data. However, few expenditures have been devoted to developing the human infrastructure, except for one round of funding by the statewide longitudinal data systems (SLDS) grant program. For example, the Oregon Data Project (n.d.) attempted to improve data literacy across the state. Montana is trying to enhance educators' capacity (Armstrong & Seifert, 2020). Wisconsin is working with its teacher preparation programs (Halverson et al., 2017). The conclusion drawn from policy is that data for both accountability and continuous improvement have had differing emphases across administrations. While incentives to misuse data will always remain, it is important to equip educators with the needed skill set to use data appropriately and responsibly, although this topic has not been a priority for funders.

Human Capacity—Data Literacy

Essential to responsible data use is data literacy; that is, educators must have the right skills, knowledge, and dispositions to use data effectively (Data Quality Campaign, 2014; Mandinach & Gummer, 2016). Responsible data use extends beyond data literacy to also include related skill sets, such as basic assessment and statistical literacy, to use the principles of assessment and statistical analyses appropriately. Here we consider the construct data literacy for teachers (DLFT; Mandinach & Gummer, 2016) where many skills pertain to the ethical use of data.

Data literacy skills are essential to data ethics. Human capacity extends beyond the data interpretation and application to the use of research evidence. Research evidence is a form of information that educators must know how to transform into practice. Further, one of the dispositions of data literacy is the knowledge of the legal aspects of data ethics and FERPA in particular. Part of the issue is where educators obtain such knowledge. Educator preparation programs do not typically address the topic of data ethics, and there is limited specification in state standards and codes of ethics that might stimulate programs to include the topic in curricula (Mandinach & Wayman, 2020). It is unclear how prevalent in-service training on FERPA and data ethics is in districts. We do know that there are a few states that require training through the Privacy Technical Assistance Center (PTAC) of the U.S. Department of Education (B. Rodriguez, personal communication, February 2018). Thus, widespread development for educators that spans preservice throughout educators' careers is sorely needed.

Data, Validity, and Interpretations

Cronbach (1988) and Messick (1989) discuss validity in terms of interpretations and the consequences of decisions. We mentioned the importance of using diverse data sources that can inform the kinds of decisions that are to be made. This alignment is essential to proper data use, data ethics, and validity. This assumes that there is appropriate alignment so that the interpretations made from the data can render valid decisions. That said, the same data can yield different decisions. Different users view the same data from their own particular perspectives with their own lenses, which can elicit very different interpretations and courses of action. This happens in many disciplines, not just education. It is therefore the educational actions based on the data that are the foundation for the validity argument. Decisions are followed by an evaluation of the outcomes that result from the decision-making process. Further, if educators truly believe in and engage in appropriate data-driven decision-making, they will be using an iterative and cyclical inquiry process where decisions are not necessarily the end point but a starting point for additional inquiry. Good data use is rarely a linear and sequential process; it is a cycle of continuous inquiry.

EXAMPLES

In this section, we present several examples or scenarios that illustrate aspects of data ethics found in practice. These examples are not exhaustive but illustrative. We want to balance our use of positive and negative examples because data-driven decision-making is often criticized as being negative. Certainly, there are plentiful examples of data misuse and examples that lean into what might appear deficit framing (e.g., "find-and-fix" approaches to problem solving or identifying learning gaps so they can be addressed), even if these approaches result in benefit to students. Also plentiful are examples of positive actions enabled by thoughtful uses of data and opportunities for good data practices to improve the status quo in classrooms, at campuses, and throughout district systems. To be clear, these examples are hypothetical in nature, though the authors drew on direct professional experiences and conversations with teachers and school leaders across their respective careers in crafting them in order to highlight particular issues related to data ethics. "Real-world" anchors that echo some of the same issues highlighted in this chapter can be explored in various media related to educational technology (Kharif, 2014), metrics used to determine "safest school" ratings used in the realty market (Niche, 2021), and tensions among reading improvement efforts and reading enjoyment among children (Gonzalez, 2017), among others. Note that although the examples here are drawn from composites of experiences and conversations with educators across the authors' careers, the potential for examples such as the ones presented here can be explored in stories related to educational technology (Kharif, 2014).

Accountability Pressures

Accountability systems can inadvertently promote misuse of data. There are many ways educators, parents, and students can game the system in an effort to manipulate data and outcomes. Students have been caught gaining access to student records to change grades and scores, for example. There is no question that many educators encounter pressure based on accountability metrics. Accountability systems typically have thresholds that trigger unwelcome ramifications. Teachers feel pressure to keep up with curricular pacing guides, even if they fear this will leave some students behind. Some teachers let plagiarism slip by unnoticed. Despite the extreme stories that appear in the news from time to time, most educators are well intentioned and try to balance the accountability pressures by doing right by their students, helping them to succeed.

Sometimes ethical, constructive use of data can turn around a negative situation. For example, a teacher who applies plagiarism software may determine that one student's report shows disproportionately more plagiarism than that of her fellow students. The plagiarism report drives her to examine the areas of concern highlighted by the software, and she sees a lack of citations and proper attribution. The teacher can discern what is original writing and what is lifted from other sources by the grammatical structure and writing style. Her initial hunch is that the student is under a great deal of pressure (from her parents, teachers, and coaches) to pass the honors course and, as a result, concludes the student likely cheated, and the behavior warrants a failing grade and a disciplinary referral. As one last check on her conclusion, she introduces another data point: a conversation with the student. In the process, she discovers an unexpected misunderstanding of the relationship between attribution and paraphrasing. Instead of punishing the student, she uses it as a teachable moment for the student about the importance of proper attribution and how to cite such material. She helps the student learn how to insert quotes into the paper and how to properly paraphrase by fully understanding the content of the original material. Here, an initial belief about a student was broadened with the intentional inclusion of more data points to the ultimate benefit of the student and the teacher–student relationship.

Resource Allocation/Cost-Benefits

Administrators regularly make decisions about how to allocate resources (Burkhauser, 2017). These decisions often come down to a cost-benefit analysis, especially given that funds in education are severely limited. Administrators can be torn between competing priorities, such as staffing and hiring, investments in physical infrastructure, programming and curricula, professional development, and transportation (Shoho & Barnett, 2010). Although such decisions do not directly impact student performance and other accountability and compliance metrics, they are essential to the effective functioning of the district and therefore indirectly affect teaching and learning in multiple ways. These decisions must be grounded in valid and quality data that are accurate, timely, complete, and relevant. Such decisions could well be influenced by political pressure, rather than be based on actual evidence.

In some cases, administrators fall back on symbolic uses of data as "cover" for making a decision or making decisions due to political pressure and expedience (e.g., Coburn et al., 2009). Such practices exist but hopefully are becoming less frequent with the emphasis on evidence-based decisions. Throughout decisions related to resource allocation, leaders may have to weigh competing goods and benefits to different groups. Leaders who center student benefit, align with legal guidelines and requirements, and employ data literacy will find themselves well equipped to navigate complex decision-making around such issues.

Moral Duty to Support *All* Students

Booher-Jennings (2005) notes the phenomenon of educational triage with bubble kids, that is, students on the cusp of passing high-stakes exams, with the expectation that focusing instruction primarily (or solely) on these students would help them over the cut score and into the "passing" category of performance. Beyond reifying a way of talking about children that is decidedly deficit-oriented (and which few educators would use to describe children in front of their parents), there are many problems with this approach. First, students slightly above and below a cut score may not be all that different due to error of measurement. Trying to improve the kids slightly below the cut score fails to realize that those right above may regress in the next measurement.

A second and even more important issue is that teachers need to address the needs of all students, not just a select group for the purpose of meeting accountability metrics. Related to this issue is the belief that all students can learn, which is one of the dispositions in the DLFT construct (Mandinach & Gummer, 2016) and a foundational principle in the transformation of the construct to culturally responsive data literacy (Mandinach, Warner, & Lacireno-Paquet, 2020) and professional development, such as Using Data

Solutions (Love et al., 2008). Believing otherwise harms the learning of the neglected students in the long term. Students across the continuum of performance require attention, from the most challenged to the most gifted. Some educators assume the most challenged will never succeed and therefore put little effort into changing the learning landscape for those students. Some educators assume gifted students will succeed without instructional attention, so there is less focus devoted to nurturing their talent. Further, each student is unique, with their own strengths and weaknesses, interests, and backgrounds. Using diverse data sources and taking the whole child perspective for each and every student is a way to keep equitable instructional attention centered in data-driven decisions.

Teacher Evaluation

Teacher evaluation has become a contentious topic as there is disagreement regarding what metrics should be included in supervisory and evaluative models (e.g., Corcoran, 2010; Hazi, 2017; Mette et al., 2017; Steinberg & Kraft, 2017). Some policymakers feel that because teachers are the most direct and impactful in-school influence on student performance, achievement outcome measures should play a role in teacher evaluation. At the same time, a research brief from the Educational Psychology division of the American Psychological Association (Lavigne & Good, 2020) cautions against teacher evaluations being too heavily dependent on either observation or value-added measures (VAM) as sole or predominant metrics in evaluating the complex task of teaching. Lavigne and Good note that while typical observations often delay feedback or provide feedback that is neither timely nor granular enough to support improvements in teaching, depending on VAM is risky due to several factors: measurement error, the need for multiple comparable data points to strengthen model stability, and the variability of both student *and* teacher performance in different contexts. Others assert there should be triangulation of several metrics such as observations, student growth, and peer evaluations (Steinberg & Kraft, 2017). Still others note positive prospects when student voice is included as part of teacher evaluation processes (Barile et al., 2012). And, of course, the whole tension between supervision and evaluation (and data used in/for each) is still debated (Hazi, 2019; Mette et al., 2017).

In light of these complexities, school districts are approaching this issue using different models, but the underlying logic remains the same: Teachers are the most impactful school-based factor when it comes to student learning, and therefore student outcomes should be part of the evaluation. However, ethical data use requires more of educators, as rendering a high-stakes judgment (e.g., teacher evaluation) requires consideration of multiple quantitative and qualitative data points. For example, evaluators must balance considerations of the impact of differential inputs (makeup of the class, poverty, ability/disability, quality of prior learning opportunity, etc.) with efforts to provide high-quality instructional experiences to every student, regardless of student or teacher background. Teacher evaluation based solely on student performance as demonstrated by standardized exams is likely to experience the same kind of accountability pressures and gaming of the system as we discussed previously. Failure to take context or other data points into consideration could deter teachers from accepting particularly challenging teaching assignments or from seeking/accepting employment in challenged schools or districts where teachers feel they are bound to fail despite their best efforts (Clotfelter et al., 2004; Feng et al., 2018).

Statistical Significance Versus Practical Significance

Statistical significance refers to the existence of an effect determined through the use of appropriate statistical procedures. Practical significance from a technical perspective indicates the magnitude of an effect size. To us, practical significance is also about whether results are meaningful in a particular context. There are many ways we could focus this discussion, such as using evidence where there is statistical significance but low effect sizes impacting outcomes and practical significance or significant results that fail to move the needle much in terms of practice.

If we think about the variety of tests, assessments, and student performance measures more generally construed, we envision a pyramid that ranges from summative measures on the top to classroom-based activities on the base (Love et al., 2008). Summative assessments are subject to psychometric examination to determine reliability and validity, which is not the case for teacher-made classroom activities and quizzes. Considering a hierarchy of assessments as a pyramid (with locally developed and deployed assessments—because they are most numerous and frequent—located at the base, with more infrequent but formally developed assessments located at the top), assessments at the top likely have more psychometric rigor, although locally developed assessments are closer in proximity to other classroom-based data points (e.g., observations, other assessments, performance tasks). In other words, there are value trade-offs to using one or another type of assessment.

Psychometric rigor may or may not equate to practical utility; that is, summative tests may not have the most impact to inform instruction and, therefore, have less practical significance, but they may prove valuable in determining student progress as compared to a broader sample of peers in an age group. In contrast, the classroom-based activities might have the most practical impact and significance as they are most closely aligned to instructional objectives and decisions, as well as closest in proximity to the student. Thus, there can be an inverse relationship between psychometric and practice utility and significance (Mandinach, 2012).

The lesson drawn from the example is that leaders have to use multiple data points and judgment to ascertain the balance between statistical or research significance and practical significance, which is the meaningfulness to the particular context. A study may have shown significant results (internal validity) but may not generalize to other situations (external validity). A standardized test may not have a valid use in making certain instructional decisions. SAT or ACT scores should not be used as proxies for real estate values by claiming that high scores translate into higher property value by virtue of better schools. Tests and other data should be used for their intended purposes. This is what Messick (1989) refers to as "pitting proposed tests use against alternative uses" (p. 86). Research results may or may not be generalized to other samples and locations. Educators must be literate consumers of data, information, and evidence to responsibly translate those results into decisions for their specific contexts and practices.

Checking Ethical Positionality in Classroom Decision-Making

Data-driven decisions that warrant awareness of ethical positionality can occur at the classroom, school, and district level. Take, for example, a scenario in which a teacher implements a computer-based reading program to build comprehension skills. The program shows that students are improving related to fluency (speed) and accuracy of response to comprehension questions. However, observations and parent feedback suggest an unintended outcome: Several students are reading fewer books or magazines on their own, and student-reported interest in pleasure reading has declined. This is an unintended consequence. Students are quicker to say "I don't like reading" than they were previous to the program's implementation. The teacher is faced with a dilemma: Students are doing well in terms of performance, but his approach has resulted in some negative side effects that require consideration. Should the teacher adjust his approach? The teacher needs to consider all "feasible options" that will benefit students. However, the teacher must also interrogate *why* he makes the decision he does: Is it to benefit students or to augment his own class test results (regardless of how his current approach may render negative consequence to students in the future)? Is there an option that can be reached that helps students continue to progress while mitigating negative attitudes toward reading? Maintaining an awareness of *why* the teacher makes the decision he makes provides an ethical compass to the decision-making process.

To explore the concept of ethical positionality at a campus level, consider a principal who is concerned about improving academics in her school. She is aware that local realtor sites and web ratings have mentioned that the high school is not safe. The principal has a school safety report due. How behavioral issues are coded in the discipline system can make the incidents look less problematic, depending on if the code used is "disruptive behavior" rather than "fight." The principal feels the campus is relatively safe and that adjusting the coding would present a more accurate portrait of the school, but she also is concerned about coding incidents accurately. She wonders whether she would be considering adjusting the coding if she were not also worried the data would reflect on her poorly as a leader. One option here is for the principal to accurately code and report the incidents but provide more granular descriptions of campus safety when talking with community groups and parents, emphasizing that in pursuit of a safe school, incidents at the campus are reported rather than ignored. The heart of maintaining ethical positionality in the data using process is an intentional focus on the question: Who benefits most from the decision she ultimately makes—the principal herself, the students, or (possibly) both?

We now move to a district-level example of the application of ethical positionality. A superintendent must make a decision about the purchase of a data warehouse for which the vendor offers a steep discount. In a conversation with the vendor, the superintendent realizes that the discount has been offered because the vendor expects to be able to extract de-identified student data to further develop the product and that the de-identified data will be resold to other vendors. "That way," the vendor explained, "we make up the money we lose on the discount." The superintendent is torn because the district will get a great system at a low cost, and he sees no issue with the vendor capturing and reselling de-identified data. But he is worried that if the full details are known, parents may opt their children out of the system. Too many opt-outs would mean the kinds of data reports the superintendent thinks would be useful to the district could be inaccurate, resulting in errant decisions about curriculum, instruction, and assessment. In terms of ethical positionality, the superintendent must not only wrestle with the best decision to make on behalf of the children in his district, but he must also wrestle with his rationale for (potentially) failing to be transparent about the conditions of purchase with parents in the district.

Confirmation Bias

Standardized tests have been attacked for years as being biased and producing results that fail to capture students' knowledge and ability. Such criticisms come from test fairness groups, advocacy groups, and the general public, despite testing companies using sophisticated algorithms to examine differential performance on items. Yet when tests are able to produce useful information, accurate interpretations by educators remain an essential component in moving data to equitable and ethical action. However, an essential ingredient in the interpretive process is examining test results within the context of the entire student body, with the test scores being only one of many data sources to help teachers understand the student.

Datnow and Park (2018) note that equity is fundamental to data use. All too often, educators make assumptions about students based on their backgrounds, contexts, characteristics, and demographics. And such perceptions about their students are affirmed through what is called *confirmation bias*; that is, they select, examine, and interpret data through the lens of their own existing and personal beliefs and prejudices, rather than through a lens of data and evidence. Ascribing to stereotypes can lead educators to engage with data in closed-minded ways to the detriment of their students. Work on stereotype threat (Spencer et al., 2016; Steele & Aronson, 1995) is particularly relevant, as the messages conveyed to students—and messages about themselves they subsequently internalize—can impact student performance. Using data in such confirmatory ways is a form of unethical data use in that interpretations educators make from data are wrongly influenced by their biases, beliefs, perceptions, and prejudices.

We pose a positive and hypothetical example that demonstrates how constructive data use practices can help counter confirmation bias and racism. A 3rd-grade student reveals she wants to be a videogame developer when she grows up and has a love of both math and science. This student is female and African American—both very underrepresented demographics in the field of videogame development. Rather than dissuading the student from this career option—based solely on the status quo of the field at the moment—the teacher has used an interest inventory as a "beginning-of-year" data point and so is aware of the career interest as well as several of the student's favorite games and hobbies. Because she has this information, she helps to nurture the student's interests through targeted activities that can enhance her knowledge and encourages her interest in the discipline. Her efforts to connect through the student's interest also feed a stronger teacher–student relationship that supports learning in other areas.

Focus Only on Test Data

Ask educators to define data, and they will most likely equate data with test results (Jimerson, 2014). Parents and other stakeholders may believe this even more strongly. But data are much more than test results or even other student performance indices. Mandinach and Gummer (2016) have long advocated for a broad definition of educational data, and more recently, support has arisen for emphasis on the whole child, an asset-based model, and culturally responsive practices (Mandinach & Mundry, 2021; Mandinach, Warner, & Lacireno-Paquet, 2020; Mandinach, Warner, & Mundry, 2019).

Limiting the view of what are relevant data severely constrains educators' abilities to gain a comprehensive view of their students. Without a range of data, educators will struggle to see the whole child in the puzzle pieces that can encompass essential factors such as motivation, strengths/weaknesses, interests, home context (homelessness, shelter, foster care, military family, highly mobile), special program status (Gifted/Talented, ELL or Emergent Bilingual, or Special Education), or other issues such as bullying, poverty, and long transportation commutes. Atwood and colleagues (2019) provide a salient example about making assumptions based on the obvious rather than looking for root causes. In this case, a student is found stealing food in school. Some teachers leapt to the conclusion that the student had behavioral problems, whereas one teacher collected more data (including from the student) and discovered a deeper problem rooted in persistent food insecurity and poverty. The broader view of data use in shaping and responding to the problem helped educators find a solution to help the student, rather than take the easier procedural steps about behavior that would have resulted in a different conclusion.

Using multiple and diverse data sources is an essential component of ethical data use, and data points must go well beyond student performance indices so that they enable educators to gain a comprehensive understanding of the whole child. This issue is related to other examples we have given. Using limited data from which to make a decision is just bad practice. It can skew interpretations and subsequent actions, and it can produce absolute inaccuracies and misconceptions, as shown in the Atwood and colleagues (2019) article. Educators must use multiple measures that can be triangulated and aligned to the decision. However, educators must also contend with the fact that some data sources may be difficult or impossible to access (e.g., some medical and justice system data). A desire to use all possible data to address the needs of the whole child will inevitably exist in tension with the need to safeguard data privacy and confidentiality in certain circumstances.

WHAT NEEDS TO HAPPEN

We have covered a lot of territory and have hopefully helped you consider scenarios that are essential to data ethics but which move beyond traditional cornerstone issues around the protection of privacy and confidentiality of student data. We have cast data ethics broadly to include using data responsibly, in a valid manner, and in alignment with espoused core beliefs about equity and the centering of student good in educational decision-making. There are many ways educators can use data inappropriately, despite good intentions. Educators talk about doing what is right for the students but may be tempted to cut ethical corners if they think their efforts are unnecessarily hampered. This could lead to well-intended but unethical (or at least questionable) acts such as trying to access data without proper authorization or communicating about a student outside of the "educational-need-to-know" parameters of FERPA. Most educators try to do good, but without appropriate education and awareness of data ethics, they may run afoul of legal and ethical guidelines in pursuit of their goals.

We draw from some recommendations that districts can implement to creature a data privacy culture (CatchOn, 2020):

- Develop a data use vision and strategy
- Adopt and promote privacy principles
- Offer innovative training and resources
- Engage parents to earn trust
- Ensure local privacy policies properly integrate federal and state requirements (p. 2)

We now turn to some ideas that may help to enhance more responsible data use in districts.

Grow Awareness

Targeting awareness about FERPA and responsible data use, we know that data ethics are not readily addressed in educator preparation or state standards (Mandinach & Wayman, 2020) or in professional development. It is also unclear what districts do in terms of in-service training specific to data ethics. Whose responsibility is it? We maintain that it is a shared responsibility: Educator preparation should introduce data ethics in their curricula, and districts should tailor broad expectations around data ethics to district-specific policies and technology platforms and then continue to reinforce the topic throughout educators' careers. Data ethics go beyond educational staff who work directly with students to anyone who has access to student data, including data clerks, food service workers, transportation employees, attendance officers, and others. We strongly advocate for a required onboarding process that provides training on data ethics. For districts that do not have the internal capacity to provide such training, resources available through PTAC can prove invaluable supports. Educators need to be aware of data ethics more broadly construed, and they must acquire the necessary skills and knowledge. Resource development is underway for educator preparation (Mandinach, Cotto, et al., 2020; Mandinach et al., 2021), but more must be done.

Validity of Data Alignment

We have discussed the importance of validity and aligning data to the specific decision. Our position here is to ensure that professional learning from preservice through in-service is structured to broaden the notion of what constitutes appropriate data use. That means expanding beyond FERPA to responsible and ethical data use, including understanding data quality, data alignment, and validity of interpretation. This must also include helping educators practice self-interrogation so they can develop awareness of ethical positionality as it intersects with the decisions they make in any data-driven process. To reiterate, data must be complete, accurate, and timely, as well as aligned to the decision. Interpretations must be valid based on the decision. And decisions must center the good of all students in the decision-making process (although this does not necessitate marginalizing benefits to teachers and leaders, as these can potentially coexist). School districts must reinforce these notions to have them become foundational to everyday practice.

Support *All* Students

Education is for *all* students, regardless of demographics, characteristics, special status, ability, and performance. To focus educational efforts on subsets of students is bad practice. Data can help provide invaluable information about every student—they can help educators not only identify academic strengths and weaknesses but also get to know students and their families better. Contextual data can provide the needed background information to address the whole child through an asset-based model. This premise must be reinforced throughout educators' careers. Districts have an essential role to play in affirming that message and supporting educators to carry out educational practice with an equity lens. Data can inform such culturally responsive practice.

Mitigate Confirmation Bias

Relatedly, the tendency to seek out information and data that confirm existing bias is a real issue in education. When this is the case, processes become less about using data and more about justifying what may be sexist, ableist, or racist beliefs, assumptions, and perceptions. Such processes are a misuse of data. Appropriate and valid data use is at the heart of increasing awareness of and working toward mitigating confirmation bias. Districts need to play an active role in preventing such practice and must increase awareness of the inappropriateness of such actions. They can instead promote the use of culturally responsive practices and, in particular, culturally responsive data literacy (Mandinach, Warner, & Lacireno-Paquet, 2020).

Focus on Growing People, Not Sorting Them

This issue pertains to the distinction between data use for continuous improvement and data use for accountability. Continuous improvement must happen at all levels within a district, from working with individual students, to the classroom, to the school, and throughout the district. Data should not be used as a sorting mechanism nor punitively by administrators to admonish educators. Messaging is essential. There is a robust body of literature on the importance of leadership in effective data use (see

Anderson et al., 2010; Firestone & Gonzales, 2007; Hamilton et al., 2009; Jimerson et al., 2019; Louis et al., 2010; Schildkamp et al., 2019). Leaders make it possible for educators to use data effectively and responsibly. They set the expectation, provide the resources, and message how data are to be used and for what purposes. It is incumbent on leaders to explicitly communicate about data use for continuous improvement to help all students grow.

Data as a Road Map, Not as Destiny

Data use is not a panacea. It is not the answer to all of education's problems, questions, or issues. Data use can be flawed, even destructive, and it must be appropriately combined with educator experience and the all-important context in which a decision is being situated. Data use should be used as a road map that lays out the evidence toward which actionable steps can be taken. Data have inherent limitations that may be grounded in interpretations and context. They are not definitive, but they are necessary alternatives to anecdotes and gut feelings.

CONCLUSION

Make no mistake, data ethics are an essential skill set that must be developed, nurtured, and sustained across educators' careers. Data use more generally is a complex enterprise and becomes even more complex as the definition of data expands to include more diverse sources. Data ethics continue to evolve. Other data regulations also come into play. Data systems, data applications, and other technologies present challenges, as do firewalls and interoperability. Social media now play a significant role in data ethics in educational settings, when students and teachers post to sites where the public can view things that should not be made public. Devices need to be protected and locked down, sometimes even encrypted. But the issues transcend technology to more traditional, face-to-face communications. Educators talk to other educators, to parents, to students, and to other stakeholders. They must know how to communicate with data and understand what can be shared. And different protection regulations pertain to different data. It is complicated and nuanced, with many gray areas. We do not expect educators to understand it all. Even lawyers and policymakers sometimes struggle with the nuances. But we do hope to build awareness of the importance of data ethics. We hope to stimulate movement to better preparing educators and then sustaining knowledge throughout their careers. Data use and data ethics will only get more complex over time. The time to begin was yesterday in helping to build a data literate education workforce that can use data effectively and responsibly.

REFERENCES

Anderson, S., Leithwood, K., & Strauss, T. (2010). Leading data use in schools: Organizational conditions and practices at the school and district levels. *Leadership and Policy in Schools*, 9(3), 292–327.

Armstrong, C., & Seifert, T. (2020, September). *Stakeholder engagement and the evolution of a partnership* [Webinar]. https://nces.ed.gov/programs/slds/webinars.asp

Atwood, E. D., Jimerson, J. B., & Holt, B. (2019). Equity-oriented data use: Identifying and addressing food insecurity at Cooper Springs Middle School. *Journal of Cases in Educational Leadership*, 22(3), 1–16. https://doi.org/10.1177/1555458919859932

Au, W. (2007). High-stakes testing and curricular control: A qualitative metasynthesis. *Educational Researcher*, 35(5), 258–267.

Barile, J. P., Donohue, D. K., Anthony, E. R., Baker, A. M., Weaver, S. R., & Henrich, C. C. (2012). Teacher–student relationship climate and school outcomes: Implications for educational policy initiatives. *Journal of Youth and Adolescence*, 41(3), 256–267.

Berliner, D. C. (2011). Rational responses to high stakes testing: The case of curriculum narrowing and the harm that follows. *Cambridge Journal of Education*, 41(3), 287–302.

Bertrand, M., & Marsh, J. A. (2015). Teachers' sensemaking of data and implications for equity. *American Educational Research Journal*, 52(5), 861–893.

Bocala, C., & Boudett, K. P. (2015). Teaching educators habits of mind for using data wisely. *Teachers College Record*, 117, 1–20.

Booher-Jennings, J. (2005). Below the bubble: "Educational triage" and the Texas Accountability System. *American Educational Research Journal*, 42(2), 231–268.

Burkhauser, S. (2017). How much do school principals matter when it comes to teacher working conditions? *Educational Evaluation and Policy Analysis*, 39(1), 126–145. https://doi.org/10.3102/0162373716668028

CatchOn. (2020). *Establishing a robust student data privacy culture: Action ideas for school districts*. https://www.setda.org/wp-content/uploads/2020/03/establishing-a-robust-student-data-privacy-culture.pdf

Clotfelter, C. T., Ladd, H. F., Vigdor, J. L., & Diaz, R. A. (2004). Do school accountability systems make it more difficult for low-performing schools to attract and retain high-quality teachers? *Journal of Policy Analysis and Management*, 23(2), 251–271.

Coburn, C. E., Honig, M. I., & Stein, M. K. (2009). What's the evidence on district's use of evidence? In J. Bransford, D. J. Stipek, N. J. Vye, L. Gomez, & D. Lam (Eds.), *Educational improvement: What makes it happen and why?* (pp. 67–86). Harvard Educational Press.

Corcoran, S. P. (2010). *Can teachers be evaluated by their students' test scores? Should they be? The use of value-added measures of teacher effectiveness in policy and practice*. Education Policy for Action Series. Annenberg Institute for School Reform at Brown University (NJ1). https://files.eric.ed.gov/fulltext/ED522163.pdf

Cronbach, L. J. (1988). Five perspectives on validity argument. In H. Wainer & H. Braun (Eds.), *Test validity* (pp. 3–17). Lawrence Erlbaum.

Daly, A. J. (2012). Data, dyads, and dynamics: Exploring data use and social networks in educational improvement. *Teachers College Record, 114*, 1–38.

Data Quality Campaign. (2014). *Teacher data literacy: It's about time.* https://dataqualitycampaign.org/resource/teacher-data-literacy-time/

Datnow, A. (2017). *Opening or closing doors for students? Equity and data-driven decision-making.* https://research.acer.edu.au/cgi/viewcontent.cgi?article=1317&context=research_conference

Datnow, A., Choi, B., Park, V., & St. John, E. (2018). Teacher talk about student ability and achievement in the era of data-driven decision making. *Teachers College Record, 120*, 1–34.

Datnow, A., & Park, V. (2018). Opening or closing doors for students? Equity and data use in schools. *Journal of Educational Change, 19*(2), 131–152.

Datnow, A., Park, V., & Kennedy-Lewis, B. (2013). Affordances and constraints in the context of teacher collaboration for the purpose of data use. *Journal of Educational Administration, 51*, 341–362.

Diamond, J. B., & Spillane, J. P. (2004). High-stakes accountability in urban elementary schools: Challenge or reproducing inequality? *Teachers College Record, 106*, 1145–1176.

Duncan, A. (2009, March 10). Federal leadership to support state longitudinal data systems. *Comments made at the Data Quality Campaign Conference, Leveraging the Power of Data to Improve Education.* Washington, DC.

Farrell, C., & Marsh, J. (2016). Contributing conditions: A qualitative comparative analysis of teachers' instructional responses to data. *Teaching and Teacher Education, 60*, 398–412.

Feng, L., Figlio, D., & Sass, T. (2018). School accountability and teacher mobility. *Journal of Urban Economics, 103*, 1–17.

Firestone, W. A., & Gonzalez, R. A. (2007). Culture and processes affecting data use in school districts. In P. A. Moss (Ed.), *Evidence and decision making* (pp. 132–154). Blackwell Publishing.

Garner, B., Thome, J. K., & Horn, I. S. (2017). Teachers interpreting data for instructional decisions: Where does equity come in? *Journal of Educational Administration, 55*(4), 407–426.

Gonzalez, J. (2017, December 3). *How to stop killing the love of reading.* Cult of pedagogy. https://www.cultofpedagogy.com/stop-killing-reading/

Halverson, R., Hackett, S., Kallio, J., Rawat, R., & Zellmer, L. (2017, August). *The practice of personalized learning and promoting a strategic assessment system* [Presentation]. STATS-DC Data Conference, Washington, DC. https://nces.ed.gov/whatsnew/conferences/statsdc/2017/session_I.asp

Hamilton, L., Halverson, R., Jackson, S., Mandinach, E., Supovitz, J., & Wayman, J. (2009). *Using student achievement data to support instructional decision making* (NCEE 2009–4067). National Center for Education Evaluation and Regional Assistance, Institute of Education Sciences, U.S. Department of Education. http://ies.ed.gov/ncee/wwc/publications/practiceguides

Hazi, H. M. (2017). VAM under scrutiny: Teacher evaluation litigation in the states. *The Clearing House: A Journal of Educational Strategies, Issues and Ideas, 90*(5–6), 184–190.

Hazi, H. M. (2019). Coming to understand the wicked problem of teacher evaluation. In S. J. Zepeda & J. Ponticell (Eds.), *Handbook of educational supervision* (pp. 183–207). Wiley-Blackwell.

Hess, F. M. (2009). The new stupid. *Educational Leadership, 66*(4), 12–17.

Honig, M. I., & Coburn, C. (2008). Evidence-based decision making in school district central offices: Toward a policy and research agenda. *Educational Policy, 22*(4), 578–608.

Hubbard, L., Datnow, A., & Pruyn, L. (2014). Multiple initiatives, multiple challenges: The promises and pitfalls of implementing data. *Studies in Educational Evaluation, 42,* 54–62.

Ingram, D., Louis, K. S., & Schroeder, R. G. (2004). Accountability policies and teacher decision-making: Barriers to the use of data to improve practice. *Teachers College Record, 106,* 1258–1287.

Jimerson, J. B. (2014). Thinking about data: Exploring the development of mental models for "data use" among teachers and school leaders. *Studies in Educational Evaluation, 42,* 5–14.

Jimerson, J. B., Garry, V., Poortman, C. L., & Schildkamp, K. (2019, April). *Implementing a data use intervention in a United States context: Enabling and constraining factors* [Conference presentation]. Annual conference of the American Educational Research Association, Toronto, Canada.

Kahneman, D., & Klein, B. M. (2009). Conditions for intuitive expertise: A failure to disagree. *American Psychologist, 64,* 515–526.

Kharif, O. (2014, May 2). Privacy fears over student data tracking lead to InBloom's shutdown. https://www.bloomberg.com/news/articles/2014-05-01/inbloom-shuts-down-amid-privacy-fears-over-student-data-tracking

Lavigne, A. L., & Good, T. L. (2020, January). *Addressing teacher evaluation appropriately.* APA Division 15 Policy Brief Series (Vol. 1, No. 2). https://apadiv15.org/wp-content/uploads/2020/01/Addressing-Teacher-Evaluation-Appropriately.pdf

Louis, K. S., Leithwood, K., Wahlstrom, K. L., Anderson, S. E., Michlin, M., & Mascall, B. (2010). *Learning from leadership: Investigating the links to improved student learning.* Center for Applied Research and Educational Improvement; Ontario Institute for Studies in Education.

Love, N., Stiles, K. E., Mundry, S., & DiRanna, K. (2008). *A data coach's guide to improving learning for all students: Unleashing the power of collaborative inquiry.* Corwin Press.

Mandinach, E. B. (2012). A perfect time for data use: Using data-driven decision making to inform practice. *Educational Psychologist, 47*(2), 71–85.

Mandinach, E. B., Cotto, J., Wayman, J. C., Rastrick, E., Vance, A., & Siegl, J. (2020). *Data ethics scenarios: Second deliverable in privacy training resources project*. WestEd.

Mandinach, E. B., & Gummer, E. S. (2016). *Data literacy for educators: Making it count in teacher preparation and practice*. Teachers College Press.

Mandinach, E. B., Jimerson, J. B., Cotto, J., Vance, A., & Siegl, J. (2021). *User's guide for data privacy and data ethics scenarios for leaders*. WestEd.

Mandinach, E. B., & Mundry, S. E. (2021). Data-driven decision making and its alignment with educational psychology: Why data are more than student performance results. In S. L. Nichols & D. Varier (Eds.), *Teaching on Assessment* (pp. 269–291). Information Age Publishing.

Mandinach, E. B., Penuel, W. R., Shepard, L. A., Hamilton, L. S., Miller, S. R., & Gummer, E. S. (2018, April). *Data-driven decision making: Does it lack a theory of learning to inform research and practice?* [Facilitated discussion]. Annual meeting of the American Educational Research Association, New York, NY.

Mandinach, E. B., & Schildkamp, K. (2021). Misconceptions about data-driven decision making in education: An exploration of the literature. *Studies in Educational Evaluation, 69*, 1–10. https://doi.org/10.1016/j.stueduc.2020.100842

Mandinach, E. B., Warner, S., & Lacireno-Paquet, N. (2020, September). *Culturally responsive data literacy: Integration into practice in schools and districts* [Webinar]. Regional Educational Laboratory Mid-Atlantic. https://ies.ed.gov /ncee/edlabs/regions/midatlantic/app/Docs/Events/RELMA_culturally _responsive_data_literacy_webinar_slides_508.pdf

Mandinach, E. B., Warner, S., & Mundry, S. E. (2019, November). *Using data to promote culturally responsive teaching* [Webinar]. Regional Educational Laboratory Northeast & Islands. https://ies.ed.gov/ncee/edlabs/regions/northeast /Docs/Events/CRDL_Workshop_Sep_30_2019_508c.pdf

Mandinach, E. B., & Wayman, J. C. (2020). *Survey of curriculum: First deliverable in privacy training resources project*. WestEd.

Messick, S. J. (1989). Validity. In. R. L. Linn (Ed.), *Educational measurement* (3rd ed., pp. 13–103). Macmillan Publishing Company.

Mette, I. M., Range, B. G., Anderson, J., Hvidston, D. J., Nieuwenhien, L., & Doty, J. (2017). The wicked problem of the intersection between supervision and evaluation. *International Electronic Journal of Elementary Education, 9*(3), 709–724.

Niche, Inc. (2021). Safest school districts methodology. https://www.niche.com /about/methodology/safest-school-districts/

Nichols, S. L., & Berliner, D. C. (2007). *Collateral damage: How high-stakes testing corrupts America's schools*. Harvard Education Press.

Oregon Data Project. (n.d.). *Data project*. https://www.oregon.gov/ode/about-us /Pages/Data%20Partnerships/DATA-Project.aspx

Penuel, W. R., & Shepard, L. A. (2016). Assessment and teaching. In D. H. Gitomer & C. A. Bell (Eds.), *Handbook of research on teaching* (5th ed., pp. 787–850). American Educational Research Association.

Schildkamp, K., & Kuiper, W. (2010). Data-informed curriculum reform: Which data, what purposes, and promoting and hindering factors. *Teaching and Teacher Education, 26*(3), 482–496.

Schildkamp, K., Poortman, C. L., Ebbeler, J., & Pieters, J. M. (2019). How school leaders can build effective data teams: Five building blocks for a new wave of data-informed decision making. *Journal of Educational Change, 20*, 283–325. Advanced online publication. https://link.springer.com/article/10.1007/s10833-019-09345-3

Schildkamp, K., & Tedlie, C. (2008). School performance feedback systems in the USA and the Netherlands: A comparison. *Educational Research and Evaluation, 14*(3), 255–282.

Schneider, A., & Ingram, H. (1993). Social construction of target populations: Implications for politics and policy. *American Political Science Review, 87*, 334–347.

Shoho, A. R., & Barnett, B. G. (2010). The realities of new principals: Challenges, joys, and sorrows. *Journal of School Leadership, 20*(5), 561–96. https://doi.org/10.1177/105268461002000503

Spellings, M. A. (2005, June 14). *Seeing the data, meeting the challenge* [Speech transcript]. U.S. Department of Education. Indiana High School Summit: Redesigning Indiana's High Schools, Indianapolis. http://www.ed.gov/news/speeches/2005/06/06142005.html

Spencer, S. J., Logel, C., & Davies, P. G. (2016). Stereotype threat. *Annual Review of Psychology, 67*, 415–437.

Starratt, R. J. (2012). *Cultivating an ethical school*. Routledge.

Steele, C. M., & Aronson, J. A. (1995). Stereotype threat and the intellectual test performance of African Americans. *Journal of Personality and Social Psychology, 69*, 797–811.

Steinberg, M. P., & Kraft, M. A. (2017). The sensitivity of teacher performance ratings to the design of teacher evaluation systems. *Educational Researcher, 46*(7), 378–396.

Strauss, V. (2015, April 1). How and why convicted Atlanta teachers cheated on standardized tests. *The Washington Post.* https://www.washingtonpost.com/news/answer-sheet/wp/2015/04/01/how-and-why-convicted-atlanta-teachers-cheated-on-standardized-tests/

Vanlommel, K., Van Gasse, R., Vanhoof, J., & Van Petegem, P. (2020). Sorting pupils into their next educational track: How strongly do teachers rely on data-based or intuitive processes when they make the transition decision? *Studies in Educational Evaluation*, 1–10.

Wiliam, D. (2011). What is assessment for learning? *Journal of Studies in Educational Evaluation, 37*(1), 3–14. https://doi.org/10.1016/j.stueduc.2011.03.001

CHAPTER 6

The Role of Professional Development in Preparing Educators for Data Ethics

Ellen B. Mandinach and Diana Nunnaley

INTRODUCTION

Professional development providers, particularly those that focus on data use, are uniquely positioned to provide an introduction to the basics of data ethics. A question has always arisen about whose responsibility it is to provide training not only on the Family Educational Rights and Privacy Act (FERPA) but also on data ethics and responsible data use. Is it teacher preparation, districts in their onboarding process, state education agencies, professional organizations, or professional development? We do know that the Privacy Technical Assistance Center (PTAC) provides resources for FERPA with which several states have required training (B. Rodriquez, personal communication, February 28, 2018). We also know that some state education agencies do not believe such training is their responsibility. The National Forum on Education Statistics (2010) long ago advocated for role-based training in schools for all educators and educational staff who deal with data. However, a question looms as to whether districts have the internal capacity to provide the needed training. Professional development providers, especially those that focus on data use, have a unique opportunity by integrating the data ethics into training and modeling appropriate behavior. They can include examples, case studies, and scenarios of appropriate data use.

In this chapter, we set the stage for what we know about the complexity of students and requisite teacher knowledge. Second, we explore what professional development is doing to better prepare educators to use data ethically. Third, we focus on Using Data Solutions (Love et al., 2008) because of its implicit emphasis on data use for *all* students. We link this model to the data literacy for teachers construct (DLFT; Mandinach & Gummer, 2016a, 2016b) and the extension of DLFT, adding culturally responsive practices and thereby creating culturally responsive data literacy (CRDL; Mandinach & Mundry, 2021; Mandinach et al., 2019; Mandinach, Warner, & Mundry, 2020) to illustrate how data ethics can be emphasized in professional development. Finally, the chapter explores what activities might be included by providers to enhance the importance of data ethics. This final section posits recommendations for professional development that focus on data use and extend to other professional development topics and how they might integrate responsible data use. The extension to more general professional development recognizes that effective data use is fundamental to educational practice.

A Parenthetical Note

In preparation for writing this chapter, we did our due diligence to be inclusive in understanding how the major data professional development providers handle data ethics. In our quest to be comprehensive, we reached out to other providers. We know about Using Data Solutions (Love et al., 2008). Only one, Kathy Boudett of Data Wise, graciously responded with targeted information about its model (Boudett et al., 2013). We thank her for directing us to informative resources. We reviewed a report (Mandinach & Gummer, 2012) that surveyed the landscape of research, practice, and training around data-driven decision-making. The outcome was the initial definition of data literacy and laying out the skills and knowledge that would evolve into the DLFT construct. Mandinach and Gummer (2012) examined existing data use books and materials that were then available. The examination yielded an analysis of how each provider dealt with data-related skills and knowledge. Given that the analyses were conducted in 2011, many more resources have since become available, existing models have been updated, and the definition of data has evolved with the times to be more inclusive. Yet that analysis still provides informative insights into how authors and professional development looked at the components of responsible data use.

EXPANDING OUR KNOWLEDGE OF STUDENTS

It became clear that other forms of teacher knowledge influence data literacy. Mandinach and Gummer (Gummer & Mandinach, 2015; Mandinach & Gummer, 2016a, 2016b) looked to Shulman's (1986, 1987) view of content knowledge and pedagogical content knowledge. Mandinach and Gummer (2013) realized that teacher preparation was positioned to address these topics while professional development could help sustain and strengthen the knowledge acquired in preservice. As Shulman (1986) said, "The ultimate test of understanding rests on the ability to transform one's knowledge into teaching" (p. 14). The later version of the construct includes all seven of Shulman's (1987) forms of teacher knowledge. The two that are especially relevant to data ethics are (1) knowledge of learners and their characteristics and (2) knowledge of educational contexts (including communities and cultures).

DLFT and CRDL are essential for educators to understand their students and gain a comprehensive understanding of the whole child (Mandinach & Mundry, 2021; Mandinach, Warner, & Lacireno-Paquet, 2020; Mandinach, Warner, & Mundry, 2020). Students present with increasing complexities of contexts and circumstances that create the need for educators to look to diverse data sources well beyond academic performance indices. Note Berliner (2006), who said that teachers cannot be held accountable for things beyond their control, such as poverty, childhood disease, hunger, and many other situational factors. Environmental and equity factors present deeply systemic problems that impact students, teachers, and schools. Educators must understand and account for such issues and use them to inform their decision-making.

Because of the complexity of students, it is essential that educators become aware of the diversity of circumstances that may impact their students. Take, for example, Dr. Biden (2016), who spoke about students from military families and what data and information educators need to be able to serve these students. Military students may be transient, moving regularly from school to school, which not only impacts academic performance but also social interactions, psychological well-being, stability, and social-emotional learning. Students may be dealing with anxiety about a parent being deployed, injured, or even deceased. As Jacobson (2020) notes, the data to support military students are sometimes a challenge, depending on if there is a military identifier.

Having a military identifier is a special status indicator that may help educators make informed data-driven decisions. Figure 6.1 presents a list of data points or categories of data that can inform educators to gain a more comprehensive understanding of their students. Professional development can bring awareness and may help provide some actionable steps.

One interesting data collection strategy for understanding home context is informal home visits by teachers. In Washington, DC, there is a program called Parent Teacher Home Visits (Stein, 2019). The program is used in 27 other states as well. Before school begins, teachers pay informal visits, called "relationship-building home visits," to meet parents or guardians. The purpose is to establish rapport while gaining insights about the students. It gives them opportunities to learn things about the student and the home circumstances. This program can provide invaluable information about students that can inform teachers' practice and help them to better adapt to students' unique needs and circumstances.

Figure 6.1. Data to Address the Whole Child

Homelessness	Incarcerated parent or guardian	Foster care
Military family (including Gold Star)	Transportation	Attendance/truancy/excessive absenteeism
Victim of abuse	Health/medicine	Emancipation status
Poverty	Undocumented status	Psychological issues
Trauma	Special education designation	Language status/barriers
Food insecurity/hunger		Family restraining order
Gang membership	Victim of gang violence	LGBTQ status
Religion	Political affiliation	Ethnicity
Bullying	Gifted and talented	Disability
Unemployed family	Student employment	Adopted
Displaced	Drug addiction	Pregnancy or birth parent
Suicide or harm risk	Unstable home environment	Behavioral/justice/arrests
Parental education level		
Migrant status	Aspirations/interests	Home connectivity

MODELS OF PROFESSIONAL DEVELOPMENT—WHAT WE KNOW AND DO NOT KNOW

We review two models of data-oriented professional development and how they address responsible data use. We then take the high-capacity data use strategies from Using Data Solutions and link them to DLFT and CRDL, explicitly noting responsible data use. We then turn to what we know about other models of professional development. Finally, we discuss in-service training provided by the vendors of data systems.

Using Data Solutions

Using Data Solutions (Love et al., 2008) consists of a five-phase process for collaborative inquiry. It focuses on the use of multiple types of data and diverse data sources with the objective to enhance educators' ability to draw sound inferences about the data. The first phase is designed to build the capacity of school teams and data coaches to engage in a process of collaborative inquiry based on an understanding of school context and student diversity. An emphasis is placed on examining decisions through the lens of cultural proficiency by learning to examine educators' own personal contexts and experiences, potentially resulting in unrecognized biases toward some groups of students. Using Data Solutions developed tools to help teachers surface and examine their assumptions, values, and commitments to student learning. The core work of Using Data Solutions is focused on helping teams create the conditions and capacity to use data.

The Using Data Solutions phases are informed by a set of assumptions to be used as a catalyst for teams to deeply reflect on their own thinking processes and ultimate decisions. These assumptions serve to promote responsible data use. The first assumption pertains to the moral responsibility to close the achievement gap. The second assumption is reflective of Cronbach's (1988) notion of validity in the form of meaningful interpretation. According to the Using Data Solutions model, data teams must examine their frames of reference, which help teams make meaning from the data and serve as an ethical checkpoint of interpretations. Other assumptions include the importance of collaborative inquiry and that good teaching is grounded in cultural proficiency and the investigation of root causes.

Using Data Solutions engages teams in drilling down into multiple types of data and multiple levels of each data type. To help teachers recognize when their inferences and decisions might be veering into unethical conclusions, Using Data Solutions introduced *Data Safety Regulations* of which *don't use data to punish* and *don't use data to blame students or their circumstances* were highlighted to draw teachers' attention to when they are using data irresponsibly (see Love et al., 2008, p. 137). The process notes the importance of triangulating data and not jumping to quick fixes based on a superficial examination of too little data. The process highlights the need for teachers to be aware of patterns in data over time, and the notion of "meaningful differences" when examining results that are based on small numbers.

Using Data Solutions has developed a focus on helping teams make the data actionable, transforming what teams learn into classroom action plans in which teachers consider the pedagogy and content knowledge needed to support all students' learning. Classroom Action Plan templates assist teachers in identifying specific learning problems, specific groups of students, and possible instructional strategies.

Another resource is a technique called My Culture (see Love et al., 2008, pp. 90–103), which helps to elicit how educators' cultures and backgrounds may differ from those of their students and therefore may skew their assumptions about their students. Many educators, especially those whose backgrounds differ from their students, most certainly can benefit from building their level of awareness and how that may shape assumptions and interpretations.

Data Wise

Data Wise (Boudett et al., 2013) is composed of an eight-step process of inquiry that is based on three tenets—prepare, inquire, and act. The model focuses on building assessment literacy as outlined in the second step of the process. This distinction is important as the focus is on test results, not data more broadly construed. This is not meant to be a criticism; it is a statement of emphasis. Price and Koretz (2013) wrote a chapter entitled "Building Assessment Literacy" in which they lay out Data Wise's principles of responsible data use about foundational assessment concepts. The chapter deals with sampling, discrimination, measurement error, reliability, and score inflation. In alignment with Cronbach's (1988) notion of validity residing in interpretation, Price and Koretz (2013) note that "inference is supported by performance on the test" (p. 37).

Price and Koretz (2013) also note the importance of responsible reporting. How results are reported can be a trade-off between detail and reliability. Educators will find importance in the details as they can be translated into instructional action. The trade-off lies in fewer items associated with lower reliability. Good measurement relies on the triangulation of multiple measures, but often even a single item may require several skills. Another caveat is the understanding of what is a meaningful difference. Booher-Jennings' (2005) findings about a focus on "bubble kids" is an important concept here. The difference between just passing and just failing may be miniscule. Thus, Price and Koretz (2013) emphasize three main principles: *Act*, that educators must act on multiple measures from which to make decisions; *Intentional Collaboration*, teams of educators come together to examine and discuss data; and *Relentless Focus on Evidence*, there are structures to enable educators to devote time to examining data and evidence to inform their practice. Bocala and Boudett (2015) note that the three principles or habits of mind can lead to effective data use but, done poorly, can lead to less responsible data use. They caution about having a narrow focus on data, which will ultimately constrain interpretations as well as overlooking valuable data sources; conclusions made based on unfounded evidence; and accountability pressures influencing assumptions.

According to Kathy Boudett (personal communication, November 26, 2019), the professional development model does not deal with FERPA but firmly emphasizes responsible data use through the use of scenarios as concrete examples of responsible data use. Data teams are given a worksheet developed by Dillman (n.d.) that outlines guiding questions for responsible data use around validity, reliability and measurement error, score inflation, sampling error, and keeping scores in perspective.

Other Professional Development Models

Because we only know about Using Data Solutions and Data Wise, we turn to a somewhat dated but also comprehensive analysis conducted by Mandinach and Gummer (2012). This analysis sought to identify the skills, knowledge, and dispositions that comprise data literacy. The outgrowth was the beginning of the definition that resulted in the DLFT construct.

Mandinach and Gummer amassed all the existing books, how-to guides, reports, and documents that addressed data use at that time. Some documents were strictly about data, whereas others veered toward assessment and formative assessment.

There are a few caveats about our review of the Mandinach and Gummer (2012) analysis. First, the analysis did not specifically examine data ethics. Thus, we have to extrapolate from the data provided to infer explicit attention to data ethics. We can only draw from the coding of what the documents addressed. Second, the analyses were conducted in 2011. Much has changed in the field of data use since that time, and extensive research has been done. Some resources have been updated and may or may not include data ethics. We know that the Data Wise documents have been updated. So short of conducting a similar analysis, our comments here address only those found in the comprehensive analysis from 2011.

One topic that pertains to data ethics is data quality. The analysis indicated that the coverage of data quality was superficial. Some resources addressed test fairness, test bias, and the timeliness of data. Similarly, reliability was addressed superficially. Some resources mentioned data sufficiency in terms of the need to use multiple sources of data and to triangulate them. Many documents mentioned interpretations, but they did not deal with implications of informing actions and the validity of such interpretations. Data Wise (Boudett et al., 2005) and Using Data Solutions (Love et al., 2008) were unique in addressing responsible data use. Surprisingly, some of the 33 resources failed to address any of the topics that are aligned with responsible data use. In hindsight of the analysis, this is an increasingly important topic, a missed opportunity, and one that we hope revisions and new resources will begin to address.

Relevant to future professional development is the work of Mandinach and colleagues (Mandinach, Warner, & Lacireno-Paquet, 2020; Mandinach, Warner, & Mundry, 2019, 2020), which transforms culturally responsive practices and data literacy into CRDL. As part of the webinars, Mandinach and colleagues developed three information domains to which educators should attend to gain a comprehensive picture of their students: Academic Performance and Schooling Experiences; Personal Story and Experiences; and Examining and Interpreting Bias. The authors have developed an extensive set of guiding questions that educators can use to better understand students' academic background and home circumstances. The resources also seek to stimulate introspection about potential biases that may interfere with sound understandings and interpretations.

Vendor-Based Training

Districts buy technology applications to support data use. As Hamilton and colleagues (2009) noted, a district should make a technological purchase to align with its educational objectives. Technologies include data warehouses, learning management systems, assessment systems, early warning indicator systems, dashboards, student information systems, and all sorts of customized applications. Each kind of technology comes with its own risks and caveats. The relevance to this chapter pertains to the training that districts receive around these technologies.

Typically, vendor in-services are one-time introductions on how to use the system. Specifically, they focus on how to access the data and specifics on using the technology, not using the resulting data. This is an essential distinction. The training is sporadic, going against recommendations by Hamilton and colleagues (2009) and Means and colleagues (2010), who promote the need for sustained and ongoing training on data use. The training fails to help the educators know how to use the data to inform their practice, therefore potentially leading to misuse. And as noted later, many data displays tend to oversimplify results in a way that can cause educators to either misinterpret or take away superficial interpretations from the displays (Penuel & Shepard, 2016). This is a major concern and one with no easy solutions because it is inextricably linked to data literacy and the ability to understand data representations and data displays. What the vendors are teaching are technical skills such as how to log in and how to access the data, whereas they need basic data literacy skills that include how to read the reports and understand the information produced by the systems to then translate that information into instructional action.

ALIGNMENT OF ONE PROFESSIONAL DEVELOPMENT MODEL WITH DATA ETHICS

For the purposes of discussion, we will analyze the Using Data Solutions (Love et al., 2008) metrics for high-capacity data use in conjunction with relevant DLFT (Mandinach & Gummer, 2016a, 2016b) and CRDL skills (Mandinach, Warner, & Lacireno-Paquet, 2020; Mandinach, Warner, & Mundry, 2019, 2020). The Using Data Solutions model outlines 13 data use strategies and compares low-capacity versus high-capacity data use. These strategies are particularly relevant to data ethics because they lay out processes that undergird the model and are seen as being necessary for both effective and responsible data use.

Love and colleagues (2008) note that "high-capacity uses are those that actually translate into improved instruction, expanded opportunities to learn for diverse learners, and improved outcomes for students" (p. 135). These strategies align with DLFT, including collaborative inquiry, Shulman's (1986) content knowledge, pedagogical content knowledge, and CRDL's cultural proficiency. We analyze each of the high-low data use contrasts found in Love and colleagues (2008, see p. 136 for quoted material).

These contrasts are telling as one can interpret that high-capacity data use should translate to responsible data use, and low-capacity data use should be not only ineffective but also irresponsible. As Love and colleagues (2008) and Mandinach and Gummer (2016a, 2016b) note, effective data use is composed of an iterative inquiry cycle, and, therefore, the strategies and skills are interrelated and are all part of the inquiry process.

The Contrasts

The first contrast pertains to interpretation. High-capacity interpretation is defined as "accurately interprets data and discerns what they mean," whereas low-capacity "misinterprets and misunderstands data." According to Cronbach (1988), interpretation is an essential component of validity. Interpretation goes to the heart of responsible data use. It is a key DLFT/CRDL skill, relating to confirmation bias and equity. Datnow and Park (2018) describe the tendency to make interpretations based on preconceived beliefs and assumptions, leading to bias and inequity. Spillane (2012) notes that educators will make interpretations based on their own views and contexts. Interpretations and data use require role-based decisions most often and impact interpretations (Mandinach & Gummer, 2016a). The issue around interpretations is that the same data can yield different interpretations—some legitimate, some ill-founded based on implicit biases. It is therefore essential for professional development to instantiate the importance of considering the legitimacy and accuracy of interpretations, being mindful of implicit biases and assumptions. Responsible data use must include accurate and unbiased interpretations on data so that the ensuing actions are grounded in sound practice.

Three strategies focus on the forms and formats of data. First is the level. High-capacity data use "regularly uses item-level data and student work," whereas low-capacity data use "uses aggregated and disaggregated data only." Second is the need to triangulate among different data sources. Thus, the high-capacity strategy "uses multiple sources of data before drawing conclusions," whereas the low-capacity strategy "uses single measures to draw conclusions." Relatedly, the third high-capacity strategy "uses formative and summative measures" whereas the low-capacity strategy "uses only summative measures." A fundamental premise of DLFT is to use multiple measures rather than single measures to make decisions. The triangulation of data and drill-down facilitate a comprehensive understanding of the phenomena that a superficial review of the data might overlook. There is more validity and reliability to the analysis. Additionally, the farther away from instruction the data are, the less relevant they are to aligning data to instructional decisions. Thus, using only summative results to make more proximal instructional decisions is not an effective practice. Linking the strategies to DLFT, good professional development will help educators gain an understanding of and appreciation for the importance of using diverse, deep dives into data sources and ensuring that the data sources are aligned to the kinds of decisions being made.

Four of the strategies pertain to data use to inform instruction that promotes equity: (1) "responds to achievement gaps with immediate concern and corrective action" versus "accepts achievement gaps as inevitable"; (2) "differentiates instruction; provides extra help and enrichment for all who need it" in contrast to "tutors only those students just missing the cutoff for proficiency; bubble kids"; (3) "increases the rigor of the curriculum for all students; assigns the best teachers to those who need them most" versus "tracks students into classes by perceived ability"; and (4) "chooses strategies that are culturally proficient and research-based and have a logical link to the intended outcome" as opposed to "chooses strategies based on instinct or the latest educational fad." These strategies reflect responsible data use. The first pertains to the disposition and belief that all students can learn and that achievement gaps and inequities are serious and in need of attention. In a related manner, attention to only the bubble kids is gaming the system and unethical practice (Booher-Jennings, 2005). All students, whether the most challenged or the most advanced, need attention, however different that attention might be. This is a fundamental principle of adaptive instruction (Corno, 2008). The third strategy follows from adaptive instruction. Finally, evidence-based practice is essential to effective education. The use of gut feelings, instinct, and anecdotes cannot and should not replace data and information as credible sources of evidence. These four strategies can and must be foundational parts of effective professional development.

The remaining strategies are a combination of good practices around what might be considered the inquiry process and differences between data for accountability versus continuous improvement. First, "aligns curriculum with standards and assessment; implements research-based improvement in curriculum, instruction, and assessment" versus "prepares for tests by drilling students on test items." Second, "looks for causes for failure that are within educators' control" as opposed to "blames students and external causes for failure." Third, "uses student work and data about practice and research to verify hypotheses" versus "draws conclusions without verifying hypotheses with data." Fourth, "regularly monitors implementation and student learning; no surprises" in contrast to "fails to monitor implementation and results; big surprises at the end." Lastly, "responds in teams and as a system" versus "responds as individual administrators and teachers." Nichols (see Chapter 4) enumerates issues around a sole focus on tests and outcomes. The first low-capacity strategy of drilling students on test items is bad educational practice that does not result in lasting learning. It games the system and negatively impacts students all in the name of higher accountability indices. The second low-capacity strategy is one of shaming and blaming. It promotes a deficit model, rather than an asset model

(Datnow, 2017). When one takes a whole child perspective and invokes CRDL, the goal is to understand the circumstances and contexts as well as student strengths and interests (Mandinach & Mundry, 2021; Mandinach et al., 2019). Blaming not only impacts students but also teachers where teachers are held responsible for student failures. Teachers are shamed and blamed. Attributions are relevant here. Bertrand and Marsh (2015) linked data use to attributions to instruction, student understanding, assessment, and student characteristics. If attributions of failure are made to unmalleable student characteristics, then this is an example of confirmation bias. In contrast, attributions can be made to instruction—that instruction needs to be modified to address student learning needs or to assessments where the tests do not adequately align to instruction. The second high-capacity strategy is one that promotes the examination of root causes, rather than the use of superficial data.

The third and fourth strategies promote the use of hypotheses to guide the inquiry process and regular monitoring of implementation. These are fundamental principles of data-driven decision-making. And combining the fifth strategy of responding in teams firmly places these last three strategies as part of collaborative inquiry. Hypotheses help to drive inquiry and target the needed data sources (Hamilton et al., 2009). Monitoring implementation pertains to taking proximal steps in examining the continuous improvement process, rather than working toward a distal goal and finding out much later that an intervention was not effective. It helps to eliminate surprises and wasted time. The collaborative aspect of data use is key, and there is a large amount of literature on data teams (Datnow et al., 2018; Earl & Katz, 2006; Hamilton et al., 2009; Jimerson et al., 2019; Marsh et al., 2015; Schildkamp & Poortman, 2015). Means and colleagues (2011) found that educators working in teams can help compensate for an individual's lack of data skills. Data teaming enables educators to discuss data in ways that yield more meaningful understanding of student strengths and weakness. Teaming is an effective data use strategy, and collaboration is one of DLFT's main dispositions. Professional development models promote these strategies, but of course there are concerns about whether educators understand the constraints and parameters to communicate about and with data.

DLFT and CRDL Skills and Dispositions

We now link the DLFT construct and its skills, knowledge, and dispositions as they relate to responsible data use and how they might be addressed within professional development. We draw from Mandinach and Gummer (2016b) because the article provides succinct definitions of the skills. We also apply the whole child view and the asset-based model of CRDL in this examination. By definition, to use data effectively and responsibly, educators must be data literate. Data ethics are part of data literacy. With more than 50 individual skills, we highlight the ones that are deemed most essential to responsible data use.

DLFT's first component is to *identify problems and frame questions*, and one of the embedded skills is to articulate a problem of practice. As Mandinach and colleagues (2019; Mandinach & Mundry, 2021) began to merge DLFT with culturally responsive practices to create CRDL, we became more mindful of negativism. Using the term, "problem" is a challenge to an asset-based model. No doubt, there are educational issues and problems, but the terminology remains negative. Professional development can help to better frame this definitional concern. Also embedded in the first DLFT component is understanding the context of the student and the context of the school, as well as involving relevant stakeholders. These are essential in terms of understanding the whole child and gaining a comprehensive picture of the circumstances. Knowledge of student privacy is explicitly mentioned as a skill here.

DLFT's second component is *use data*, which is an amalgam of skills related to actual data use. Several relevant skills are embedded here that speak to responsible data use: identify possible sources of data; understand the purposes of different data sources; develop sound assessments; understand data properties; use multiple data sources; use qualitative and quantitative data; understand the specificity of data to the question; understand what data are appropriate; understand data quality; understand the elements of data accuracy, appropriateness, and completeness; and understand how to drill down into data. Each of these skills and knowledge must be made explicit in professional development on data. Using Data Solutions addresses many of these skills, but the link to data ethics can be made emphasized.

The third DLFT component is *transform data into information*. Many of the skills are relevant to responsible data use, including the following: consider the impact and the consequences, generate hypothetical connections to instructions (actions), test assumptions, understand how to interpret data, probe for causality, and articulate inferences and conclusions. These actions rely on using the inquiry cycle in a way that is grounded in sound evidence and responsible practice.

The fourth component, *transform information into a decision*, pertains to the instructional or pedagogical actions educators take. For teachers, it is the pedagogy, yet not all decisions teachers make are solely about instruction. They may be behavioral, motivational, and beyond. For administrators, there is a parallel set of actions that pertain to administrative decision-making. Because of this, we extrapolate. The skills involve how to determine (instructional steps), monitor performance, make adjustments, and understand the context for the decision. Professional development around data typically falls short of this component. It does not deal with the instructional actions teachers or other educators should be taking, relying more on their existing pedagogical content knowledge.

The final component is to *evaluate outcomes*. This component involves how to monitor changes in performance, reexamine the original question, and compare pre- and post-results. The essential part of this component is the recognition that the inquiry process is cyclical or iterative; that is, the movement across the components is not linear. Effective decision-making is recursive by nature. The determination that a decision has been made and that it is finite is both ineffective and irresponsible. Most all professional development models for data and theories also recognize that the inquiry process is cyclic (see Mandinach & Jackson, 2012).

In addition to the knowledge and skills embedded within the five components, DLFT recognizes dispositions or habits of mind that are more generic skills directly related to effective data use and professional development beyond data. They include a belief that all students can learn; belief in thinking critically; educational improvement requires a continuous improvement cycle; ethical data use, including the protection of privacy and confidentiality; collaboration; and communication. The belief that all students can learn goes to the heart of an equity model on which CRDL is founded. To think otherwise is irresponsible. Educators must be able to think critically, introspecting about their own practice in their own evaluative feedback loop. Collaboration and communication go to the heart of both data use and the professional development to support effective data use. Most professional development models focus on collaborative inquiry. Data teaming participants must understand the ethics of communicating collaboratively and beyond about and with data. Thus, professional development has an essential role to play in supporting and enhancing these dispositions that contribute to effective and responsible data use.

RECOMMENDATIONS—WHERE THE FIELD NEEDS TO GO

We have taken a broad view of the meaning of data ethics and how the topic is being addressed or not being addressed in professional development. We are not necessarily advocating for FERPA-specific professional development, although we do think that schools and districts should have an onboarding process for all staff who deal with data that specifically pertains to protecting data privacy and confidentiality—sort of a FERPA 101 course. We now turn to possible solutions and recommendations for professional development on data and more general suggestions as well. We also recognize that the systemic nature of districts will impact some of the recommendations as they speak to issues around policy, structure, practice, and the general functioning of educational agencies.

Because of the systemic nature of education, a first suggestion is for states and professional organizations to modify standards and codes of ethics to explicitly include data ethics. In a review by Mandinach and Wayman

(2020), few states (only two) explicitly mention FERPA, the protection of privacy and confidentiality, or even take a broader view of data ethics. Most states have codes of ethics but they vary widely in how they deal with data, if at all. Nineteen states mention privacy and confidentiality, while a handful mention disclosure, communication, disposal of tests, and falsification. Instead, state codes of ethics typically deal with broader ethical problems such as respecting students and professional learning. The codes may sometimes discuss disposing, communicating, or securing data, but in no way do they adequately or explicitly address data ethics. Even the most comprehensive document, the *Model Code of Ethics for Educations* (MCEE) developed by the National Association of State Directors of Teacher Education and Certification (NASDTEC, n.d.) lacks explicitness in terms of data ethics. Thus, our recommendation is that there is outreach to NASDTEC, its state members, and associated staff in state departments of education to work to educate them about the importance of data ethics. Further, it would be possible to develop comprehensive wording that can be shared with these agencies for inclusion in their standards and codes. These documents will impact teacher preparation, local education agencies, and subsequent professional development.

A second recommendation is the creation of a set of guidelines that builds from documents such as the Institute of Education Sciences (IES) practice guides. The data-oriented practice guide (Hamilton et al., 2009) is now dated and requires updating, given the large amount of relevant research over the past decade. Data ethics should be included in such a revision. While data ethics have not been a focus for the rigorous research typically reviewed in the practice guides, there must be a way to include ethical data use in the recommendations.

A third recommendation is about messaging. Data-driven and evidence-based practices in education have been emphasized for nearly 2 decades. The messaging could be modified to merge language about equitable and ethical decisions. Given the complexity of students today and in the future, invoking the whole child perspective and one where there is an overarching theme of data ethics and equity could be helpful. The messaging should include that all decisions educators make should seek to enhance all students' opportunities to build on their strengths, backgrounds, interests, and aspirations. The messaging should provide the notion of the value of students as individuals and learners, rather than data points that contribute to better performance on accountability indices. Professional development can help frame discussions around data in terms of what data should be used, for what purpose, and how. Professional development can also help frame the discussion in terms of the inherent value of each student and that the use of data can contribute to improving the teaching and learning process by providing diagnostic indicators to address student needs (J. B. Jimerson, personal communication, August, 19, 2019).

A fourth recommendation, and one that is in progress by Mandinach and colleagues (Mandinach, Cotto, et al., 2020; Mandinach et al., 2021; Mandinach, Warner, & Mundry, 2019, 2020) is to build materials that explicitly promote data ethics that can be used across educators' careers to build understanding and capacity such as the questions in the three informational domains mentioned previously. Materials should be used in educator preparation programs and in professional development. They should be realistic and authentic, using scenarios and case studies that illustrate various components of responsible data use. Such materials should be based on DLFT and CRDL and look across the developmental continuum of skills (Beck & Nunnaley, 2021). The materials should highlight the impact of unethical or inequitable decisions, and show how such practice can be eliminated through consistent and responsible practices.

A fifth set of recommendations pertains to data system vendors. Penuel and Shepard (2016) criticize data systems for distorting and dumbing down the presentation of data to what is called a stoplight—passing is green, on the cusp is yellow, and failing is red. The stoplight fails to provide educators with a theory of learning and overly simplifies student performance. The stoplight presents many problems around ethical data use. Vendors must seek to find more responsible ways of presenting data. Further, they can provide hover-over capabilities and prompts that could lead educators to examine data through an equity and culturally responsive lens. Such prompts could provide suggestions about additional data to examine before drawing conclusions. They could suggest further analyses and explorations. It is not about knowing how to access the data but what to do with the data.

A sixth recommendation is highly systematic and not easily addressed. As Nichols (see Chapter 4) and her prior work (Nichols & Berliner, 2007) note, accountability pressures cause educators, rightly or wrongly, to game the system. Some gaming is just plain cheating and illegal. Other gaming has ethics at the heart. Accountability pressures will not disappear, but messaging can emphasize the importance of meeting the needs of *all* students through continuous improvement. If educational leadership take seriously the need to address all students, rather than just look good through domestic and international test scores, then educators on the front lines may be able to modify their focus in a fundamental way.

A seventh recommendation is also systemic and goes to the heart of leadership. Leaders must create cultures where it is unacceptable to engage in shaming and blaming of teachers and the same for teachers of their students. As Berliner (2006) so eloquently notes, you cannot blame teachers for things that are beyond their control. Leadership must have realistic expectations for what teachers can accomplish and provide them the latitude and tools to help students, particularly those who are most challenged. Relying solely on standardized test scores to determine what success looks like only seeks to do more damage. Adopt an equity model, rather than a deficit model.

The eighth suggestion is to consider expanding the notion of relevant data to diverse sources and bring into the mix professional development that trains on trauma, growth mindset, social-emotional learning, school improvement, and other topics. Have these providers highlight and integrate the concepts of ethical data use into their models to uncover unconscious bias. Such inclusion will expand not only the notion of what data are but also begin to raise awareness in other forms of professional development.

The ninth recommendation is about data teaming and expertise. As Bocala and Boudett (2015) and Jimerson and colleagues (2020) note, putting people together in teams to pursue collaborative inquiry is not a trivial matter. There are enabling factors and necessary structures that must be in place, including strong leadership, a safe and trusting culture, appropriate resources, focused inquiry, and routine processes. Without these structures, teaming will not be productive. Creating teams without effective and knowledgeable expertise is problematic. Professional development for leaders to help them create trusting and nonpunitive data and inquiry cultures is important. Professional development can help provide the needed expertise that can spread across a school through observation, modeling, and turnkey learning.

A final recommendation is about the need for foundational data literacy. Educational agencies suffer from limited resources and competing priorities. Training on data-driven professional development often is not prioritized. But data use and, foremost, ethical and responsible data use, is at the heart of almost every action educators take. If educators do not have at least some fundamental amount of data literacy or better yet, CRDL, this is a very real problem. District leadership must recognize the potential negative impact there could be if educators make poor decisions based on unethical and even illegal data practices. Consider what happened in Atlanta with the cheating scandal as one extreme example. Educators need to be aware, understand data ethics, and gain the skills, knowledge, and dispositions of DLFT and CRDL. It is incumbent upon districts, in conjunction with educator preparation programs, to ensure that their staff receive sufficient training (Mandinach & Gummer, 2013; Mandinach, Cotto, et al., 2020; Mandinach et al., 2021). We are not talking about a one-time, quick in-service to check a box. We are talking about the sustained enhancement of educators' skills and knowledge pertaining to ethical data use that runs throughout their careers as a process of continuous professional learning. Data ethics are becoming more and more nuanced as regulations evolve and are modified. Districts need to exercise flexibly to adapt and make sure that their staff stay current and understand how these changes can impact their practice. Professional development providers, both those who focus on data-driven decision-making and others, must integrate the notions of responsible data use into their models. This should be a realistic task in data-related professional development, but it may be a harder fit for more generic providers.

Although this is a systemic enterprise with awareness building and a steep learning curve for many, we firmly believe it is both important and necessary. It is the ethical and moral thing to do.

REFERENCES

Beck, J. S., & Nunnaley, D. (2021). A continuum of data literacy for teaching. *Studies in Educational Evaluation*, *69*, 1–8. https://doi.org/10.1016/j.stueduc.2020.100871

Berliner, D. C. (2006). Our impoverished view of education. *Teachers College Record*, *108*(6), 949–995.

Bertrand, M., & Marsh, J. A. (2015). Teachers' sensemaking of data and implications for equity. *American Educational Research Journal*, *52*(5), 861–893.

Biden, J. (2016, April). *Operation educate the educators: Recognizing and supporting military-connected students through university-based research, community partnerships, and teacher education programs* [Speech transcript]. Annual conference of the American Educational Research Association, Washington, DC.

Bocala, C., & Boudett, K. P. (2015). Teaching educators habits of mind for using data wisely. *Teachers College Record*, *117*, 1–20.

Booher-Jennings, J. (2005). Below the bubble: "Educational triage" and the Texas Accountability System. *American Educational Research Journal*, *42*(2), 231–268.

Boudett, K. P., City, E. A., & Murnane, R. J. (Eds.). (2005). *Data Wise: A step-by-step guide to using assessment results to improve teaching and learning.* Harvard Education Press.

Boudett, K. P., City, E. A., & Murnane, R. J. (Eds.). (2013). *Data Wise: A step-by-step guide to using assessment results to improve teaching and learning* (Rev. & Exp. Ed.). Harvard Education Press.

Corno, L. (2008). On teaching adaptively. *Educational Psychologist*, *43*(3), 161–173.

Cronbach, L. J. (1988). Five perspectives on validity argument. In H. Wainer & H. Braun (Eds.), *Test validity* (pp. 3–17). Lawrence Erlbaum.

Datnow, A. (2017). *Opening or closing doors for students? Equity and data-driven decision-making.* https://research.acer.edu.au/cgi/viewcontent.cgi?article=1317&context=research_conference

Datnow, A., Choi, B., Park, V., & St. John, E. (2018). Teacher talk about student ability and achievement in the era of data-driven decision making. *Teachers College Record*, *120*, 1–34.

Datnow, A., & Park, V. (2018). Opening or closing doors for students? Equity and data use in schools. *Journal of Educational Change*, *19*(2), 131–152.

Dillman, M. (n.d.). *Tips for using data responsibly*. Boston Public Schools.

Earl, L. M., & Katz, S. (2006). *Leading schools in a data-rich world: Harnessing data for school improvement*. Corwin Press.

Gummer, E. S., & Mandinach, E. B. (2015). Building a conceptual framework for data literacy. *Teachers College Record*, *117*(4), 1–22. http://www.tcrecord.org/PrintContent.asp?ContentID=17856

Hamilton, L., Halverson, R., Jackson, S., Mandinach, E., Supovitz, J., & Wayman, J. (2009). *Using student achievement data to support instructional decision making* (NCEE 2009–4067). National Center for Education Evaluation and Regional Assistance, Institute of Education Sciences, U.S. Department of Education. https://ies.ed.gov/ncee/wwc/PracticeGuide/12

Jacobson, L. (2020, March 9). Would Jill Biden's interest in military families influence ed policy in a Biden White House? *Education Dive*. https://www.educationdive.com/news/would-jill-bidens-interest-in-military-connected-families-influence-ed-pol/573547

Jimerson, J. B., Garry, V., Poortman, C. L., & Schildkamp, K. (2019, April). *Implementing a data use intervention in a United States context: Enabling and constraining factors* [Conference presentation]. Annual conference of the American Educational Research Association, Toronto, Canada.

Love, N., Stiles, K. E., Mundry, S., & DiRanna, K. (2008). *A data coach's guide to improving learning for all students: Unleashing the power of collaborative inquiry*. Corwin Press.

Mandinach, E. B., Cotto, J., Wayman, J. C., Rastrick, E., Vance, A., & Siegl, J. (2020). *Data ethics scenarios: Second deliverable in privacy training resources project*. Future of Privacy Forum and WestEd.

Mandinach, E. B., & Gummer, E. S. (2012). *Navigating the landscape of data literacy: It IS complex*. WestEd; Education Northwest.

Mandinach, E. B., & Gummer, E. S. (2013). A systemic view of implementing data literacy into educator preparation. *Educational Researcher*, *42*(1), 30–37.

Mandinach, E. B., & Gummer, E. S. (2016a). *Data literacy for educators: Making it count in teacher preparation and practice*. Teachers College Press.

Mandinach, E. B., & Gummer, E. S. (2016b). What does it mean for teachers to be data literate: Laying out the skills, knowledge, and dispositions. *Teaching and Teacher Education*, *60*, 1–11.

Mandinach, E. B., & Jackson, S. (2012). *Transforming teaching and learning through data-driven decision making*. Corwin Press.

Mandinach, E. B., Jimerson, J. B., Cotto, J., Vance, A., & Siegl, J. (2021). *User's guide for data privacy and data ethics scenarios for leaders*. WestEd.

Mandinach, E. B., & Mundry, S. E. (2021). Data-driven decision making and its alignment with educational psychology: Why data are more than student performance results. In S. L. Nichols & D. Varier (Eds.), *Teaching on Assessment* (pp. 269–291). Information Age Publishing.

Mandinach, E. B., Warner, S., & Lacireno-Paquet, N. (2020, September 15). *Culturally responsive data literacy: Integration into practice in schools and districts* [Webinar]. Regional Educational Laboratory Mid-Atlantic. https://ies.ed.gov/ncee/edlabs/regions/midatlantic/app/Docs/Events/RELMA_culturally_responsive_data_literacy_webinar_slides_508.pdf

Mandinach, E. B., Warner, S., & Mundry, S. E. (2019, November 6). *Using data to promote culturally responsive teaching* [Webinar]. Regional Educational Laboratory Northeast & Islands. https://ies.ed.gov/ncee/edlabs/regions/northeast /Docs/Events/CRDL_Workshop_Sep_30_2019_508c.pdf

Mandinach, E. B., Warner, S., & Mundry, S. E. (2020, June 4). *Using data to promote culturally responsive teaching: Workshop 2* [Webinar]. Regional Educational Laboratory Northeast & Islands.

Mandinach, E. B., & Wayman, J. C. (2020). *Survey of curriculum: First deliverable in privacy training resources project.* WestEd.

Marsh, J. A., Bertrand, M., & Huguet, A. (2015). Using data to alter instructional practice: The mediating role of coaches and professional learning communities. *Teachers College Record, 117,* 1–40. https://www.tcrecord.org/content .asp?contentid=17849

Means, B., Padilla, C., & Gallagher, L. (2010). *Use of education data at the local level: From accountability to instructional improvement.* U.S. Department of Education, Office of Planning, Evaluation, and Policy Development.

National Association of State Directors of Teacher Education and Certification. (n.d.). *Model code of ethics for educators.* https://www.nasdtec.net/page /MCEE_Doc

National Forum on Education Statistics. (2010). *Forum guide on data ethics* (NFES 2010-801). U.S. Department of Education, National Center for Education Statistics.

Nichols, S. L., & Berliner, D. C. (2007). *Collateral damage: How high-stakes testing corrupts America's schools.* Harvard Education Press.

Penuel, W. R., & Shepard, L. A. (2016). Assessment and teaching. In D. H. Gitomer & C. A. Bell (Eds.), *Handbook of research on teaching* (5th ed., pp. 787–850). American Educational Research Association.

Price, J., & Koretz, D. M. (2013). Building assessment literacy. In. K. P. Boudett, E. A. City, & R. Murnane (Eds.), *Data Wise: A step-by-step guide to using assessment results to improve teaching and learning* (pp. 35–63). Harvard Education Press.

Schildkamp, K., & Poortman, C. (2015). Factors influencing the functioning of data teams. *Teachers College Record, 117,* 1–42. https://www.tcrecord.org/content .asp?contentid=17851

Shulman, L. S. (1986). Those who understand: Knowledge growth in teaching. *Educational Researcher, 15*(2), 4–14.

Shulman, L. S. (1987). Knowledge and teaching: Foundations of the new reform. *Harvard Educational Review, 57*(1), 1–22.

Spillane, J. (2012). Data in practice: Conceptualizing the data-based decision-making phenomena. *American Journal of Education, 118,* 113–141.

Stein, P. (2019, September 15). D.C. schools try to meet students where they live. *The Washington Post.* https://www.washingtonpost.com/local/education /dc-has-the-biggest-parent-home-visit-program-in-the-country-is-it-working /2019/09/15/21d06124-d56d-11e9-86ac-0f250cc91758_story.html

The Role of Educator Preparation Programs to Teach About the Ethical Use of Data

Edith S. Gummer, Norman Paul Gibbs, and Sherman Dorn

Developing the capacity to use education data ethically is an important element of educator preparation, and educator preparation programs (EPPs) must integrate data literacy into early programming. This chapter encourages educators to pay attention to the quality and ethics of the goals they set, how they are measuring those goals, and how they are using data to improve performance across educational systems (Brighouse et al., 2018; Darling-Hammond et al., 2019). Preparing educators to ethically use data involves integrating data use and ethics in program coursework and clinical experiences that are already filled with the range of knowledge, skills, and dispositions expected of effective educators. The increasing importance of data and the growing volume of information available pressure institutions of higher education to determine how ethical data literacy fits into already overburdened programs.

Institutions must also determine what data will be addressed. A narrow curricular focus on data as assessments alone may prepare educators who do not recognize how frequently unethical data use can occur in informal discussions about children within and outside of school. While education leaders have local authority on the use of data systems and practices, they have less authority over determining what data are collected and used, the design of systems and practices for data use, and the curtailment of the unethical data reporting that influences public perceptions.

In this chapter, we examine the preparation of teachers and education leaders for ethical data use. In the first section, we begin with a review of the research on initial teacher preparation in data use and ethics, overviewing the evidence on learning experiences for teachers in data literacy and then examining teacher preparation in ethical literacy. We conclude the first section with an example of what it might look like to integrate the ethical use of data across a teacher preparation program. In the second section, we turn to leader preparation in ethical data use in a similar fashion.

TEACHER PREPARATION

Preservice teacher education does not have a deep well of research on either data literacy or ethical literacy. We here draw from threads of research on assessment literacy, data literacy, and preparation in ethics to identify curricular interventions that address data use in order to provide a practical perspective on how teacher preparation programs might better address these concerns. Recognizing the debate on whether assessment and data literacy are separate constructs (Beck et al., 2019; DeLuca & Bellara, 2013; Mandinach & Schildkamp, 2021; Penuel & Shepard, 2016), we have chosen in this chapter to use the term "data literacy," both because the concepts and skills overlap and because we believe that teachers' use of data must expand beyond the assessment of students' academic performance to the overall improvement of instruction. Nevertheless, in reporting specific research studies and their interventions, we use the term adopted by the author.

Research on Teacher Candidate Preparation in Assessment and Data Literacy

Nearly 2 decades ago, Stiggins (1999) asked teacher preparation programs to move beyond teaching measurement concepts alone toward broader assessment literacy. Then, only half of the state teacher licensing and certification requirements required that a teacher be competent in assessment (Stiggins, 1999). At that time, the American Federation of Teachers (1990) had developed standards in educational assessment for teachers, but few teacher preparation programs had substantive preparation in assessment. Much has changed since, with increased calls for the establishment of teacher standards for assessment being issued in both the United States and internationally (DeLuca et al., 2016). These calls have arisen in an era marked by expanding accountability expectations, as the proportion of a teacher's professional life that is consumed with data management has grown over time (e.g., Dorr-Bremme, 1983, in contrast with Rentner et al., 2016; Robelen, 2016)—and there is little indication that this is likely to change anytime soon (Sahlberg, 2011, 2016). Accordingly, professional standards have come to accommodate these expectations, as the introduction to the Council for the Accreditation of Educator Preparation (CAEP, 2018) standards for K–6 teacher preparation programs explains:

> New K–6 teachers are expected to demonstrate greater knowledge, understanding, and skill in developing and using a range of formative and summative

assessments; use assessment data to understand each student's progress; guide and revise instruction based on assessment data; and provide feedback to learners about their achievement, development, and engagement. (p. 2)

Revisions in the Interstate New Teacher Assessment and Support Consortium (InTASC) standards have likewise reflected this movement toward assessment literacy. Standard 6 of the InTASC Model Core Teaching Standards directly addresses teacher assessment competency (Council of Chief State School Officers [CCSSO], 2013), and a focus on data literacy is evidenced in the InTASC learning progressions for teacher preparation programs (CCSSO, 2013). Furthermore, in the InTASC standards, educators are encouraged to move beyond classroom assessment data toward broader sources of data that can inform instruction: "The teacher gathers, synthesizes and analyzes a variety of data from sources inside and outside of the school to adapt instructional practices and other professional behaviors to better meet learners' needs" (CCSSO, 2013, p. 43). The call for assessment literacy was likewise issued by the Joint Committee for Standards on Educational Evaluation, whose 2015 publication of the *Classroom Assessment Standards: Practices for PK–12 Students* included a focus on unbiased and fair assessment, reliability and validity, and reflective practices in assessment for teachers, particularly in the areas of cultural and linguistic diversity, exceptionality, and special education (Klinger et al., 2012). Similarly, state-created standards documents provide additional indicators that may inform the development of preservice curricula.

Yet research on teacher preparation programs has found that, while programs incorporate these standards within their course syllabi, training in assessment nevertheless remains thin. While Beck and colleagues' (2019) recent review of research identified a number of promising practices in teacher preparation programs—including the introduction of explicit courses on assessment as well as the integration of assessment across the curriculum—numerous studies over the past 2 decades have found that preservice teachers often feel unprepared for the measurement challenges of the profession and are unclear on how to use data to improve instruction (Campbell & Evans, 2000; DeLuca & Klinger, 2010; Graham, 2005; MacLellan, 2004; Mertler, 2004).

Reflecting this state of affairs, Greenberg and Walsh's (2012) expansive study of 180 teacher preparation programs found that 83% failed to provide what the authors believed to be an adequate treatment of assessment, with the greatest weaknesses found in data use–related instructional decision-making and analytical skills. These findings were echoed in DeLuca and Bellara's (2013) study of the alignment of Florida state standards on assessment and Florida EPP curricula in which the researchers concluded that "mandatory assessment education is too short to lead to significant changes in candidates' conceptions and practices of assessment [or] to engage in deep and complex learning about the linkages between assessment, teaching, and learning" (p. 367). Similarly, Xu and Brown (2016) found that the emphasis of EPPs on a single three-credit course allowed too little time to connect theory with practice. And there is evidence that data literacy has fared no better than assessment literacy: Mandinach and colleagues' (2015) study found that EPP course syllabi prioritized measurement practice with little emphasis on data literacy, while Beck and colleagues (2020) found that an underemphasis on data literacy left program graduates insufficiently prepared to read and interpret data. Thus, despite a 2-decades-long call for change, the constricted EPP curricula continue to offer little programming beyond foundational measurement processes.

Interventions to Promote Assessment and Data Literacy

Despite this overarching state of affairs, some EPPs and individual teacher educators have, in fact, sought to introduce into their courses a greater emphasis on assessment and data literacy. A number of these interventions have been described in the literature and are instructive on what might be done to heed the call for change and better prepare teachers who know how to read and use data in their professional work.

Critical Reflection. DeLuca and colleagues (2013) argued for a process-based focus on assessment that engaged preservice teachers in experiential learning, with components of critical reflection and interactions with their peers and other colleagues. Their study focused on four pedagogical approaches in teaching assessment literacy: (1) fostering substantive classroom conversations that surfaced the teacher candidates' multiple perspectives on assessment, (2) embedding authentic learning tasks in the class structure and activities, (3) developing a portfolio of assessments over the course of a semester, and (4) modeling good assessment literacy practices in the course itself. Throughout these approaches, the teacher educators paid explicit attention to the role of reflective practice in assessment practice.

Guided Use of Authentic Data. Piro and colleagues (2014) described an intervention that developed educators' data literacy by examining standardized testing and end-of-course assessment data. Using data collected from local school districts, Piro and colleagues de-identified student performances and guided teacher candidates through the interpretation of these data sets using appropriate statistical techniques in simulated grade level teams. The teacher candidates then used those analyses to support inferences they made about students' levels of performance across a number of domains. The teacher candidates then developed instructional strategies to address perceived student weaknesses and crafted formative and summative assessment procedures based on their initial analyses. Teacher candidates presented their data analyses and instructional plans as the final part of the intervention. The authors concluded that teacher candidates were more confident as a result of the classroom experiences (Piro et al., 2014).

Similarly, Reeves and Honig (2015) used authentic student data in an intervention that combined teacher candidate collaboration, support from an expert facilitator, opportunities for data use and reflection, and a close link between data use and the classroom context. In a pre-clinical assessment course, the authors designed a two-session module using Microsoft Excel tools to support data analysis and interpretation, together with a protocol to use the data to support instructional decisions. In the final 2 weeks of the semester-long course, preservice teachers scored real-world assessment data collected from K–12 students, examined student responses for patterns, and experienced the challenges of inter-rater reliability by double-scoring students. In addition, the preservice teachers examined the statistical information generated by the assessment analysis; reflected on the performance of selected students by item and test overall; reflected on class strengths, weaknesses, and misconceptions; and indicated the next instructional steps that would address feedback to students. Reeves (2017) provides more details about the intervention, including implementation challenges.

Identifying Problems and Framing Questions. Reeves and Chiang (2018) employed a parallel intervention that expanded the one used in their prior study by including an opportunity for preservice teachers to identify problems and frame questions, aligning the intervention with the Mandinach and Gummer (2016) data literacy for teaching framework. Seeking to help preservice teachers develop a data use schema, the researchers engaged their students in exploring data, generating questions, and analyzing standardized test score data sets at different levels, including individual, subgroup, whole class, grade, and school levels. The intervention was structured so that the preservice teachers could work individually and collaboratively in class sessions scaffolded by a protocol and supported by the expert instructor. The preservice teachers indicated on questionnaires that they found the course effective, though the results of other instruments were mixed.

Teacher Inquiry. Several researchers have demonstrated the potential for preservice teachers to develop data literacy in courses that were not specifically identified as assessment literacy or data literacy courses. Athanases and colleagues (2012) described the ways that preservice teachers examined data on the identification of culturally and linguistically diverse learners in an EPP capstone course and in field experiences—rare in the literature. Throughout a 10-week intervention with postbaccalaureate preservice teachers, Athanases and colleagues used an inquiry framework to support three series of inquiries in which preservice teachers collected their own students' work to address a particular inquiry question. The authors discussed the ways in which the preservice teachers used this data to reframe their inquiry questions, to identify patterns in student work, and to expand the data collected from students. This final theme was further explored in Athanases and colleagues (2015) in which they examined the difficulties preservice teachers had with identifying relevant data for a specific inquiry question.

Demographic Exploration of NAEP Data. Also working outside the context of a discrete course in assessment, Fitchett and Heafner (2013) led preservice teachers in a social studies methods course exploring "instructional strategies, student demographics, and school contexts associated with student learning outcomes" (p. 297). They scaffolded the identification of demographic variables the preservice teachers used to determine relationships with National Assessment of Educational Progress (NAEP) scores from the NAEP Data Explorer. Discussions of data literacy concepts include statistical tests of significance in the comparisons, test item difficulty, scaling of scores, and normal distributions, such as limitations of the normalized data to make predictive learning outcomes based on student characteristics (e.g., gender, race, opportunity to learn, and family background). The preservice teachers included characteristics such as race/ethnicity, accommodation and socioeconomic status, and family and community factors that influenced the NAEP scores.

Conceptual Change Theory. Some interventions have sought to generate a theory that EPPs might use in preparing teachers for data literacy. In an educational psychology course, Dunn and colleagues (2019) examined a theoretical framework that could be useful in shaping preservice teachers' belief systems on data-driven decision-making. Using a cognitive affective model of conceptual change (Gregoire, 2003), the researchers developed a series of online modules designed to address misconceptions, improve understanding, and decrease anxiety and resistance toward data-driven decision-making. Topics addressed included (1) the use of multiple types of data, (2) Family Educational Rights and Privacy Act (FERPA), (3) using data to set goals and guide instructional decisions, (4) multiple forms of assessment, (5) issues in the technical quality of assessments, (6) grading and psychometric issues around scoring, and (7) the state value-added assessment system used to evaluate teachers and schools. Post-intervention changes in knowledge and perceptions indicated that the preservice teachers developed a better understanding of data-driven decision-making, more confidence in its use, an awareness of their own knowledge gaps, and a willingness to learn more.

Absence-of-Bias Assessments. Few interventions have been explicitly framed around ethics in data use. One such intervention is described in Whitesides and Beck's (2020) report on an equity-focused data literacy course for elementary teachers that included a module on test bias and featured weekly assignments called "absence-of-bias assessments." Using an iterative concept-mapping process to examine preservice candidates' emergent understanding of equity issues in data use, the researchers charted how preservice candidates' understanding of the role of equity in data use moved from simply focusing on fairness in assessment to encompassing a broader understanding of the use of data to support the learning of all students. While preservice teachers' understanding of data use improved, they still had difficulties identifying and resolving inequitable data use practices at the end of the course. The intervention required the faculty and preservice teachers to look at data use as something that informs ethically loaded instructional considerations, such as students' opportunity to learn, placement decisions, and curriculum choices. These findings illuminate the need to help teacher candidates understand the ethical nature of data use.

The studies just described are a representative sample of the ways in which teacher preparation learning experiences might support the development of assessment and data literacy. Before we examine the ways in which these interventions might be used to address teacher candidates' ethical use of data, we first examine how teacher candidates are provided with the opportunity to learn ethical literacy in general. These two areas will then be brought together in our examination of the dilemmas and constraints of preservice teacher preparation in ethical use of data and in our recommendations for practical goals for teacher preparation programs.

DILEMMAS AND CONSTRAINTS TO TEACHING ABOUT THE ETHICAL USE OF DATA IN PRESERVICE EDUCATION

Program Expectations

State expectations for teacher preparation programs include a growing number of standards related to teachers' ethical use of data. Indeed, according to Mandinach and Wayman's (2020) national survey of the expectations of states and professional associations for teachers' ethical use of data, the majority of states require some treatment of data ethics within authorized teacher preparation programs. However, states vary in the depth to which they require programs to treat data ethics, and the articulation of their expectations vary from state to state. Most states articulate an educator code of ethics, but Mandinach and Wayman found that only 34 of these state codes deal with data ethics, while six states established no code of ethics whatsoever. While the InTASC standards aim to provide a starting point for establishing common expectations among states, Mandinach and Wayman found that 30 states (60%) either adopted the common InTASC framework or maintained in-house standards that closely reflected InTASC standards.

The InTASC standards situate data ethics within the broader scope of teachers' ethical practice, asking teacher preparation programs to prepare their graduates for "the moral and ethical demands of professional practice" (CCSSO, 2013, p. 44). The standards describe graduates as professionals who are reflective in their ethical practice and understand their own value system within the context of a pluralist society: the understanding their "own frames of reference (e.g., culture, gender, language, abilities, ways of knowing), the potential biases in these frames, and their impact on expectations for and relationships with learners and their families" (InTASC standard 9m). The standards hold out the expectation that EPPs will go beyond specific ethics codes and legal requirements toward helping their graduates understand the values that govern their decision-making processes. Thus, EPPs would incorporate data-driven decision-making within a larger framework of values-driven decision-making. Such a framework has been seen as essential to supporting teachers in the gray areas that emerge in the changing contexts of educational measurement. As Green and colleagues (2007) observe, professional standards and ethics codes fall short of this ideal in that they "provide rules without an overarching ethical framework that can provide support and guidance for exercising judgment in specific situations" (p. 1000). Rather, Green and colleagues (2007) suggest orienting preservice teachers to the foundational ethical theories that underly professional standards and using classroom dialogue to help preservice teachers construct their own ethical theories. Thus, preparation of teachers for data ethics involves supporting preservice teachers as they develop the ethical beliefs and theories that will serve as heuristic guides to dispositional decision-making across a host of unforeseen professional circumstances in their future careers (Eraut, 1994).

Uncertain Role of Formal Classes in Data Literacy and Ethics

Despite the call of states and accreditors to prepare preservice teachers for both the ethical use of data and for ethical reasoning in general, cross-disciplinary reviews of professional preparation programs in American universities have found ethics to be underemphasized in education programs—and particularly so in comparison with the training provided in other professions. In Glanzer and Ream's (2007) review of 151 education programs at religious universities, the authors found that only nine (6%) programs required an ethics course or provided a program-specific ethics elective; in contrast, the study found that 46% of business programs, 43% of nursing programs, and 39% of social work and criminal justice programs required an ethics course. More recently, in a five-country study of professional preparation programs, Maxwell and Schwimmer (2016) found that ethics courses "are vanishingly rare in programs of study in teaching" (p. 356). This underemphasis on ethics appears to have a trickle-down effect on data ethics: In studying the teaching of data ethics through nine interviews with teacher educators and K–12 practitioners, Mandinach and Wayman (2020) found that only one of the interviewees was aware of any substantive curricular content in teacher preparation that addressed the ethical use of data.

It may be that the relative underemphasis on ethics programming reflects the challenge of fitting a growing number of standards into the limited number of credits available in a bachelor's level program. The steady growth of standardization leaves teacher preparation programs struggling to find space in the curriculum to incorporate hundreds of outcomes associated with InTASC, CAEP, and state learning expectations. As is the case with school leadership preparation programs, the ponderous task of addressing such a broad range of expectations leaves many programs treading water, struggling to keep afloat a curriculum waterlogged in accountability and short on time. An alternative to dedicating credits to ethics programming is to address these topics in an integrated manner across the curriculum. However, Glanzer and Ream's (2007) study indicates that this, too, is unlikely to be the case. In analyzing descriptions of courses offered in the 151 education programs surveyed, the authors found little evidence that ethics and moral decision-making were being treated systematically in an integrated fashion across courses.

Yet, whether the limited treatment of ethics in EPPs may be explained by credit limitations or by more general challenges, such as the complexity of discussing moral and ethical concerns in increasingly multicultural university classrooms, it is nevertheless incumbent upon teacher preparation programs to decide how they will support their students in the development and articulation of those ethical beliefs that will guide lifelong practice. As CAEP's Accreditation Handbook succinctly asks, "How do you know your candidates can apply appropriate professional and ethical standards in their work?" (CAEP, 2018, p. 33).

Practical Goals for Preservice Teacher Preparation

The question from the CAEP Accreditation Handbook (CAEP, 2018) is not just a rhetorical one for teacher preparation programs. Mandinach and Gummer (2013, 2016) have clearly articulated that the concerns around preparing teachers to use data involve more than just adding a data literacy course to an already packed curriculum. In the same vein, preparing teachers to navigate the ethical dilemmas in their careers as teachers will not be satisfied by presenting them with a module or course on ethical literacy. Rather, the real effort of infusing ethical literacy and data literacy requires a larger framework for both ethics and data use that can then be used to reflectively inquire about the ways in which the themes of the framework(s) can be actively connected to the courses of a program. We here present an example of how the inclusion of ethical literacy is being framed in a large teacher preparation program at Arizona State University (ASU).

Goals to Integrate Ethics and Data

An Integrated Framework to Support Ethical Literacy. At ASU, the Mary Lou Fulton Teachers College (MLFTC) began an effort in 2018 to infuse a spiraling approach to ethics into its teacher preparation programs, seeking to operationalize ASU's institutional value of innovation within an ethical framework called Principled Innovation (PI). The PI framework comprises eight practices for positive social change distributed across four dimensions of character: moral, civic, intellectual, and performance (MLFTC, 2019). For instance, within the domain of civic character, Practice C1 "Understand Culture and Context" states the following: "Use evidence-based resources, empathy, reflective questioning, and asset-based appreciative inquiry to fully understand and assess the lived and current experiences and circumstances of individuals, communities, and learning environments." Through practices such as these, the framework—which was developed by a committee composed largely of teacher educators—overlaps with many of the expectations for ethics literacy, which were outlined previously, and is designed to support the development of preservice teachers' ethical reasoning skills.

Within data ethics, the PI Practices provide ethical principles with which to approach topics of data use. For instance, Practice C1's focus on "Understand Culture and Context" provides the ethical framing to discuss cultural bias in instruments or in the interpretation of data (compare with InTASC standards 6b, 9e, and 9i). Similarly, Practice C2 "Engage Multiple and Diverse Perspectives" encourages the use of multiple sources of data for informing one's understanding of problems of practice (InTASC standards 6v and 9o). Through PI, MLFTC has rooted the ethical content of the teacher preparation standards—including those related to assessment and data literacy—within its own institutional values for educational innovation.

The introduction of PI into the college's teacher preparation programs has taken place as one component of a larger 2-year curriculum redesign process. In the redesign, the faculty reviewed and revised all of its teacher preparation programs to incorporate through PI a renewed focus on the character of teachers as agents of change. A central concern in this redesign was to integrate PI in a spiraling manner across both the classroom curriculum and, critically, into students' field experiences. Such field experiences are primary sites of ethical learning in which preservice teachers are confronted with rapid-fire problems of instruction, assessment, and teamwork—all areas in which ethical decision-making plays a frequent role. In the redesigned teacher preparation programs, a series of two-credit courses support the staged development of students' ethical understanding of the profession from multiple perspectives. The series is integrated into students' clinical field experiences and culminates in the final semester of the teacher preparation program with a course titled "The Principled Educator." In support of this implementation, an online toolkit with introductory videos, dialogue starters, and classroom activities was developed, and a series of PI Support Studio Sessions were made available to faculty members seeking support from a curriculum designer on the operationalization of the PI Practices in their courses. Finally, a team of faculty PI Ambassadors received specialized training to help create exemplar courses and model PI infusion for their colleagues.

Integration into Multiple Places in the Preservice Program. Cooper and colleagues (2017) offer a useful perspective in their study of the ways in which "embedding, and making explicit, mathematical thinking and reasoning with the courses across the programme" (p. 3) combined with mentoring and online curricular support to improve preservice teacher competencies in mathematical and statistical literacy. In the same way, an ethical framework such as PI can provide the developmental materials needed to introduce a data ethics focus to a particular course without expanding or distorting the particular course objectives.

In an integrated framework such as PI, faculty must determine how the framework might be used to scope ethical literacy proficiencies throughout the broader context of the program. Infusion requires not just a commitment to an ideal but hard work to flesh out specifics of curriculum planning. The faculty would also need to examine the components of data literacy, course syllabi, and instructional materials, and ask, "What particular set of decisions does this course prepare our teacher candidates to examine, and what data are available to them to support these decisions?" This examination and other processes would inform the development of curricular maps that situate ethical and data literacy across the program. Scenarios designed to introduce preservice teachers to teacher inquiry (Athanases et al., 2012) could be incorporated in multiple literacy or multicultural courses, such as through modules that contain important data-rich scenarios for discussion. For example, a course to prepare teacher candidates to collaborate, plan, and implement instruction in a diverse context could easily engage these preservice teachers in such a way. The intent here is not to burden the program with a separate ethical data literacy course or add modules to already developed courses, but rather to examine the ways in which these literacies can be incorporated within the existing instructional content.

Opportunities for Teacher Preparation

Collaboration and Teamwork. A common theme addressed in the preservice teacher preparation in ethics and in data literacy is the potential for collaboration and teaming to expand the abilities for teachers to learn to practice ethical data literacy. Shapira-Lishchinsky (2013) describes a four-dimensional model of learning about ethical conduct in team-based simulations. These simulations provide preservice teachers with experiences to learn about real-world situations in a simplified fashion. This model includes ensuring that the environment in which preservice teachers practice making decisions is safe, providing them with opportunities to consider caring support for students, giving them examples of inappropriate conduct, and helping them integrate multiple perspectives. This is a rich instructional practice that assessment and data literacy researchers described previously have incorporated into their classes (Fitchett & Heafner, 2013; Piro et al., 2014; Reeves & Chiang, 2018).

Use of Cases and Simulations. The use of cases as a pedagogical device is found in the literature on ethical literacy and data literacy. For example, Warnick and Silverman (2011) describe the case of a teacher taking student records from the school in order to better understand her diverse students. This is both a data use issue and an ethical issue in that the teacher is breaking school policy on the security of student records (an issue associated with FERPA regulations) and potentially infringing on student privacy (an ethical issue). Cherubini (2009) describes multiple cases in which students are confronted with ethical issues that have data implications and could be fleshed out into ethical data literacy cases. The simulations with data sets provided by cooperating school districts described by Piro and colleagues (2014) could be used not only in assessment courses but also in literacy or multicultural courses. Likewise, the simulation with external data sets such as the NAEP Data Explorer as seen in the work of Fitchett and Heafner (2013) in a social studies methods course might be used in a science or mathematics methods course.

Differing Roles of Course-Based and Clinical Experiences. This infusion of ethical data literacy provides the opportunity to move beyond teaching the technical aspects of data literacy. It encourages the consideration of the decisions that might be made in the use of data in the preservice course and of how the same decisions might be reflected in actual classroom practice. The coordination of a curriculum map that aligns courses with programmatic outcomes provides the opportunity to connect an exercise in a course with a future activity in the classroom with K–12 students. While some constraints for engaging preservice teachers in data literacy practices in clinical experiences have been documented (Carey et al., 2018.), there is much that still needs to be studied around the affordance of the clinical experiences to engage preservice teachers in the complexities of data use. With only a 5-week clinical experience, there may be little opportunity for teacher candidates to engage in studying data with mentor teachers. However, when such experiences are expanded to 12 or 16 weeks—as in the case of semester-long student teaching or even a year-long residency—more opportunities are likely to emerge.

Taking the Long View

Preparing preservice teachers for the ethical use of data may thus involve both short-term and long-term components. In the short term, incorporating data ethics into a college's discrete data literacy course or introducing case studies and dilemmas at different points in the curriculum are relatively easier approaches for addressing this evident need. Ensuring that such courses introduce students to privacy laws and state or professional codes of ethics are appropriate mid-term approaches that are essential to fulfilling most state or accreditor requirements for teacher preparation. Short-term approaches such as these allow programs to move immediately toward addressing data ethics without waiting for the coordination of full curriculum changes.

In the long term, however, institutions should seek opportunities to help their students identify their own overarching ethical beliefs, which will serve them in their professional lives. A teacher's daily life is filled with lacunas left unfilled by the normative codes of ethics that govern the profession, and preservice teachers must understand their own beliefs to support their decision-making in these areas. It is not enough to simply *use* data—it must be used ethically, in a manner suited to teachers' highest values. While it is true that programs are already piled high with InTASC, CAEP, and state expectations, institutions must nevertheless find pathways to equip teachers for decision-making in the gray areas of everyday practice.

Leader Preparation

Leader preparation programs theoretically have a deeper philosophical knowledge base for discussions of professional ethics—for example, with graduate-level texts in ethics stretching back several decades (e.g., Kimbrough, 1985). Nevertheless, the field's internal discussion of ethical frameworks does not make the incorporation of ethical data use in leader preparation programs any easier than in initial teacher education. This is in part because leader preparation faces many of the same dynamics discussed in the previous section. This section discusses the existing literature, focusing on where there is a critical mass of discussion in the field; the dilemmas and constraints in leader preparation programs; and practical goals for school leader preparation in ethical data use.

Research on Leadership Preparation in Ethical Data Use

In the modern context of intensified data use, there remains deep ambiguity about what professional ethics requires of education leaders in the context of modern accountability policies. The push of education policy in the 2000s led many to discuss the obligations of education leaders to prioritize the interest of children in an abstract sense of children's interests as opposed to considering "adults" as having special interests (e.g., Johnson & Uline, 2005). Even such an appealing concept as *children's interests* is wracked with inconsistent and sometimes irreconcilable definitions (e.g., Frick, 2001; Stefkovich & Begley, 2007). How, then, to set expectations of education leaders for the ethical ambiguities and political pressures?

Leadership's Multiple Ethical Frameworks. Educational leadership has prioritized the act of debate and deliberation as appropriate professional activity within the constructs of defined frameworks. For over half a century (e.g., Greenfield, 2004), the internal debates have converged on a deeper commitment to leadership as a combination of roles such as moral agent, educator, and community builder (Murphy, 2002). Smylie and Murphy (2018) argue that the current national standards (Professional Standards for Educational Leaders [PSEL]) encompass broader commitments rather than a focus on narrow managerial skills.

Starratt (1991, 2012) established the standard approach, what he calls multiple *ethics* of justice, critique, and care. The ethic of justice requires consideration of what is required of educational leaders to promote a just education and society. The ethic of critique requires consideration of how education leaders must challenge inequitable structures even while they serve as managers inside a system (also see Buskey & Pitts, 2009; Furman, 2012). The ethic of care requires consideration of how education leaders must care for both students and colleagues as individuals deserving respect and compassion. Starratt (2012) sees this triad as wrapped up in an overarching ethic of professionalism.

Furman (2003) proposed an ethic of community building to add to Starratt's triad, strongly arguing that the ethical moral agency of a school leader is in building a school *community* that makes ethical decisions more than being an *ethical individual leader*. This last addition is consistent with what we see as an essential role of leadership in data use; because the most serious recent threats to ethical data use have arisen out of systematic neglect and abuse of data, ethical leadership requires paying attention to the culture and systems around data use. Ethics texts written for leader preparation courses focus on either general ethical presentations (Starratt, 2012) or a case-based approach (Shapiro & Stefkovich, 2016).

Multiple Ethical Frameworks in Preparation Programs. In practice, there are two likely places where students in leadership preparation programs encounter data use and potential ethical challenges. One is in didactic presentation and discussion of published cases. Shapiro and Stefkovich (2016) includes the ethics of data use in four of the text's 37 cases. Gross and Shapiro (2016) present examples of positive ethical leadership, with at least three cases clearly tied to the ethics of data use. In the most recent 5 completed years of the *Journal of Cases in Educational Leadership* (Vols. 19–23), 36 of 151 cases (or 24%) involved some potential discussion of the ethical questions involved in data use. The issues in these published cases include examples such as disproportionate disciplinary data and the interpersonal challenges of promoting data use in instructional decision-making. In addition to presentation of ethical dilemmas in didactic cases, students might also encounter data use and ethical challenges in their supervised internship classes, where they might be responsible for analyzing school-level data and/or participating in meetings around strategies of data use and potential misuse.

Leader Preparation and Data Literacy. The Goldring and Berends (2009) work is representative of the literature from the No Child Left Behind era: Leaders need to see the use of data as an essential part of their professional responsibilities. Murphy's (2017) explanation of the PSEL largely follows this literature, emphasizing a leader's responsibility to establish an appropriate environment for discussing assessment data to guide school improvement. Anderson and colleagues' (2018) survey of leader preparation programs allied with the University Council for Educational Administration provides evidence that preparation programs more recently have devoted significantly more attention and focus to school improvement; however, that survey does not address data literacy as such.

One concern specific to advanced graduate programs is the conflation of conventional research methods with data literacy appropriate for aspiring or current leaders of education systems. Bowers (2016) argues for a reorientation of doctoral-level research classes away from "fundamental statistical research topics" and toward practitioner-scholar skills. As far as we are aware, this is the only refereed article discussing instructional practices around data literacy in preparation programs—in this case, in Bowers' classes, and in the context of a doctoral program.

In considering the combination of these factors—greater foundational discussions about ethics and values in the field, changes in preparation programs to emphasis school improvement, and the remaining separation of general ethics discussions from assessment and data literacy for leaders—we want to emphasize that these are *not* the primary barriers to improved preparation of school leaders for ethical data use. In many cases, as we discuss later, there are practical ways to address what we see as a gap between the professional framing of ethics for school leaders, on the one hand, and typical preparation programs' handling of preparing leaders for data-informed decision-making on the other hand. In particular, Furman's (2003) focus on the ethic of community-building is consistent with our emphasis here on how ethical data use must be systemic, and preparation issues must face the organizational contexts within which leader candidates work and aspire to lead. As a result, preparation must extend beyond individual reflection to preparing individuals to stand up for the ethical use of data within organizations and support important challenges when raised by external stakeholders.

Dilemmas and Constraints in School Leader Preparation

Related constraints shape education leadership preparation programs: As with initial EPPs, leadership programs face limited program time, professional standards that can appear overstuffed from a preparation program perspective, dilemmas about infusion or inoculation of foundational skills, and uncertainty about what practitioner partners model in terms of the scope of professional decision-making. In addition, leadership preparation programs face the graduate-level dilemma of how to balance theoretical material with experience in practitioner issues, though internal criticism (e.g., Murphy, 2002) and development of national standards over the past few decades has supported programs in wrestling with this dilemma and developing different curricular and pedagogical approaches to leader preparation (e.g., Orr, 2006).

Limited Program Time, Expanding Standards. Whether in master's or doctoral programs, the effective length of formal classwork is generally limited to 42 credit hours or fewer, that is, typically no more than 14 didactic classes, often considerably fewer. At the same time, national professional standards are growing in length and complexity: The 2015 PSEL contains 83 competencies across 10 areas, up from 60 competencies in six broad areas in the preceding set of standards (National Policy Board for Educational Administration, 2007, 2015).

Standards and Uncertain Role of Formal Classes. The tension between theory and practice-oriented classes is different from initial preparation programs, and different again between master's and doctoral programs in leadership. Beyond initial preparation programs, faculty often expect that students demonstrate greater mastery of academic skills such as writing and the underlying research in an area. This greater expectation often extends to subjects such as measurement and assessment, statistics, and research design. How this expectation is expressed in individual programs varies widely. Despite Levine's (2006) critique of leadership programs as overweighting the esoteric, there is a dynamic tension in leadership curricula that program faculty at many universities are well aware of. That awareness is for several reasons: Primarily, a broad coalition of state leaders, administrative organizations, and university faculty have worked over several decades to change the nature of leader preparation (Murphy, 2015).

In the area of data literacy and use, the evolution of professional standards in leadership has distributed the applications to data use across the

10 PSEL domains, even while the ethics domain is an anchor domain in itself (Shapiro & Gross, 2017). Some examples follow (National Policy Board for Educational Administrators, 2015):

- 4g: Use assessment data appropriately and within technical limitations to monitor student progress and improve instruction (p. 12).
- 6e: Deliver actionable feedback about instruction and other professional practice through valid, research-anchored systems of supervision and evaluation to support the development of teachers' and staff members' knowledge, skills, and practice (p. 14).
- 7d: Promote mutual accountability among teachers and other professional staff for each student's success and the effectiveness of the school as a whole (p. 15).
- 9g: Develop and maintain data and communication systems to deliver actionable information for classroom and school improvement (p. 17).

At the same time as the standards distribute references to data use in multiple domains, many programs teach about data use primarily in standalone courses. This is especially true at the doctoral level, where didactic classes function in significant part to prepare students for dissertation projects (Bowers, 2017). And that type of standalone preparation is often separate from ethics, perhaps reflecting the field's intellectual dispositions; in Murphy's (2017) volume explaining the foundations of PSEL, the discussion of data literacy focuses almost entirely on academic assessment, with no discussion of the ethics issues involved.

Local Professional Context. The professional experiences in a leadership preparation program are embedded in local school districts. And while there are significant benefits of building relationships between leadership programs and local school systems, there is no guarantee that local leaders or districts model ideal decision-making. In areas where the goal of leadership preparation is incremental improvement over current practice, that is not a serious challenge. On the other hand, current practices also are part of what Tyack and Cuban (1995) term the "grammar of schooling" (p. 9), or the underlying understandings of practice that can limit what future leaders understand about their role.

As with the other issues raised in this section, this is an inevitable dilemma of leadership preparation programs, and instead of avoiding the challenge, we see it as a design constraint for preparation programs. As Orr (2006) observes, leader preparation programs in this century have broadly spread the use of case- and problem-based teaching in leader preparation programs alongside increased use of clinical experiences. This pedagogical pattern layers such didactic instruction on top of the clinical experiences that modern leader preparation programs share with teacher education. Helping future leaders understand ethical decision-making using data requires their being able to work in a broad range of professional settings and with colleagues and the local public who see conflicting and contradictory roles for schooling in general, let alone debate the purpose of using data in decision-making. Framing those conflicts as a fundamental condition of working in schools is a healthy and necessary approach to leadership preparation and can help persuade future leaders that their responsibility lies not in avoiding conflicts but in rooting decision-making in solid ethical foundations.

Practical Goals for School Leader Preparation

Goals to Integrate Ethics and Data

The target for preparing future leaders to work with data is a broader range of roles than preparing a classroom educator. The historically shifting set of leadership responsibilities is a combination of at least two factors: the politics of education and the internal dynamics of leadership as a profession (e.g., Tyack & Hansot, 1986). In the past 40 years, that changing set of responsibilities has grown to include expanded responsibility for data use.

The common responsibility for data use now includes data-informed decision-making in an educational context. That is not the only role of leaders related to data—for leaders in systems-level positions, there is considerable responsibility for data collection and management of different sorts. Thus, aspiring educational leaders need to make decisions at a different level from classroom teachers, and thus their relationship with data is inherently broader than the professional responsibilities of teachers. In addition, it is highly unlikely that the responsibilities of leaders toward data management and use are going to be static in the near future. Three major considerations need to guide instruction about ethical data use.

Teach Beyond Technical Knowledge. Toward these broader ends of data use, leader preparation programs must include but not stop at instruction about technical issues of assessment and data use. Other chapters in this volume document the errors that are often made in use of data that violate fundamental principles of education research, and a program must prepare graduate students who know about those fundamental principles. But in every education system with unethical uses of data—whether fabrication, falsification, or misuse—there have been both applied research staff and leaders who were well aware that they were violating the technical standards of data use and violated them nonetheless. In this way, data use is much like driving, in that a license test that includes a test of didactic knowledge may encourage drivers to know the rules of the road, but in itself that is no guarantee that drivers will not speed, tailgate, or run red lights.

What is needed is both an explicit discussion of how to identify and address potential misuses of data, and also the opportunity to learn how to talk about data use in difficult conversations. For leaders, especially, skill-building around data conversations is more important than being able to complete problem sets in measurement and statistics.

Teach Responsibility Within and For Systems of Data Use. In the same way that technical knowledge of assessment is insufficient, a leader's responsibility is only partly around individualistic decision-making. A leader's responsibility in the recognized ethic of community is about system leadership. In the context of data use, leadership must focus on the organizational role of data use, as Murphy (2017) argued: "[W]orking on the technical and rational aspects of assessment alone is insufficient to garner important gains. Without simultaneous attention to values and norms around assessment, meaning and relevance are too easily left out of the equation, a recipe for producing formulaic work" (p. 97).

Teach Teamwork in Ethical Data Use. Professional and highly skilled data use is engaged, and an aspiring educational leader must learn essential skills related to both team membership and facilitation. The capacity of graduates to analyze school- or district-level assessment data is important, and a leader's perspective on data is generally sufficient to set an agenda for change but not guarantee agreement by educators. Graduates of leader preparation programs must be able to model effective participation in discussions of how to ask and answer important questions with data, and also prepare for and facilitate group discussions among members of an instructional team at a school or district level.

Opportunities for School Leader Preparation

Despite the tighter credit constraints of school leader preparation programs, there are more options to give future education leaders opportunities to wrestle with the practical issues of ethics in data use than in initial educator preparation. For students in leadership programs, their prior experience and current work settings provide a springboard for more complex discussion of issues through case studies, tabletop exercises that build collaboration skills, and applied or action research projects embedded in real-world contexts.

Case Studies and Role-Play Simulations. The fastest way to incorporate discussions of ethical data use in leader preparation programs is through case studies and case simulations, which already have a role in programs. They exist in several contexts: classes in school law where both school law texts and assignments occasionally mirror the typical case-analysis approach of legal instruction; so-called "inbox exercises" where students are faced with professional dilemmas; and in some programs in live simulations where community members or practitioners play roles in a simulated conversation to set up class discussion. Several of the examples in this volume would serve as logical cases for encouraging explicit discussion of the ethical dilemmas of data use, and more examples of dilemmas can be found in standard ethics case texts (Shapiro & Stefkovich, 2016) or in the *Journal of Cases in Educational Leadership*.

Case-based instruction promises to develop individual understandings of the ethical issues embedded in the cases, and thus to help future leaders tease out the potential issues for discussion and resolution in practice. What they do not necessarily engage is the development of skills in difficult conversations when the ethical challenges of practice engage direct professional opportunities and threats. For this purpose, leader preparation skills need additional forms of activities, such as tabletop exercises and critical-friends protocols.

Tabletop Exercises and Critical-Friends Protocols. To develop skills in collaboration under fraught circumstances, leader preparation programs can embed the teaching of important collaborative skills and group processes within the topic of ethical data use. For this purpose, longer activities such as tabletop exercises around a year's worth of decision-making moments can add the reality of local consequences to class-based discussions. What may be a moment of decision in a simulation or case study leads to a consequence and another moment for decision, followed by additional consequences. At each decision point, the preparation program can guide discussion through structured protocols, giving a decision-making role to a subset of the class and a consultative role to others. McDonald and colleagues (2015) provide both a rationale and structure for using protocols in professional practice.

The literature on such critical-friends protocols in a leadership context often focuses on their use to promote collaborative decision-making among teachers, such as in the structure of a professional learning community (Bambino, 2002; Kuh, 2016; Stolle et al., 2019) or the support of school improvement (O'Brien, 2014). In addition to promoting effective decision-making among classroom educators, it is essential to support aspiring and current leaders in the development of skills for difficult conversations not just within teams of educators but also in discussions with district leadership, governing boards, and community members. It is rare that a classroom teacher can pressure a school to make inappropriate or unethical decisions around data use, and the examples of unethical conduct in this volume generally are not at the classroom level; it is therefore essential to enable leaders to raise and discuss ethical issues at the district and community levels.

An important side benefit of tabletop exercises and critical-friends protocols is that they help build collaboration and teamwork in activities and assignments that do not require group projects, and they can be used in single-session contexts. This structure enables their use not only in degree programs but also within program personnel development and single-session workshops.

Applied Data Projects. Assignments can require that students in leader preparation programs collect, analyze, and sometimes act on data relevant to the students' current professional context or internship setting. Such applied projects are common in education master's programs (sometimes in an action research context), and can be part of a capstone project or as a standalone assignment in an individual class. (For a broad survey of instructional approaches current in leader preparation programs, see Anderson et al., 2018.)

An applied data project can address ethical dimensions of data use by requiring that leader candidates incorporate both individual formal analysis of ethical use in a written form and also the facilitation of group discussion of data, using assignment requirements to help leader candidates demonstrate the type of skills discussed throughout this section and push beyond the first-line analysis of data to ask, "so what?" and "what next?" questions. Such an assignment has several benefits. It connects formal knowledge to practice settings by embedding the discussion of data collection and use in a real-world context. It is efficient; it combines both technical and organizational competencies that are directed by standards components. It pushes leader candidates to take responsibility for organizational dynamics; reflection in such an assignment can and should be about both individual candidate positionality and the limits of organizations and data in the assignment's context. It incorporates teamwork and critical-friends protocol skills if it requires facilitation of meetings with both internal and external stakeholders. And it both respects and leverages the local context of programs without necessarily endorsing existing practices in terms of data use.

One example of such an assignment that embeds consideration of ethics is the applied research sequence in Notre Dame's leader preparation program (Holter & Frabutt, 2012). The philosophical underpinning of this choice is the preparation of leaders in a Catholic school context who are responsible for a broad sense of Catholic education and community. In an instructional sense, this four-semester sequence follows conventional approaches to action research, and specifically Mertler's (2019) approach. Another example of this type of assignment would be an extended version of an equity audit assignment that is described by Skrla and colleagues (2004) and advocated by Boske (2012) and Capper and Young (2015). What we propose is introducing an equity audit in a case setting as Skrla and colleagues (2004) describe and then putting the responsibility in the hands of students in leadership programs to compose internal or external (or combined) stakeholder groups as Skrla and colleagues (2004) describe, gather and organize the data to present, and facilitate the group discussion in the context of the leader candidate's clinical experience context. In both an action-research project as Holter and Frabutt (2012) describe or a stakeholder-facilitation equity audit, leader candidates become actively responsible for the ethical implications of data analysis, either in the sense of advancing an existing mission of schools as in Catholic education and Notre Dame's preparatory program purpose, or in the sense of stepping beyond the analysis of data to facilitate discussion of what the systemic response should and can be.

CONCLUSION

EPPs at both the initial teacher and school leadership levels are flooded with state and accreditor expectations. Amid this cloud of professional standards are scattered indicators addressing data usage and, more rarely, data ethics. Teacher preparation programs often address these standards by incorporating a discrete course in assessment that often excludes broader notions of what constitutes data. Likewise, professional codes may be directly addressed throughout a program, but these are infrequently situated within a greater context of ethical theory designed to inform educator practice in the new and unexpected gray areas of professional practice. Conversely, leadership programs have a long history of thinking and writing about ethics, yet such coursework has been criticized as esoteric and disconnected from practice. Similarly, while leadership programs include discrete classes that focus on statistics and measurement, these are often disconnected from practice, and these two streams of study—ethics and data—find few intersections in most school leadership programs.

Our concluding recommendations for EPPs combine incremental modifications with suggestions for deeper change. Among these recommendations, perhaps the easiest is for program chairs to conduct an initial scan of curricula and courses to identify where data use and ethics currently exist and to identify the most obvious locations where these could be introduced or reinforced. Assessment courses or experiences in the preservice program and statistics and decision-making courses in the leadership program are prime sites for this material. Slightly more challenging, but nevertheless straightforward, would be the introduction of a required ethics course or the insertion of syllabus goals around ethics aimed at helping students reflect on and articulate their own overarching ethical beliefs about personal values and decision-making. Books such as that by Strike and Soltis (2009) can provide a road map through personal and professional ethics and facilitate dilemma-based classroom discussions. However, these materials would need to be modified to identify ways in which data literacy could be incorporated within them. Likewise, there are relatively simple ways to infuse both data literacy and ethical literacy, and there are deliberate experiences around the ethical use of data that can be modified. Specific discrete courses, assessment, statistics, and decision-making can use pedagogical examples that are identified in the preceding literature reviews. Leadership programs can employ equity audits in assignments to help leaders learn how to leverage institutional data to identify shortcomings in community ethics. Similarly, the employment of facilitated critical-friends protocols can help ensure that dialogue around community ethics addresses key ways to *use* the information, going beyond data analysis into real conversations about equitable improvements.

More challenging than any of these "easy lifts" is the spiraling infusion of ethics, data literacy, and the intersection of the two across the curriculum. Beyond bringing together faculty to revise a course, introducing a spiraling learning sequence in data ethics across all of a college's EPPs is a much greater task. In the case of ASU, a large-scale curriculum revision to focus on PI spanned multiple years and required special funding for faculty's summer work, course releases throughout the year, coordination with multiple stakeholders, and outside consulting. And it remains a work in progress. Such work requires long-term institutional commitment, but we believe it is worth the effort.

EPPs will be remiss and operating in an unethical manner if they do not pay adequate attention to these issues. The educator's daily work is a key context for the enactment of ethics within the profession. Teachers and students are in unbalanced power relationships, with the weight of assessment placing teachers' thumbs on the scale of students' lives (Bull, 1993). In the lived experience of this teacher–student relationship, data and assessment literacy play an important role in teachers' ethical use of data. Is it fair that a teacher should exercise this level of control over a student's life, based on insufficient understanding of statistical reliability or differential item functioning? Similarly, assigning assessments without providing students with sufficient opportunities to learn also raises questions of fairness—and evokes a visceral sense of violated justice in every student who argues that a teacher never taught the content of the test. In a parallel fashion, the weight of evaluation places the leader's thumb on the scale of teachers' and students' lives. On a systems level, inconsistent assessment regimes that strip away learning time and curricular content for urban students while affording suburban students fewer tests and broader learning opportunities bring equity concerns sharply into focus (Berliner, 2011). Decisions to close down neighborhood schools or implement sweeping statewide school reforms based on unreliable test data or incomplete demographic and financial data highlight the ethical implications of educational leaders' data literacy (e.g., Ewing, 2018). The unequal power relationship that exists between students and teachers is multiplied many times over at the systems level, as school leaders and district supervisors exert enormous influence over the lives of teachers, students, school personnel, and the communities they serve. Clearly, data use and ethics go hand-in-hand in the work of education, and the hazards of ethical missteps at any of these levels are far-reaching and potentially devastating. EPPs, therefore, serve the community well when they prepare their students for the sobering responsibility of data ethics.

REFERENCES

American Federation of Teachers, National Council on Measurement in Education, and National Education Association. (1990). Standards for teacher competence in educational assessment of students. *Educational Measurement: Issues and Practice*, 9(4), 30–32.

Anderson, E., Winn, K. M., Young, M. D., Groth, C., Korach, S., Pounder, D., & Rorrer, A. K. (2018). Examining university leadership preparation: An analysis of program attributes and practices. *Journal of Research on Leadership Education*, 13(4), 375–397.

Athanases, S. Z., Bennett, L. H., & Wahleithner, J. M. (2015). Adaptive teaching for English language arts: Following the pathway of classroom data in preservice teacher inquiry. *Journal of Literacy Research*, 47(1), 83–114.

Athanases, S. Z., Wahleithner, J. M., & Bennett, L. H. (2012). Learning to attend to culturally and linguistically diverse learners through teacher inquiry in teacher education. *Teachers College Record*, 114(7), 1–50.

Bambino, D. (2002). Critical friends. *Educational Leadership*, 59(6), 25–27.

Beck, J. S., Morgan, J. J., Brown, N., Whitesides, H., & Riddle, D. R. (2020). "Asking, learning, seeking out": An exploration of data literacy for teaching. *Educational Forum*, 84(2), 150–165.

Beck, J. S., Morgan, J. J., Whitesides, H., Riddle, D. R., & Brown, N. (2019, Apr. 6). *Differentiating between data literacy and assessment literacy: A systematic review of research* [Roundtable]. American Educational Research Association, Toronto, CA.

Berliner, D. (2011). Rational responses to high stakes testing: The case of curriculum narrowing and the harm that follows. *Cambridge Journal of Education*, 41(3), 287–302.

Boske, C. (2012). Sending forth tiny ripples of hope that build the mightiest of current: Understanding how to prepare school leaders to interrupt oppressive practices. *Planning and Changing*, 43, 183–197.

Bowers, A. J. (2017). Quantitative research methods training in education leadership and administration preparation programs as disciplined inquiry for building school improvement capacity. *Journal of Research on Leadership Education*, 12(1), 72–96.

Brighouse, H., Ladd, H. F., Loeb, S., & Swift, A. (2018). *Educational goods: Values, evidence, and decision making*. University of Chicago Press.

Bull, B. L. (1993). Ethics in the preservice curriculum. In K. A. Strike & P. L. Ternasky (Eds.), *Ethics for professionals in education: Perspectives for preparation and practice* (pp. 69–83). Teachers College Press.

Buskey, F. C., & Pitts, E. M. (2009). Training subversives: The ethics of leadership preparation. *Phi Delta Kappan, 91*(3), 57–61.

Campbell, C., & Evans, J. A. (2000). Investigation of preservice teachers' classroom assessment practices during student teaching. *Journal of Educational Research, 93*(6), 350–355.

Capper, C. A., & Young, M. D. (2015). The equity audit as the core of leading increasingly diverse schools and districts. In G. Theorharis & M. Scanlan (Eds.), *Leadership for increasingly diverse schools* (pp. 186–197). Routledge.

Carey, M., Grainger, P., & Christie, M. (2018). Preparing preservice teachers to be data literate: A Queensland case study. *Asia-Pacific Journal of Teacher Education, 46*(3), 267–278.

Cherubini, L. (2009). Exploring prospective teachers' critical thinking: Case-based pedagogy and the standards of professional practice. *Teaching and Teacher Education, 25*(2), 228–234.

Cooper, B., Cowie, B., Furness, J., Peter, M., & Bailey, J. (2017, June). Mathematical reasoning and knowledge in initial teacher education (MARKITE). Teaching and Learning Research Initiative. http://www.tlri.org.nz/sites/default/files/projects/Final%20formatted%20report%20_Cooper%20and%20Cowie%28v3%29.pdf

Council for the Accreditation of Educator Preparation. (2018). *CAEP handbook: Initial-level programs 2018.* http://caepnet.org/~/media/Files/caep/accreditation-resources/caep-initial-handbook-2018.pdf?la=en

Council of Chief State School Officers. (2013). *Interstate Teacher Assessment and Support Consortium (InTASC) model core teaching standards and learning progressions for teachers 1.0: A resource for ongoing teacher development.* https://ccsso.org/sites/default/files/2017-12/2013_INTASC_Learning_Progressions_for_Teachers.pdf

Darling-Hammond, L., Oakes, J., Wojcikiewicz, S., Hyler, M. E., Guha, R., Podolsky, A., Kini, T., Cook-Harvey, C. M., Jackson Mercer, C. N., & Harrell, A. (2019). *Preparing teachers for deeper learning.* Harvard Education Press.

DeLuca, C., & Bellara, A. (2013). The current state of assessment education: Aligning policy, standards, and teacher education curriculum. *Journal of Teacher Education, 64*(4), 356–372.

DeLuca, C., Chavez, T., Bellara, A., & Cao, C. (2013). Pedagogies for preservice assessment education: Supporting teacher candidates' assessment literacy development. *The Teacher Educator, 48*(2), 128–142.

DeLuca, C., & Klinger, D. A. (2010). Assessment literacy development: Identifying gaps in teacher candidates' learning. *Assessment in Education: Principles, Policy & Practice, 17*(4), 419–438.

DeLuca, C., LaPointe-McEwan, D., & Luhanga, U. (2016). Teacher assessment literacy: A review of international standards and measures. *Educational Assessment, Evaluation and Accountability, 28*(3), 251–272.

Dorr-Bremme, D. W. (1983). Assessing students: Teachers' routine practices and reasoning. *Evaluation Comment, 6*(4), 1–12.

Dunn, K. E., Skutnik, A., Sohn, B., & Patti, C. (2019). Disdain to acceptance: Future U.S. teachers' conceptual change related to data driven decision-making. *Action in Teacher Education, 41*(3), 193–211.

Eraut, M. (1994). *Developing professional knowledge and competence.* Falmer Press.

Ewing, E. L. (2018). *Ghosts in the schoolyard: Racism and school closings on Chicago's South Side.* University of Chicago Press.

Fitchett, P. G., & Heafner, T. L. (2013). Making critical connections between social studies teaching and student achievement using NAEP Data Explorer. *The Teacher Educator, 48*(4), 296–310.

Frick, W. C. (2011). Practicing a professional ethic: Leading for students' best interests. *American Journal of Education, 117*(4), 527–562.

Furman, G. C. (2003). Moral leadership and the ethic of community. *Values and Ethics in Educational Administration, 2*(1), 1–8.

Furman, G. C. (2012). Social justice leadership as praxis: Developing capacities through preparation programs. *Educational Administration Quarterly, 48*(2), 191–229.

Glanzer, P. L., & Ream, T. C. (2007). Has teacher education missed out on the "ethics boom"? A comparative study of ethics requirements and courses in professional majors of Christian colleges and universities. *Christian Higher Education, 6*(4), 271–288.

Goldring, E. B., & Berends, M. (2009). *Leading with data: Pathways to improve your school.* Corwin Press.

Graham, P. (2005). Classroom-based assessment: Changing knowledge and practice through preservice teacher education. *Teaching and Teacher Education, 21*(6), 607–621.

Green, S. K., Johnson, R. L., Kim, D.-H., & Pope, N. S. (2007). Ethics in classroom assessment practices: Issues and attitudes. *Teaching and Teacher Education, 23*(7), 999–1011.

Greenberg, J., & Walsh, K. (2012). *What teacher preparation programs teach about K–12 assessment: A review.* National Council on Teacher Quality. https://files.eric.ed.gov/fulltext/ED532766.pdf

Greenfield, W. D. (2004). Moral leadership in schools. *Journal of Educational Administration, 42*(2), 174–196.

Gregoire, M. (2003). Is it a challenge or a threat? A dual-process model of teachers' cognition and appraisal processes during conceptual change. *Educational Psychology Review, 15*(2), 147–179.

Gross, S. J., & Shapiro, J. P. (Eds.). (2016). *Democratic ethical educational leadership: Reclaiming school reform.* Routledge.

Holter, A. C., & Frabutt, J. (2012). Mission driven and data informed leadership. *Journal of Catholic Education, 15*(2).

Johnson Jr., J. F., & Uline, C. L. (2005). Preparing educational leaders to close achievement gaps. *Theory into Practice, 44*(1), 45–52.

Kimbrough, R. B. (1985). *Ethics: A course of study for educational leaders.* American Association of School Administrators.

Klinger, D. A., McDivitt, P., Rogers, W. T., Howard, B., Wylie, C., & Munoz, M. (2012). *The Classroom Assessment Standards: Our ongoing efforts to improve K–12* (Spotlight Session). Canadian Society for the Study of Education. https://cssespotlight.files.wordpress.com/2012/04/klinger-knowledge-snapshot-cera.pdf

Kuh, L. P. (2016). Teachers talking about teaching and school: Collaboration and reflective practice via critical friends groups. *Teachers and Teaching*, *22*(3), 293–314.

Levine, A. (2006). *Educating school leaders*. The Education Schools Project. The Woodrow Wilson National Fellowship Foundation. https://eric.ed.gov/?id=ED504144

Maclellan, E. (2004). Initial knowledge states about assessment: Novice teachers' conceptualisations. *Teaching and Teacher Education*, *20*(5), 523–535.

Mandinach, E. B., Friedman, J. M., & Gummer, E. S. (2015). How can schools of education help to build educators' capacity to use data? A systemic view of the issue. *Teachers College Record*, *117*(4), 1–50.

Mandinach, E. B., & Gummer, E. S. (2013). A systemic view of implementing data literacy in educator preparation: *Educational Researcher*, *42*(1), 30–37.

Mandinach, E. B., & Gummer, E. S. (2016). What does it mean for teachers to be data literate: Laying out the skills, knowledge, and dispositions. *Teaching and Teacher Education*, *60*, 366–376.

Mandinach, E. B., & Schildkamp, K. (2021). Misconceptions about data-based decision making in education: An exploration of the literature. *Studies in Educational Evaluation*, *69*, 1–10. https://doi.org/10.1016/j.stueduc.2020.100842

Mandinach, E. B., & Wayman, J. C. (2020). *Survey of curriculum: First deliverable in privacy training resources project*. WestEd.

Mary Lou Fulton Teachers College, Arizona State University. (2019). *Principled innovation in the systems of educator and leader preparation* (2nd ed.). https://education.asu.edu/sites/default/files/framework-for-principled-innovation.pdf

Maxwell, B., & Schwimmer, M. (2016). Professional ethics education for future teachers: A narrative review of the scholarly writings. *Journal of Moral Education*, *45*(3), 354–371.

McDonald, J. P., Mohr, N., Dichter, A., & McDonald, E. C. (2015). *The power of protocols: An educator's guide to better practice*. Teachers College Press.

Mertler, C. A. (2004). Secondary teachers' assessment literacy: Does classroom experience make a difference? *American Secondary Education*, *33*(1), 49–64.

Mertler, C. A. (2019). *Action research: Improving schools and empowering educators*. SAGE.

Murphy, J. F. (2002). Reculturing the profession of educational leadership: New blueprints. *Educational Administration Quarterly*, *38*(2), 176–191.

Murphy, J. F. (2015). The empirical and moral foundations of the ISLLC standards. *Journal of Educational Administration*, *53*(6), 718–734.

Murphy, J. F. (2017). *Professional standards for educational leaders: The empirical, moral, and experiential foundations*. Corwin Press.

National Policy Board for Educational Administration. (2007). *Educational leadership policy standards: ISLLC 2008.* Council of Chief State School Officers. https://www.danforth.uw.edu/uwdanforth/media/danforth/isllc-2008.pdf

National Policy Board for Educational Administration. (2015). *Professional standards for educational leaders 2015.* https://www.wallacefoundation.org/knowledge-center/Documents/Professional-Standards-for-Educational-Leaders-2015.pdf

O'Brien, S., McNamara, G., & O'Hara, J. (2014). Critical facilitators: External supports for self-evaluation and improvement in schools. *Studies in Educational Evaluation, 43,* 169–177.

Orr, M. T. (2006). Mapping innovation in leadership preparation in our nation's schools of education. *Phi Delta Kappan, 87*(7), 492–499.

Penuel, W. R., & Shepard, L. A. (2016). Assessment and teaching. In D. H. Gitomer & C. A. Bell (Eds.), *Handbook of research on teaching* (5th ed., pp. 787–850). American Educational Research Association.

Piro, J. S., Dunlap, K., & Shutt, T. (2014). A collaborative data chat: Teaching summative assessment data use in pre-service teacher education. *Cogent Education, 1*(1), 1–24.

Reeves, T. D. (2017). Pre-service teachers' data use opportunities during student teaching. *Teaching and Teacher Education, 63,* 263–273.

Reeves, T. D., & Chiang, J.-L. (2018). Online interventions to promote teacher data-driven decision making: Optimizing design to maximize impact. *Studies in Educational Evaluation, 59,* 256–269.

Reeves, T. D., & Honig, S. L. (2015). A classroom data literacy intervention for preservice teachers. *Teaching and Teacher Education, 50,* 90–101.

Rentner, D. S., Kober, N., Frizzell, M., Ferguson, M., & Aigner, B. (2016). *Listen to us: Teacher views and voices.* Center on Education Policy, George Washington University.

Robelen, E. (2016, June 3). *Testing and test prep: How much is too much?* Education Writers Association. https://www.ewa.org/blog-educated-reporter/testing-and-test-prep-how-much-too-much

Sahlberg, P. (2011). The fourth way of Finland. *Journal of Educational Change, 12*(2), 173–185.

Sahlberg, P. (2016). The global educational reform movement and its impact on schooling. In K. Mundy, A. Green, B. Lingard, & A. Verger (Eds.), *The handbook of global education policy* (pp. 128–144). John Wiley & Sons.

Shapira-Lishchinsky, O. (2013). Team-based simulations: Learning ethical conduct in teacher trainee programs. *Teaching and Teacher Education, 33,* 1–12.

Shapiro, J. P., & Gross, S. J. (2017). Ethics and professional norms. In J. F. Murphy (Ed.), *Professional standards for educational leaders: The empirical, moral, and experiential foundations* (pp. 21–35). Corwin.

Shapiro, J. P., & Stefkovich, J. A. (2016). *Ethical leadership and decision making in education: Applying theoretical perspectives to complex dilemmas.* Routledge.

Skrla, L., Scheurich, J. J., Garcia, J., & Nolly, G. (2004). Equity audits: A practical leadership tool for developing equitable and excellent schools. *Educational Administration Quarterly, 40*(1), 133–161.

Smylie, M. A., & Murphy, J. (2018). School leader standards from ISLLC to PSEL: Notes on their development and the work ahead. *UCEA Review*, *59*(3), 24–28.

Starratt, R. J. (1991). Building an ethical school: A theory for practice in educational leadership. *Educational Administration Quarterly*, *27*(2), 185–202.

Starratt, R. J. (2012). *Cultivating an ethical school.* Routledge.

Stefkovich, J., & Begley, P. T. (2007). Ethical school leadership: Defining the best interests of students. *Educational Management Administration & Leadership*, *35*(2), 205–224.

Stiggins, R. J. (1999). Evaluating classroom assessment training in teacher education programs. *Educational Measurement: Issues and Practice*, *18*(1), 23–27.

Stolle, E. P., Frambaugh-Kritzer, C., Freese, A., & Persson, A. (2019). Investigating critical friendship: Peeling back the layers. *Studying Teacher Education*, *15*(1), 19–30.

Strike, K. A., & Soltis, J. F. (2009). *The ethics of teaching* (5th ed). Teachers College Press.

Tyack, D. B., & Cuban, L. (1995). *Tinkering toward utopia: A century of public school reform.* Harvard University Press.

Tyack, D., & Hansot, E. (1986). *Managers of virtue: Public school leadership in America, 1820–1980.* Basic Books.

Warnick, B. R., & Silverman, S. K. (2011). A framework for professional ethics courses in teacher education. *Journal of Teacher Education*, *62*(3), 273–285.

Whitesides, H., & Beck, J. S. (2020). "There is subjectivity, there is bias": Teacher candidates' perceptions of equity in data literacy for teaching. *The Teacher Educator*, *55*(3), 283–299.

Xu, Y., & Brown, G. T. L. (2016). Teacher assessment literacy in practice: A reconceptualization. *Teaching and Teacher Education*, *58*, 149–162.

CHAPTER 8

Data Access, Ethics, and Use in Learning and Navigation Organizations

Wayne Camara, Michelle Croft, and Alina von Davier

Diverse data are collected in the assessment process, including test scores, demographics, aspirations, interests, behaviors, and academic information. Assessment data are combined with other educational information about the student, school, or postsecondary institution, to produce additional indicators or metrics. Data on attendance, extracurricular activities, program participation, homework, time on tasks, and interim assessments can be combined to provide indicators for accountability systems or to evaluate educational outcomes. This chapter reviews the data collected or produced by large-scale assessments, as well as the efficacies which may result from assessments and learning, future performance, and policy decisions. We examine appropriate and inappropriate uses of test scores that may create ethical dilemmas for testing organizations, as well as federal and state laws, regulations, and best practices that address release, reporting, and reuse of assessment data for additional educational purposes. We discuss data collection from learning systems with embedded assessments, called learning and assessment systems (LAS), and implications for ethical and fair data use.

In the past 2 decades, there has been increased attention on harnessing educational data to provide additional insights concerning learning and proficiency. This enthusiasm for using data to inform instruction emerged from other disciplines and was advocated by policymakers, state government, foundations, technology entrepreneurs, and curriculum marketers (McDonald, 2019). No Child Left Behind (NCLB, 2002) and the Elementary and Secondary Education Act of 2001 (ESEA) fueled much of the demand for longitudinal data to inform policy. States and districts improved their data systems in response to new reporting requirements as policymakers urged districts to use data-driven decision-making. The Data Quality Campaign was established in 2005 to promote the value of data. The American Recovery and Reinvestment Act of 2009 incentivized data use with funds contingent on assurances about the use and quality of data systems (U.S. Department of Education, 2011). Yet as of the mid-2000s, relatively little research examined the use of summative assessments for instructional decision-making (Mandinach & Honey, 2008).

Educators face pressure from accountability policies to improve student achievement, and the use of data is viewed as essential for evaluating their practices and student progress (Knapp et al., 2006; Mandinach, 2012). Measurement professionals and many educators understand that summative tests are too distal from instruction, at the wrong grain size, and administered too late to be effective instruments for instructional uses (Perie et al., 2009). The North Central Regional Educational Laboratory (2004) states the following:

> There is a growing impetus in some schools and districts for creating longitudinal student record data systems as repositories of individual student histories. These data can be used to improve curricular alignment and student transitions throughout the P–16 pipeline by identifying important variables that impact students' academic progress at key points along the way. Such data systems can also be rich informational tools to aggregate individual records for analysis at national, state, and district levels in order to inform policy, planning, and resource allocation. (p. 1)

Advances in artificial intelligence (AI) and big data influence data to inform student learning and mastery. These advances have expanded the possibilities for educational measurement and decision-making and exposed ethical and equity limitations in the use of digital data traces and AI in education (Wang, 2021). These advances led to new types of data analysis, evolving from traditional classical test theory to computational psychometrics. Simply defined, *computational psychometrics* blends traditional psychometrics (the science of measuring knowledge, skills, abilities, personality traits, attitudes) with computational techniques from AI and cognitive science fields (von Davier, 2017). Traditional methods employed by states, districts, and testing organizations to collect, store, and analyze the longitudinal data from multiple administrations does not support real-time, data-intensive computational psychometrics and analytics methods that can reveal new patterns and information about students over time.

The impetus on performance assessment led to new challenges regarding data governance: data design, collection, alignment, and storage. Learning analytics encountered similar problems: how to merge multiple data types into logfiles to provide a comprehensive picture of students' progress. Some researchers and practitioners propose solutions for the interoperability of learning data coming from multiple sources (Bakharia et al., 2016). Multimodal data analysis requires that the data from multiple sources are available and easy to align across providers and users. This led to the importance of the data exchange standards for activities and events, such as the Caliper Standards for event data from IMS Global.[1] See also the work of Project Unicorn.[2]

In the context of interoperability for learning analytics, Cooper (2014) emphasized the need for standards. Recently, von Davier and colleagues (2019) proposed the adoption of data cube data governance for educational organizations that have multiple data sets and data types. A data cube allows for an alignment of multiple databases on various dimensions (Gilbert et al., 2017). In districts with multiple data sources, one dimension on which one may want to align the information is the student. Another dimension for alignment may be a discipline. Institutions need to overcome several alignment challenges, including lack of coherence of traditional content tagging, interoperability, and computational resources. Criteria for data privacy and protection mechanisms need to be considered. A flexible data governance framework coupled with a well-versed staff has the potential to support districts in making decisions (with the caveats noted in Wang, 2021). It provides evidence-based insights on what works and what does not work over time. A careful analysis can also identify a lack of access to technology and resources at the student level or school level. Districts that manage these technologies and data well and that provide continuous professional development for the teachers, counselors, and IT support are potentially better prepared to support their students' learning. Professional development is essential for the success of technology- and data-based learning.

DATA SUPPORTING CLAIMS FROM LARGE-SCALE SUMMATIVE ASSESSMENTS

Large-scale summative assessments are generally used for a variety of purposes but are designed to provide data that (1) indicate students' status or proficiency at the culmination of a program, and (2) are predictive of future performance or proficiency. State assessments, mandated under the Every Student Succeeds Act of 2015 (ESSA), are used for accountability purposes across education levels. Data are tracked longitudinally to provide insights about student proficiency, to monitor student progress, and to show other outcomes. Consistent with requirements under ESEA (2001), Section 1111(h) requires states to report disaggregated data for all student groups, including major racial and ethnic groups, economically disadvantaged students, children with disabilities, and English learners.[3] Districts often rely on commercially available assessments, which may provide national norms or other cumulative reporting of students' skills and knowledge (Perie et al., 2009). Another class of summative assessments is used for higher education and includes admissions, course placement, and certification and licensure tests. Such assessments are used by higher education to evaluate past achievement and proficiency and predict future performance (Camara et al., 2013).

Irrespective of the original purpose and intended use, policymakers, educators, and other stakeholders often introduce additional uses for large-scale assessments. High school accountability tests are also used to confer a diploma in more than a dozen states, and several other states use Smarter-Balanced Assessment Consortium (SBAC) test scores for placement in college courses. A more glaring example of misuse was instituted by the Florida legislature, which earmarked up to $10,000 for individual teacher bonuses with high ACT or SAT scores. The intent of the program was to recruit and retain the best teachers, but using admission test scores taken as a teenager is a flawed indicator. Of course, there are multiple more recent and more direct metrics of academic achievement such as college degrees and college grades (Education World, 2015).

When policymakers adopt a test for a new purpose, it is essential that the developer raise concerns and explain that the new claim or use lacks evidence. State adoption of a test may have positive effects for students and large financial benefits for the developer. In the latter instance, the test developer should have already established the intended uses and provided evidence to support its validity argument. New claims regarding score use require direct support from the vendor. When either a state or other entity is responsible for development and contracts with the vendor to produce the assessment, it is regarded as the state's responsibility to support its claims and furnish appropriate validity evidence. In such instances where customized assessment development is contracted to a vendor, it is more difficult for the vendor to contradict claims from the sponsoring organization. The *Standards for Educational and Psychological Testing* (American Educational Research Association [AERA] et al., 2014) note that the test developer[4] should set forth how test scores are intended to be interpreted and used, including the intended population, the targeted construct(s), the context of use, and the process for administration and scoring. Supporting validity evidence is required to support the claims and prescribed uses.

Many of the most consistent criticisms of summative assessments include an overemphasis on selected-response tasks, "one and done" testing, absence of extended performance tasks, and lack of instructionally sensitive information. Yet, as noted earlier, summative assessments are primarily designed to capture student status or proficiency and not to provide instructional-relevant information for students. Stakeholders are critical of summative tests because of their limited utility in providing individual diagnostic and instructional relevant data, even when those uses are not claimed by a test developer or test user. Brookhart (2010) summarizes arguments and evidence that the evaluative and grading functions of summative tests tend to negate any instructional information and feedback. DePascale (2003) traces the evolution of criterion-referenced testing to fill the void created by the absence of statewide or national curriculum: "If it is a given that teachers are going to teach to the test, give them a test worth teaching to" (p. 5).

Criterion-referenced summative tests are widely employed in states to meet the accountability requirements of ESEA and were designed to specify a domain of content and cognitive skills codified in standards and taught by teachers. The expectation was that this design would facilitate aligned instruction, which would reduce group achievement gaps and demonstrate instructional validity and instructional sensitivity (Baker et al., 2016). There has been a general lack of empirical data regarding the tests' sensitivity to instructional differences and inconsistent results on instructional sensitivity from different data collection approaches (Ing, 2018). The University of California's Standardized Testing Task Force (2020) notes that significant portions of standards or content may also be underused in the classroom, and the relatedly flat performance in math and reading, along with persistent achievement gaps along race/ethnicity lines demonstrated by tests such as SBAC, which has been in use in California for more than a decade, undercut any argument of instruction validity.

Formative and classroom-based assessments generate other types of data used in the evaluation and support of learning. Black and Wiliam (2003) emphasize that the distinction between "formative" and "summative" applies not to the assessments themselves, but to the function they serve, and they note that assessment becomes formative only when evidence is used to adapt the teaching to meet student needs. Black and Wiliam (1998) provide evidence that formative assessment impacts learning outcomes at all grade levels.

Use of formative assessments has greatly expanded in K–12 testing and refers to an instrument such as a diagnostic test, an "interim" assessment, or an item bank from which teachers might create those tests. Formative assessments of this kind typically produce multiple scores, often claimed to have "diagnostic" value, and are used throughout the school year. Bennett (2011) notes that this definition represents the view of test publishers and varies from the view of formative assessment as a process that may lead to insights that help direct further refinement in instruction. Perie and colleagues (2009) distinguish between classes of assessments such as formative, interim, and summative, but emphasize that each class of assessment is bound to a validity argument requiring evidence to support claims. Formative and interim assessments, by design, are brief and short, but the trade-off can be score precision and accurate information. Ethical issues can emerge in formative assessments despite their focus on learning and reputation as "low-stakes assessments." For example, if formative assessment products lack sufficient instructional sensitivity, alignment, or precision, they may provide misinformation about prior learning. Unreliable information about prior learning can point the learner in the wrong direction and waste valuable instructional time. According to Shepard (2005), "because of the grossness of the information from reliable subtest scores, interim assessment results can only be used to make relatively gross instructional-program-level decisions" and that such focusing of effort can do more harm than good (p.6). The decision to use any assessment can create ethical dilemmas that compromise quality for other purposes, and such trade-offs must be weighted. Selection of assessments involves trade-offs, but the test user has an ethical responsibility to evaluate available evidence to ensure it supports the claims, intended uses, and appropriateness for the local population (AERA et al., 2014).

Often, test scores are appropriated for purposes outside their intended purpose to promote a policy position. In such instances, additional claims about test scores may be promoted by test users. For example, large-scale summative assessments were proposed as a principled method for evaluating the quality of teachers, schools, and teacher-preparation programs under NCLB (2002). Several scientific societies (AERA, American Statistical Association [ASA]) issued statements cautioning policymakers about the widespread use of changes in the large-scale test scores of students in value-added models (VAM) of teacher and program effectiveness. The law was intended to identify and reward highly effective teachers, but even officials at the testing companies argued against the use, citing the lack of evidence (Travis, 2015). Policymakers, education leaders, and other stakeholders often burden large-scale assessments with purposes, claims, and uses that were never intended and may often constitute misuses. Such parties, labeled "secondary test users," are not traditional test users trained in measurement, but they may have controlling authority over how an organization, institution, or government entity uses test scores (Camara, 1997). These secondary users have no general training in assessment and no prescribed responsibilities for assessment. Some of these individuals can influence the interpretation of results, may misuse assessments and results, and may have political incentives to selectively use results to support certain values or beliefs (Berliner & Biddle, 1995).

Standards 1.1 to 1.6 of the *Standards for Educational and Psychological Testing* provide guidance on the responsibilities of test developers and users to identify how test scores are interpreted and provide evidence to support each use. Table 8.1 illustrates the shifting burdens when new uses are proposed by a test user responsible for an assessment program based on the Standards (AERA et al., 2014). The table illustrates how the burden to produce evidence and support claims may shift when new claims are made concerning outcomes related to the test or additional uses for scores. Standard 1.6 cites relative to the claim that summative testing can advance classroom instruction: "evidence for such a claim should be examined—in conjunction with evidence about the validity or intended test score interpretation and evidence about unintended negative consequences of test use—in making an overall decision about test use" (AERA et al., 2014, p. 24).

Table 8.1. Responsibilities of Test Developers and Users

Task (Standard)	Primary Responsibility	Timeline
Clearly specify the intended use of the assessment. (1.1)	Test developer	During test design and development
Provide a rationale for each intended interpretation along with a summary of evidence and theory to support each use. (1.2)	Test developer	During test design and development
Identify any likely interpretation or use that is not supported. (1.3)	Test developer and test user	During test design, development, and implementation
Provide a rationale and evidence to support any additional uses or interpretations proposed or resulting from the implementation. (1.4)	Test user	During implementation
When claims are made or implied that test use will result in a specific outcome, supporting evidence should be provided. (1.5)	Test user or whoever is making and supporting the claim	During test design, development, and implementation
When test use is recommended because it will result in some benefits, such recommendations should be made explicit along with the rationale and supporting evidence. (1.6)	Test user or whoever is making and supporting the claim	During test design, development, and implementation

Developers are responsible for identifying intended uses and purposes, and collecting and sharing validity evidence supporting those claims. The test user or test sponsor[5] may assume primary responsibility for all statements about the intended use and claims associated with scores from customized assessments. Many states and institutions issue a request for proposal that identifies the intended uses, claims, and responsibilities of all parties in supporting the collection of evidence.

Misuses of Standardized Test Data

Third parties often bear no responsibility to the development or use of assessments. Examples of misuse with admissions test scores include employers who require scores from applicants, realtors' use of test scores to market homes, and services that use test scores in ranking institutions. The National Association of College Admissions Counseling (2008) released a report on the use of standardized tests in undergraduate admissions that identified a number of practices that raise ethical concerns:

- Cut scores or minimum scores to determine eligibility for merit-based financial aid
- Reliance on a test score as the sole criterion for an initial screen for scholarships
- Use of admission test scores for college ranking
- Bond ratings that rely on admissions tests or other indicator of institutional financial health

The most common misuse of test scores seems to result from the insistence of test sponsors (e.g., legislators, state departments of education, institutions) to use a single test score as the sole determinant of high-stakes decisions (e.g., graduation, promotion to the next grade) even against the recommendations of the testing organizations (Rhoades & Madaus, 2003). Most off-the-shelf testing programs include statements concerning the intended purpose and appropriate uses of their tests and test scores. The College Board (2018b) issued comprehensive guidelines that address how test scores should be used as well as the use of scores for various purposes such as recruitment, marketing, admissions, scholarship eligibility, placement, credit, and aggregate purposes. The Guidelines caution against reproduction of admissions scores on transcripts and to establish standards regarding the length of time that scores are considered valid for institutional decisions. The Guidelines also cite usage examples for test scores (Table 8.2).

Median test scores account for much more of the differences in the *U.S. News & World Report* professional school rankings than rankings of undergraduate institutions, which leads to overemphasis on test scores by programs attempting to maintain or achieve a high ranking. Institutional rankings may inadvertently result in programs overweighting test scores and de-emphasizing other factors such as fit, diversity, and ability to benefit.

Test-Optional Policies and COVID-19

The decision on whether to use a test or other data for important decisions such as retention, graduation, placement, scholarship, and admissions carries ethical implications. More than 1,100 colleges and universities were identified as test optional at the beginning of 2020. Test-optional policies have increased across undergraduate institutions due to the increasing diversity of applicants and matriculants (Camara, 2021; Lucido, 2018). Two recent studies found that test-optional institutions saw an average increase of 8 to 26 SAT score points (on a 1600-point scale), which enhanced their

Table 8.2. Usage Examples for Test Scores

Encouraged Uses of Test Scores	Discouraged Uses of Test Scores
1. Using test scores to provide additional context to better understand other information (e.g., grades and courses taken) in a student's transcript	1. Encouraging the belief that tests measure a person's worth as a human being
2. Reviewing student performance on tests with individual students, parents, and teachers in order to help everyone understand the student's strengths and challenge areas	2. Using test scores as the sole basis for important decisions affecting the lives of individuals, when other information of equal or greater relevance and the resources for using such information are available
3. Using test results to identify, in advance, students at risk, to assist with retention and persistence support	3. Using minimum cut scores on tests without proper validation
4. Helping students understand how their scores on standardized assessments relate to all other test takers on the same assessment and to the applicant pools at institutions the student is considering	4. Making decisions about otherwise qualified students based only on small differences in test scores
5. Using standardized assessment scores to conduct unique, institutionally based research to identify which of those characteristics used in decision-making are the best predictors of success in course placement or in freshman or long-term performance	5. Using scores without appropriate consideration to their validity
6. Using placement test results to ensure that students enroll in appropriate courses and that developmental support is provided to students who need it	6. Providing inadequate or misleading information about the importance of test scores in making judgments or decisions
7. Incorporating information about student performance high school profiles to provide a context in which to understand students' scores and transcript information in addition to data about students' socioeconomic status	7. Failing to recognize differences in admission standards and requirements that may exist among different schools or departments within many institutions when providing information to prospective applicants

(continued)

Table 8.2. (continued)

Encouraged Uses of Test Scores	Discouraged Uses of Test Scores
8. Providing information about institutional test scores in print, online, and through other communications, so students and families understand the full range of characteristics of applicants and admitted and enrolled students	8. Discouraging certain students from taking tests in an effort to increase a school's or district's average score
9. Sharing score reports, especially aggregate reports that assess specific academic performances, with teachers to assist instructional needs and planning	9. Rejecting a student's application for transfer on the basis of scores received 2 or 3 years prior when the student has since maintained a strong academic record
10. Using test scores and accompanying proficiency information as an early identification system for college-bound students or as an early intervention tool for students in need of additional academic preparation	10. Using as a sole indicator of the overall performance of students, teachers, educational institutions, districts, states, and other groups, except for those states in which all students are tested
11. Using multiple criteria when advising students about advanced courses opportunities (e.g., prior grades and courses, test scores, teacher recommendations, and student motivation)	11. Ranking states, districts, schools, and other institutions solely by aggregate advanced course grades and admission test scores, except for those states in which all students are tested

Note: Edited and adapted from *Guidelines on the Uses of College Board Test Scores and Related Data* by College Board, 2018b.

selectivity and college ranking, and had a small increase in applications, but did not find a difference in ethnic, racial, or economic diversity of total applicants or enrolled students (Belasco et al., 2014; Sweitzer et al., 2018). It would be a disservice to imply that institutions adopting test-optional or test-blind policies are engaging in unethical practices, but the results of such policies clearly produce significant advantages in selectivity and rankings, calling into question the fairness of rankings that influence perceptions of institutional quality. One solution is for test-optional colleges to obtain scores for all enrolled students. Test-optional policies also introduce a "gaming" component that may disadvantage more naïve or first-generation applicants. While professional admissions coaches are available to provide individually tailored advice to more privileged students, less-fortunate students will have difficulty determining the efficacy of submitting or withholding their test score from different institutions in a competitive admissions environment that lacks transparency.

In 2020, COVID-19 was responsible for closing U.S. schools as early as March. It created unique circumstances surrounding admissions testing and test-optional policies. By mid-May, all public schools in 43 states and most schools in other states had been closed for some period of time, affecting more than 55 million students (*Education Week*, 2020). National administrations of college admissions tests were canceled, and when they were restored in the summer and fall of 2020, they had greatly reduced seating capacity. The College Board estimated that at least 1.5 million students missed the test because of cancellations and a similar figure could be estimated for the ACT. Given this closure of schools and colleges and limited access to the SAT and ACT, more than 1,600 4-year colleges waived the test score requirement for admissions in 2021. Many of these institutions are extending the policy into 2022 and beyond, and, for the first-time, several institutions adopted a test-blind policy, meaning they will not consider test scores for any applicants (Adams, 2020). COVID-19 was responsible for the emergence of many new ethical dilemmas for students, institutions, and testing organizations (Camara, 2020), such as the following:

- Should schools open for testing? Should students attend a test center where health concerns exist?
- Should testing organizations provide access to tests in some states and regions that permit schools to open even when safety concerns exist?
- Should testing organizations prioritize access to tests for seniors or students who have not previously tested, and can they implement such policies effectively?
- Who is responsible if students or test center staff contract the virus? Who is responsible for ensuring social distancing and other safety guidelines are implemented in local testing centers?

Perhaps the biggest dilemma to emerge from COVID-19 was the decision of graduate and professional admissions testing programs to offer at-home testing with remote-proctored administrations and the barriers that prevented undergraduate admissions tests to forgo this solution. Camara (2020) identified significant requirements for at-home testing (e.g., video quality Internet connection for several hours, a quiet and uninterrupted testing space), which are clearly not universally available for all students. At-home proctoring also raises the ethical issue of having students choose between their own privacy and the opportunity to have a test score for admissions or scholarships purposes. This is particularly of issue if students do not have control over how their personal information may be stored or later used. There are also legal concerns related to remote proctoring for both people of color and people with disabilities. The Consortium for Citizens with Disabilities and the Lawyers' Committee for Civil Rights Under Law (2020) outlined concerns such as having less access to the technology and space requirements needed for testing; reports that some of the software used for remote proctoring has difficulty identifying people of color; and remote proctoring may inappropriately flag a student with a disability such as attention deficit hyperactivity disorder (ADHD) or Tourette's Syndrome who exhibits unpredictable body movements—or require the student to disclose a medical condition.

Errors in Standardized Testing

Rhoades and Madaus (2003) describe two types of errors that occur in large-scale assessments: active errors and latent errors. *Active errors* include systemic errors in processes or human errors. *Latent errors* stem from poorly conceived legislation or policy mandates, or from flawed decisions by a testing sponsor; they were also described earlier as misuses of test data. Examples include the following:

- Legislation requires a single test be used to determine graduation.
- A state department of education demands that test scores be reported faster than can be dependably accomplished by the contractor.
- Policymakers use tests to track achievement trends without any external confirmation of validity.
- A mandate requires that school test scores increase by x percent per year. This directive fails to take measurement errors into account, and projects growth estimates that are not realistic. (p. 6)

The National Commission on Testing and Public Policy (1990) noted that despite widespread reliance on testing for critical decisions in education and employment, the testing industry lacked oversight or independent audit processes, making it difficult to detect errors and misuse, and to protect the consumer or test taker. One of the most well-documented errors occurred between 1976 and 1980 with the Armed Services Vocational Aptitude Battery (ASVAB) due to a test-score calibration error that resulted in acceptance of more than 300,000 army recruits who did not score above the cut-score and should have been rejected (Camara & Means, 1986). In 1999, CTB McGraw Hill found a programming error that resulted in using the wrong conversion table for the TerraNova reading comprehension test and an additional error that caused students who scored at the top and bottom of the scale—about 250,000 students—to receive incorrect percentiles. Students in New York City and Nevada were most impacted because the test was used for high-stakes decisions, and approximately 8,700 students whose corrected percentiles would have passed the test were mistakenly compelled to complete summer school.

ASSESSMENT DATA: COLLECTION, ACCESS, AND RELEASE

Ethical issues and controversy often surround the release, sale, and use of ancillary data that are collected as part of national testing programs. Data on test takers may be collected from students prior to the test administration. National testing programs often include voluntary surveys as part of the registration process that students complete weeks or days prior to testing. Testing organizations frequently sell the names and other personally identifiable information (PII) to colleges, scholarships, and other educational service organizations. Students typically must opt in to such services but have no control over who receives their information and how it is stored and protected in secondary databases. While test publishers generally restrict access to individuals' financial status, most other demographic and self-report interests are fair game. Some of the controversy emanates from the lack of transparency with such arrangements, while others express concern with the millions of dollars of revenue generated from such data exchanges.

In the past 2 decades, there has been an increased demand by colleges to identify high achievers who are also from low-income families or underrepresented minorities and student search services. However, there is also concern that institutions could misuse such data to identify students from wealthy families with no financial need and who can be expected to enroll as "full pay" matriculants. The same data used to identify and recruit low-income or minorities could be sorted and selected differently to identify applicants from privileged backgrounds.

Different Types of Data

Data from a large range of different types are collected in advance of, during, and subsequent to testing. One special use of such data for admissions tests is to provide colleges, universities, and select third parties, such as scholarship organizations, access to applicants based on a profile or specific factors that they select. Admissions tests for undergraduate, graduate, and professional degrees routinely provide a service for institutions to purchase the names and PII of applicants based on some combination of characteristics. Test takers must either opt in or opt out of such services when they register or complete the test in order to allow third-party access to their PII. The language used to communicate how the information will be shared and used is particularly important as it may constitute a sale of the student's personal information (Struett, 2019).

Although these special uses are designed to benefit students and post-secondary institutions through sharing the student data, it is important that testing programs are judicious in the type of information that is collected and shared. For instance, a recent lawsuit challenged the inclusion of an optional ACT registration item asking if the student has a disability requiring special provisions from the educational institution where the data were shared with postsecondary institutions (*Bloom et al. vs. ACT, Inc.,* 2020). The lawsuit alleged that sharing the information was a violation of the Americans with Disabilities Act, among other laws. ACT removed the question from the registration survey and ultimately settled for $16 million without admitting wrongdoing (Jaschik, 2020). The legal challenge illustrates that testing programs should narrowly tailor registration surveys and clearly articulate to examinees how the information is shared with others.

The collection and sharing of data are further complicated by who pays for the test. When the examinee pays for the test, the examinee is entering into a contract with the test provider, and by registering, the examinee is agreeing to the terms and conditions specified by the test provider, including the test provider's privacy policy. In recent years, however, there has been an increase in the number of states and districts that administer national tests during the school day. When a state entity is funding the assessment, states are required to ensure that schools comply with federal laws such as the Family Educational Rights and Privacy Act (FERPA, 20 U.S.C. § 1232g) and the Protection of Pupil Rights Amendment (PPRA, 20 U.S.C. § 1232h) (U.S. Department of Education, 2018).

FERPA applies to schools that receive federal funding and has specific requirements for instances when schools can share information from a student's educational record. This sharing is relevant to test providers as states and districts provide student information, such as name and gender, prior to testing for administration purposes. The district's ability to share this information with the test provider is permissible under multiple FERPA exceptions, such as the "school official" exception (34 C.F.R. § 99.31) and the "directory" exception (34 C.F.R. § 99.3.) Although states/districts are able to share student information with test providers, FERPA does limit resharing of the student educational records that are provided by the state to the test providers, unless the resharing fits within an FERPA exception. Absent other contract provisions, test providers may share information that has been provided directly from students, as those are not FERPA-protected educational records.

In addition to FERPA, PPRA also influences what information can be collected when the test is administered by a state or district. Among other requirements, the PPRA has certain restrictions on the type of survey data schools can collect from students. Parental notice and the ability to opt their student out of the survey is required if the survey asks questions about PPRA-protected information such as religion or family income.

Federal laws are not the only laws guiding the collection, access, and release of data. State laws may prevent the collection, use, and/or sharing of data as well. Since 2013, there have been numerous data privacy bills introduced and enacted (Data Quality Campaign [DQC], 2017, 2019). Many of the state laws are modeled after California's Student Online Personal Information Protection Act (SOPIPA, California Business and Professions Code § 22584), which was written to regulate educational technology companies that collect student data. SOPIPA (and SOPIPA-like statutes) apply to websites, applications, and online services that focus on K–12 services. SOPIPA primarily prohibits the sale of student information and targeted advertising, which has implications for students who want to participate in programs that sell student names to college and scholarship organizations. SOPIPA also limits the ability to use or share student data for research purposes unrelated to the improvement of the tests, unless the research is at the direction of the state or district. Other aspects of testing programs that can be impacted by state data privacy laws include data retention policies as well as the collection of certain types of data (Croft, 2018).

Even without state law restrictions, states may decide to include more stringent data privacy restrictions within a contract with the test provider. For example, states may request that data not be used for research purposes, not be shared with third parties, or not be included in national reports (even in aggregated form). Similarly, states where laws would otherwise allow for the sale of student data may decide not to permit their students from participating in the postsecondary institution/scholarship organization opt-in programs when the test is administered through a state contract.

The American Psychological Association (APA, 2019) has produced guidance to assist psychologists in navigating release of test data and defines test data as including, but not limited to, all test results, raw test data, records; written/computer-generated reports; and global scores or individual scale scores. APA cautions that disclosure of test data requires consideration of several issues: (1) maintaining confidentiality of testing data, as appropriate; (2) disclosing information as part of the process of informing the test taker of the purpose, use, and results of testing; (3) releasing test data with the consent of the test taker; (4) releasing test data and materials to qualified persons; (5) releasing test data without impairing test security; (6) releasing test data without impairing copyright or other intellectual property interests of third parties (e.g., test publishers); (7) disposing of test data in an appropriate and timely manner so that test security is not compromised; and (8) conforming to legal mandates and rules pertaining to test data and test materials.

There are various ways testing data can be classified:

- Test scores and subscores (raw or scaled scores, percentiles, proficiency levels, classifications)

- Item-level data (e.g., actual responses selected, item correct/incorrect indices, item latency, item omission/completion, item content classification, item difficulty)
- Testing experience (e.g., form code or item codes, mode of administration, device and platform, seating charts, accommodations, language tested in, test center ID, date and time of testing, retesting and score change history, flags for irregularity of security concerns)
- Demographic and background data (e.g., gender, ethnicity/race, age, grade, language, parental income and educational level)
- Self-report data on background, interests, aspirations, plans, attitudes (e.g., courses completed, grades in course, school activities, postsecondary plans, interests in majors or occupations, plans to apply to colleges or for financial support, degree aspirations, interests in activities, number of books in the home, hours spent on digital media)
- Institutional characteristics (e.g., size, geographical location, number of students, curriculum, and percent of students going onto postsecondary or graduate degrees)

Much of this data can further be classified in terms of privacy concerns or risk of identifying the test taker or institution:

- Individual data, which includes PII (name, digital identifiers, date-of-birth, address, email, telephone number, credit card or financial identifiers), other sensitive data (health or medical information, accommodations, citizenship, religious affiliation), and other data that would not identify an individual (scores, percentiles, grade) (Educational Testing Service [ETS], 2011)
- Institutional data, which includes both institutionally identifying data (name, number or code, address, location) and data which would not necessarily identify an institution
- Aggregated data, which would combine data across students (in a school, district, state, nationally) or data across institutions

Publicly Available Data

The release and protection of test scores and PII present additional challenges to testing organizations. The Standards (AERA et al., 2019) address protections for maintaining the security and confidentiality of all test data and PII in a database, other types of records, or when data are transmitted to authorized parties.[6]

State assessment programs and several national testing programs provide aggregate data to the public on their websites. First, ESEA addresses the type of aggregate data and subgroups that should be publicly available, and many states or districts may exceed these requirements in their reporting. As previously mentioned, ESSA requires states to establish a minimum sample size for reporting, so caution is required when reporting aggregate data to ensure individual test takers cannot be identified. Similarly, testing organizations need to carefully review data requests from third parties to ensure both that they have authority to release the data (e.g., control, ownership) and that they are not releasing aggregate data that could be used to identify individual students or educators. The FERPA requirements highlighted earlier provide guidance about resharing when there is a state or district contract.

The ACT and SAT also release aggregate data at the state and national levels each fall, and results include the number of test takers and their scores by demographic background, educational experience, and many other characteristics.[7] Testing entities that house such data need to maintain heightened security to protect it and carefully scrutinize all posted or requested results to ensure PII of students or educators are not discoverable from subgroup data. Aggregated data can often result in unethical and inappropriate uses such as when scores are used to determine real estate values or the establishment of new businesses and services.

A separate challenge is data maintenance. States, districts, and institutions who are responsible for the education of students often have additional historical and trend data on students. When such data exist in large relational databases, they can easily be matched with new data collected from an assessment program. Consistent with FERPA, states and districts must ensure that only those with legitimate educational interests have access to the data. Likewise, test providers must limit access to only those with a need for the data. Similar protections must be afforded to institutionally identifiable data in many instances. Data that can be used to compare institutions receiving scores is typically protected to avoid misuse and to protect the confidentiality of data for those institutions. Examples of institutional-level data include the total number of students taking AP Biology, the mean SAT scores for a district, and the mean ACT math score for African American students at a district.

The same principle generally applies to school and district data, especially nonpublic institutions, but all states generally provide access to data at the school or district level for state assessments, and some will allow similar access to data from third-party assessments. Some school- and district-level aggregate data are generally available on public websites, but requests for additional data require review and may not be available to any third party without consent. Some testing entities may release data to a qualified requester as well as in response to third-party requests that are approved by the institution or district, but districts often lack the resources to process special requests. Data for cities and counties will not be routinely provided according to *Guidelines for the Release of Data* (College Board, 2018a) because the data often come under the control of multiple parties (public schools, private schools, home schools). One promising method that can both facilitate independent research and protect institutional and district data is to aggregate data across multiple similar institutions into two or three different categories based on the selected condition (e.g., open admissions vs. selective institutions; test-optional vs. test-required institutions). These Guidelines also note that appropriate statistical disclosure limitations (e.g., cell suppression, random noise addition) are used, and all requests are monitored to protect the confidentiality of data aggregated at the institutional or district levels.

ACT, the College Board, and ETS have established policies and procedures that attempt to provide access to non-PII data for researchers, policymakers, and the public, within the constraints of any contract or other legal agreements. ETS has a specific policy pertaining to the release of data from ETS-controlled assessments. ETS data are classified into three categories: (1) wholly owned by ETS, (2) maintained by ETS but permission for release of the data must be granted by another entity, and (3) maintained by ETS but cannot be released due to contractual requirements. Some data maintained by a testing contractor, such as ETS, may require additional permission from an external or governing body (e.g., state, certifying agency). Some data (e.g., state assessments or assessments provided under contract to a state or district) may be owned by the entity and cannot be released by the testing organization. Similar considerations are needed for systems that blend assessment and learning through feedback loops.

EQUITY OF ACCESS AND FAIRNESS IN LEARNING AND ASSESSMENT SYSTEMS

In designing virtual learning and assessment systems (LAS), one needs to consider a framework that is flexible, inclusive, and rooted in the science of learning (Arielli-Attali et al., 2019). An LAS is a virtual system that provides interactive and personalized learning opportunities blended with quizzes and interim assessments, which in turn identify the learner's strengths and weaknesses alongside actionable recommendations for the next steps. An LAS is usually more focused on providing personalized tutoring than on being a learning management system (LMS), but it may connect with the LMSs. See von Davier and colleagues (2019) for an overview of the development of a holistic LAS. An LAS aims to adapt to the goals, abilities, and preferences of each learner, which may address equity and fairness from different perspectives. An LAS requires the blend of many data sources, such as those from formal and informal learning, and may consider variables that describe the context for learning. LAS examples include ASSISTments[8] and the Duolingo Learning App.[9]

Unfortunately, we have learned that personalization algorithms that depend on training data are likely to reflect the same bias that may exist in the large training data sets. Some of these problems were recently discussed at a panel focused on Fairness in Machine Learning in Educational Measurement (von Davier & Burstein, 2016).

In education, we need to stay abreast of these new approaches that can complement the standards for assessment described in this chapter. Researchers and practitioners need to consider inclusive models for learning pathways for a diverse population of learners: culturally and linguistically diverse, neurodivergent, geographically diverse, and socioeconomically diverse populations. As with the exposure to bad teachers over time, ongoing algorithmic use of invalid learner experiences occurs, and the impact may compound. Therefore, it is imperative that research on LAS efficacy, equity, and fairness, as well as adoption of the best practices from assessment, focuses on the validity of the tools for learning.

Another issue to consider is the validity and security of an LAS. If the data from an LAS will be used for eventual summative decisions such as certification, credentialing, admissions, hiring, or accountability, it is likely that people will attempt to game the LAS. The literature on detection of cheating within an LAS is growing (Baker et al., 2005). As with standardized assessments, one type of security incident that invalidates the evidence collected through an LAS is the involvement of a proxy (a different person, teacher, parent, etc.) during unproctored use of the system. Fortunately, AI-based technologies are improving for ensuring that the results are fair (Madnani et al., 2017).

User guides and other materials, as well as learning support, need to be considered for fairness. The amount of ancillary information an individual has access to while working in an LAS will also influence the learning experience and outcomes. For a better learning experience, an LAS may not limit an individual's access to external material at all times; it may be relevant though to capture the other sources of information that were perused by the learner because it offers critical context for proper interpretation of results. This is obviously just as difficult to do in a virtual environment as it is for the brick-and-mortar schools to account for the opportunities (or lack thereof) to learn that their students have at home.

While these new challenges related to ethics in a virtual LAS may have seemed futuristic a few months ago, now in the middle of the COVID-19 experience and with schools' attempts to continue the instruction in virtual settings, the awareness of pitfalls is more relevant than ever. Moreover, we are experiencing a paradigm shift: Some changes are happening in education, some old teaching and learning models coexist with new (mostly virtual) teaching and learning models, and the perspectives on ethics and data are shifting too.

CONCLUSION

This chapter traced the expanding role played by educational data to both inform and direct learning, as well as measure performance and growth in accountability systems. ESEA has driven much of the demand to use longitudinal data to evaluate the status and growth of students for accountability purposes, and *Race to the Top* further fueled the use of longitudinal data in the evaluation of educators. States subsequently expanded their data systems to better capture and combine different data elements to provide insights into learning and proficiency within major subgroup classifications and across grades. A variety of data elements (demographics, course taking, engagement, latency, solution behavior) have been combined with test scores and item-level responses to provide additional insights into learning. Progress in AI and the availability of big data have resulted in new types of data analyses evolving from traditional classic test theory to computational psychometrics. As in other fields, such advances have exposed ethical lapses and overreliance on data to address new and emerging needs.

Many ethical issues emerge from limitations of summative assessments and the desire to use test scores for new purposes and uses that were not originally envisioned or supported by evidence. Examples include using test scores to appraise housing values, reward or penalize educators, award scholarships, or allow entrance into honors programs. Policymakers and other secondary users of assessment data often overstate the precision of scores and often propose new and novel uses for assessment data without providing evidence to support such uses. Admission test scores are often used when ranking graduate or law schools, as well as when hiring interns or entry-level professionals, despite cautions against such issues by the testing organizations. Test developers remain ultimately responsible and should anticipate common misuses and guard against them. When new uses are proposed for an existing test, they are responsible for providing supporting evidence, but the burden may shift when states contract for such services, and the vendor is working for hire.

Summative assessments are not alone in the potential for misuse. The term "formative assessment" has generally been misappropriated by many of the commercial vendors and rarely fits these definitions proposed by Black and Wiliam (1998), Perie and colleagues (2009), and Shepard (2005). Ethical issues can similarly emerge in the use of such formative assessments despite their focus on learning and reputation as "low-stakes assessments." Formative assessment products may lack sufficient instructional sensitivity, alignment, and score precision, providing misinformation about prior learning and misdirecting the learner. The choice of an assessment or other measure involves trade-offs that must be evaluated in terms of costs and benefits to the student as well as the school or district. The test user has an ethical and professional responsibility to evaluate available evidence on assessments to ensure it supports the claims, intended uses, and appropriateness for the local population.

Many testing organizations and professional associations (e.g., the National Association of College Admissions Counselors) have promulgated their own guidelines on test use, which should be adhered to, and, of course, the Standards (AERA et al., 2014) provide broad direction on these issues, but suffer from limited dissemination, measurement illiteracy, and lack of enforcement.

There are also legal and ethical issues related to the sharing of the assessment and learning data. FERPA and ESEA provide some protections, such as limiting the sharing of data and requiring a minimum n-size for reporting. State data privacy laws provide additional protections. However, there are ethical issues such as the sale of data from students taking the ACT and SAT given the limited transparency in how colleges use this information in recruitment and admissions, as well as the profit generated from the sale of PII by testing companies. Similarly, errors in processing, scoring, and reporting can result from aggressive timelines, lack of quality control, or efforts to reduce costs, representing other types of choices made by test users. Both the test developer and test user are responsible for minimizing such risks.

NOTES

1. http://www.imsglobal.org

2. https://www.projectunicorn.org

3. Note that states are not required to report disaggregated data if the number of students in the subgroup at a school, district, or state are insufficient to yield statistically sound and reliable information or results could reveal PII. The U.S. Department of Education does not prescribe a minimum number, but if a state uses a value of more than 30 students to withhold reporting, a rationale is required.

4. A test developer is the person(s) or organization responsible for the design and construction of a test and for the documentation regarding the technical quality for an intended purpose (AERA et al., 2014).

5. A test sponsor is an organization, association, or other entity that mandates the use of tests for a specific purpose, such as a licensure, accountability, and so on, and may create policies and procedures regarding how the test is used, scored, and interpreted.

6. See Chapters 5–6.

7. See, for example, SAT results at https://research.collegeboard.org/programs/sat/data/2019-sat-suite-annual-report, and ACT results at https://www.act.org/content/dam/act/unsecured/documents/cccr2018/P_99_999999_N_S_N00_ACT-GCPR_National.pdf.

8. https://new.assistments.org

9. https://www.duolingo.com

REFERENCES

Adams, S. (2020, September 30). How the SAT failed America. *Forbes*. https://www.forbes.com/sites/susanadams/2020/09/30/the-forbes-investigation-how-the-sat-failed-america/amp/

American Educational Research Association, American Psychological Association, & National Council on Measurement in Education. (2014). *Standards for educational and psychological testing.* https://www.apa.org/science/programs/testing/standards

American Psychological Association. (2019, April 11). *FAQs: Disclosure of test data and test materials.* https://www.apa.org/science/programs/testing/data-disclosure-faqs

Arieli Attali, M., Ward, S., Thomas, J., Deonovic, B., & von Davier, A. A. (2019). The expanded evidence-centered design (e-ECD) for learning and assessment systems: A framework for incorporating learning goals and process within assessment design. *Frontiers Psychology, 26.* https://www.frontiersin.org/articles/10.3389/fpsyg.2019.00853/full

Baker, E. L., Chung, G. K. W. K., & Cai, L. (2016). Assessment gaze, refraction, and blur: The course of achievement testing in the past 100 years. *Review of Research in Education, 40,* 94–142.

Baker, R. S., Corbett, A., Koedinger, K., & Roll, I. (2005). Detecting when students game the system, across tutor subjects and classroom cohorts. In L. Ardissono, P. Brna, A. Mitrovic (Eds.), *User modeling 2005* (pp. 220–224). Springer.

Bakharia, A., Kitto, K., Pardo, A., Gašević, D., & Dawson, S. (2016). Recipe for success: Lessons learnt from using xAPI within the connected learning analytics toolkit. In *Proceedings of the Sixth International Conference on Learning Analytics & Knowledge* (pp. 378–382). Association for Computing Machinery. https://doi.org/10.1145/2883851.2883882

Belasco, A. S., Rosinger, K. O., & Hearn. J. C. (2014). The test-optional movement at America's selective liberal arts colleges: A boon for equity or something else? *Educational Evaluation and Policy Analysis, 36,* 1–18.

Bennett, R. E. (2011). Formative assessment: A critical review. Assessment in education: *Principles, Policy & Practice, 18*(1), 5–25.

Berliner, D. C., & Biddle, B. J. (1995). *The manufactured crisis: Myths, fraud, and the attack on America's public schools.* Addison-Wesley.

Black, P., & Wiliam, D. (1998) *Inside the black box: Raising standards through classroom assessment.* King's College London School of Education.

Black, P., & Wiliam, D. (2003). In praise of educational research: Formative assessment. *British Educational Research Journal, 29*(5), 623–637.

Bloom et al. vs. ACT Inc. (2020). *Settlement Agreement and Proposed Consent Decree.* http://www.actclassactionsettlement.com/media/3058483/bloom_settlement_agreement__final_.pdf

Brookhart, S. M. (2010). Mixing it up: Combining sources of classroom achievement information for formative and summative purposes. In H. L. Andrade and G. J. Cizek (Eds.), *Handbook of formative assessment* (pp. 279–296). Routledge.

Camara, W. J. (1997). Use and consequences of assessments in the USA: Professional, ethical, and legal issues. *European Journal of Psychological Assessment, 13*(20), 140–152.

Camara, W. J. (2020). Never let a crisis go to waste: Large-scale assessment and the response to COVID-19. *Educational Measurement: Issues and Practice*, 39(3), 10–18.

Camara, W. J. (2021). *Admissions testing impact on access and alternative opinions* [Manuscript submitted for publication]. Law School Admissions Council.

Camara, W. J., Mattern, K. M., Croft, M., Vispoel, S., & Nichols, P. (2019). A validity argument in support of the use of college admissions test for federal accountability. *Educational Measurement: Issues and Practice*, 38(4), 12–26.

Camara, W. J., & Means, B. (1986). *Status of low-aptitude accessions following military service* [Conference presentation]. The 94th Annual Convention of the American Psychological Association, Washington, DC.

Camara, W. J., Packman, S., & Wiley A. (2013). College, graduate and professional school admissions testing. In K. Geisinger (Ed.), *Handbook of testing and assessment in psychology* (pp. 297–318). American Psychological Association.

College Board. (2018a). *Guidelines for the release of data*. https://research.collegeboard.org/pdf/rd-guide-release-data.pdf

College Board. (2018b). *Guidelines on the uses of College Board test scores and related data*. https://research.collegeboard.org/pdf/guidelines-uses-college-board-test-scores-and-data.pdf

Consortium for Citizens with Disabilities/Lawyers' Committee for Civil Rights Under Law. (2020, October 5). *Letter to Honorable Nathan L. Hecht regarding civil rights concerns with administration of bar examinations*. https://lawyerscommittee.org/wp-content/uploads/2020/10/2020-Bar-Exam-Response-10-6-20.pdf

Cooper, A. (2014). *Learning analytics interoperability—the big picture in brief*. Learning Analytics Community Exchange.

Croft, M. (2018). Potential effects of student data privacy legislation on assessment. *NCME Newsletter*, 26(1), 13–14.

Data Quality Campaign. (2017, September 26). *Education data legislative review: 2017 state activity*. https://dataqualitycampaign.org/resource/2017-education-data-legislation/

Data Quality Campaign. (2019, May 7). *2019 legislative update part I*. https://dataqualitycampaign.org/2019-legislative-update-part-one/

DePascale, C. A. (2003). The ideal role of large-scale testing in a comprehensive assessment system. *Journal of Testing Technology*, 5(1), 1–10. http://www.jattjournal.com/index.php/atp/article/view/48343

Educational Testing Service. (2011, July 22). *ETS policy on the release of data to external researchers*. https://www.ets.org/s/research/pdf/ets_research_data_policy.pdf

Education Week. (2020, May 15). *Map: Coronavirus and school closures*. https://www.edweek.org/ew/section/multimedia/map-coronavirus-and-school-closures.html

Elementary and Secondary Education Act of 1965, as amended by the Every Student Succeeds Act, Negotiated Rulemaking Committee (2016,

April 6–8). *Issue Paper #3*. https://www2.ed.gov/policy/elsec/leg/essa/session/nrmissuepaper34182016.pdf

Elementary and Secondary Education Act of 2001, H.R. 1, 107th Congress. (2002).

Every Student Succeeds Act of 2015, 20 U.S.C. § 1111. (2015).

Gilbert, R., Lafferty, R., Hagger-Johnson, G., Harron, K., Zhang, L. C., Smith, P., Dibben, C., & Goldstein, H. (2017). GUILD: guidance for information about linking data sets. *Journal of Public Health*, *40*, 191–198. https://doi.org/10.1093/pubmed/fdx037

Ing, M. (2018). What about the "instruction" in instructional sensitivity? Raising a validity issue in research on instructional sensitivity. *Educational and Psychological Measurement*, *78*, 635–652.

Jaschik, S. (2020, October 26). ACT settles class action for $16 million. *Inside Higher Ed*. https://www.insidehighered.com/admissions/article/2020/10/26/act-settles-class-action-16-million

Knapp, M. S., Swinnerton, J. A., Copland, M. A., & Monpas-Huber, J. (2006). *Data-informed leadership in education*. University of Washington, Center for the Study of Teaching and Policy.

Lucido. J. A. (2018). Understanding the test-optional movement. In J. Buckley, L. Letukas, and B. Wildavsky (Eds.), *Measuring success: Testing, grades and the future of college admissions* (pp. 146–170). Johns Hopkins University Press.

Madnani, N., Loukina, A., von Davier, A. A., Burstein, J., & Cahill, A. (2017). Building better open-source tools to ensure fairness. In *Proceedings of the First ACL Workshop on Ethics in Natural Language Processing* (pp. 41–52). Association for Computational Linguistics.

Mandinach, E. B. (2012). A perfect time for data use: Using data-driven decision making to inform practice. *Educational Psychologist*, *47*(2), 71–85.

Mandinach, E. B., & Honey, M. (2008). Data-driven decision making: An introduction. In E. B Mandinach and M. Honey (Eds), *Data-driven school improvement: Linking data and learning* (pp. 1–12). Teachers College Press.

McDonald, J. P. (2019, February 25). Toward more effective data use in teaching. *Phi Delta Kappan*, *100*(6), 44–50.

National Association for College Admissions Counseling. (2008). *Report of the commission on the use of standardized tests in undergraduate admissions*.

National Commission on Testing and Public Policy. (1990). *From gatekeeper to gateway: Transforming testing in America*. Author.

No Child Left Behind of 2002, Pub.L. 107–110, 115 Stat. 1425. (January 8, 2002).

North Central Regional Educational Laboratory. (Fall, 2004). Using data to guide school improvement. *Notes and Reflections*, *7*. https://files.eric.ed.gov/fulltext/ED518630.pdf

Perie, M., Marion, S. F., & Gong, B. (2009). Moving towards a comprehensive assessment system: A framework for considering interim assessments. *Educational Measurement: Issues and Practice*, *28*(3), 5–13.

Rhoades, K., & Madaus, G. (2003). *Errors in standardized tests: A systemic problem*. National Board on Educational Testing and Public Policy (NBETPP), Boston College.

Shepard, L. (2005, October). *Formative assessment: Caveat emptor* [Conference presentation]. 2005 ETS Invitational Conference, New York, NY.

Standardized Testing Task Force. (2020). *Report of the UC Academic Council Standardized Testing Task Force*. University of California Academic Senate. https://www.universityofcalifornia.edu/ press-room/university-california-board -regents-approves-changes-standardized-testing-requirement

Struett, D. (2019, December 10). CPS parent sues College Board for allegedly selling students' personal data for profit. *Chicago Sun Times*. https://chicago.suntimes .com/education/2019/12/10/21009843/college-board-lawsuit-student -personal-data-student-search-service-university-sat-psat

Sweitzer, K., Blaock, A. E., & Sharma, D. B. (2018). The effect of going test-optional on diversity and admissions: A propensity score matching analysis. In J. Buckley, L. Letukas, & B. Wildavsky (Eds.), *Measuring success: Testing, grades and the future of college admissions* (pp. 288–307). Johns Hopkins University Press.

Travis, S. (2015, July 17). Teachers hoping for $10,000 bonus caught in Catch-22. *Sun Sentinel*. https://www.sun-sentinel.com/local/broward/fl-test-score-bonus -follow-20150717-story.html

U.S. Department of Education. (2011). *Teachers' ability to use data to inform instruction: Challenges and supports*. Office of Planning, Evaluation and Policy Development.

U.S. Department of Education. (2018). *Technical assistance on student privacy for state and local educational agencies when administering college admissions examinations*.

von Davier, A. A. (2017). Computational psychometrics in support of collaborative educational assessments. *Journal of Educational Measurement, 54*, 3–11. https://doi.org/10.1111/jedm.12129

von Davier, A. A., & Burstein, J. (2016). *Fairness in machine learning in educational measurement* [Symposium]. National Council on Measurement in Education, Washington, DC.

von Davier, A. A., Chung Wong, P., Yudelson, M., Polyak, S. (2019). The argument for a "data cube" for large-scale psychometric data. *Frontiers in Education, 18*. https://www.frontiersin.org/articles/10.3389/feduc.2019.00071/full

von Davier, A. A., Deonovic, B., Yudelson, M., Polyak, S., & Woo, A. (2019). Computational psychometrics approach for holistic learning and assessment systems. *Frontiers in Education, 17*. https://www.frontiersin.org/articles/10.3389 /feduc.2019.00069/full

Wang, Y. (2021). When artificial intelligence meets educational leaders' data-informed decision-making: A cautionary tale. *Studies in Educational Evaluation, 69*, 1–9. https://doi.org/10.1016/j.stueduc.2020.100872

The Cyclical Effects of Ethical Decisions Involving Big Data and Digital Learning Platforms

Edward Dieterle, Beth Holland, and Chris Dede

Around the world, learners seeking to upskill or reskill, including students in pre-K–12, higher education, and informal learners, access digital learning platforms to prepare for success in school, work, and life. When humans engage with such platforms through immersive simulations, cognitive tutors, interactive videos, and massive online open courses, the technology generates enormous amounts of data that can answer instructional and administrative questions, discover patterns, predict outcomes, and automate low-level decisions.

Although the platforms have promising and positive impacts (Pane et al., 2017a), complex ethical questions underpin the stages associated with generating, analyzing, and interpreting data. We first offer a definition of learning platforms and the big educational data they produce as well as a discussion of the security and privacy issues they create. We then discuss the cyclical effects of ethical decisions involving big data and learning platforms and how each stage of the cycle can benefit learning and teaching, how it can introduce bias and further inequity, and how it might increase life outcome disparities among subpopulations. The conditions necessary to support equitable learning—learning that occurs irrespective of race, gender, ethnicity, language, disability, sexual orientation, family background, or family income (Council of Chief State School Officers, 2018) through the platforms—require ongoing reflection and improvement by educators, designers, and policymakers.

The COVID-19 pandemic has heightened the implications and urgency of understanding this cycle and its related ethical questions. As remote and hybrid learning become our new normal, and reliance on platforms grows, the stakes are high. Inequitable divisions leave vulnerable populations without access to the resources they need to advance their learning journey toward more positive and productive life outcomes such as greater proficiency in literacy, numeracy, and 21st-century skills (Kirsch et al., 2021).

LEARNING PLATFORMS

Table 9.1 summarizes learning platforms, a collection of integrated tools designed to improve learning and teaching while facilitating the administration of schools, universities, or other educational and workforce development organizations (Passey & Higgins, 2011). Richards and Dede (2012) reveal three primary qualities of robust learning platforms:

- Learners and educators interface with the platform through broadband connectivity and a one-to-one person-to-device ratio.

Table 9.1. URLs and Primary Audiences of Common Digital Learning Platforms

Digital Learning Platform and URL	Elementary School	High School	Higher Education	Workforce
ALEKS https://www.aleks.com		X		
Axonify https://axonify.com				X
Canvas Learning Management Platform https://www .instructure.com	X	X	X	X
Cerego https://www.cerego .com			X	X
Coursera https://www.coursera .org			X	X
edX https://www.edx.org			X	X
Fulcrum Labs https://www .fulcrumlabs.ai		X	X	X
Knewton https://www.knewton .com	X	X	X	
Realizeit https:// realizeitlearning.com			X	X

- The platform contains a fully digital curriculum with embedded measures of learning.
- The platform has tools for managing, assigning, and facilitating whole- and small-group activities and discussions; monitoring a learner's progress; and displaying content, learner work, and other artifacts. Educators can develop and assign lessons and experiences that allow learners to work independently and in groups.

BIG EDUCATIONAL DATA

In their synthetic literature review on big educational data, Fischer and colleagues (2020) differentiate data at micro- (i.e., clickstream and log file data), meso- (i.e., user developed digital text data), and macro- (i.e., institutional and administrative data) levels. At each of these levels, data are characterized as "big" because of their (1) *volume*, the size and scale of data and data sets; (2) *variety*, the production of data from different data sources and in different formats and grain sizes; (3) *velocity*, the speed at which data are created; (4) *veracity*, the noise, bias, and uncertainty in data; and (5) *value*, the administrative, instructional, monetary, and knowledge produced by analyzing big data (European Economic and Social Committee, 2017). Before the dawn of big data in education, collecting data was hard, time-consuming, and resource intensive. Educators are now awash in a continuous flow of data generated by technologies, and they need to understand key ethical questions associated with the cyclical nature of how data are generated, analyzed, and interpreted as well as how those activities influence behavior and outcomes.

THE CYCLE OF BIG EDUCATIONAL DATA AND LEARNING PLATFORMS

As learning platforms have advanced over the past decade, historical inequities, societal-level conditions, cultural norms, and institutional practices have altered their evolution, introducing and perpetuating systematic bias. This bias widens the digital divide, resulting in conditions that unduly constrain the opportunities, resources, and well-being of different subpopulations (Friedman & Nissenbaum, 1996; Hatzenbuehler & Link, 2014; Mitchell et al., 2020). At this juncture, we explore divides associated with access, data, algorithmic, interpretation, and citizenship, and how those divides contribute to the interwoven and reinforcing cycle that Figure 9.1 illustrates. We provide examples and propose key ethical questions that educators, developers, and policymakers should consider to best make wise

Figure 9.1. The Cyclical Effects of Ethical Decisions Involving Big Data and Learning Platforms

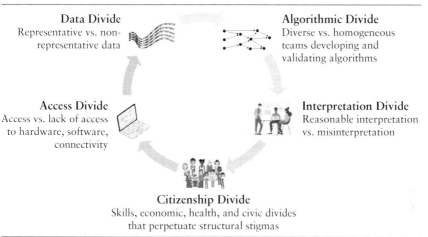

Data Divide
Representative vs. non-representative data

Algorithmic Divide
Diverse vs. homogeneous teams developing and validating algorithms

Access Divide
Access vs. lack of access to hardware, software, connectivity

Interpretation Divide
Reasonable interpretation vs. misinterpretation

Citizenship Divide
Skills, economic, health, and civic divides that perpetuate structural stigmas

instructional, administrative, design, and policy decisions regarding their use of digital learning platforms.

Our entry point into the cycle is the *access divide*: Who does and does not have access to the hardware, software, and connectivity necessary to access and engage with digital learning platforms? In turn, we explore the *data divide*: What factors make data representative of populations or over-representative of a subpopulation's preferences, preventing objectivity and influencing understandings, outcomes, or both? While much has been written about the access and data divides and their impacts, less has been written about the *algorithmic divide*, the next segment in the cycle. This divide warrants additional exploration as we consider the following: How do teams of humans plan for and mitigate bias when using the tools of artificial intelligence (AI; e.g., machine learning, natural language processing, computer vision) to model and inform instructional decisions and predict learning outcomes? Next, we explore the *interpretation divide*: How do learners, educators, and others understand the outputs of algorithms and use them to make decisions? We then consider the *citizenship divide*: How do the additive divides impact accurate and inaccurate interpretations by learners, educators, and others, which then influence behaviors and potentially longer-term skills, culture, economic, health, and civic outcomes? We conclude the chapter by looking forward and discussing how to increase opportunity and equity while mitigating bias. Success for all learners requires constant reflection by educators, educational leaders, designers, and policymakers on the ethical questions raised in this chapter in addition to a constellation of investments and actions.

The Access Divide

Educational technologies have helped redefine and strengthen the relationship learners have with their curriculum, peers, and instructors (Dieterle, 2010). When implemented by well-trained educators, these technologies have developed and enhanced the following for learners: (1) knowledge within academic disciplines; (2) cognitive skills such as problem solving, critical thinking, and systems thinking; (3) interpersonal skills such as communications, social skills, teamwork, and cultural sensitivity; and (4) intrapersonal skills such as self-management, time management, self-regulation, adaptability, and executive functioning (Clark et al., 2016; D'Angelo et al., 2014; Díaz et al., 2019; Fishman & Dede, 2016; National Academies of Sciences, 2018).

The benefits of educational technologies accrue to those learners and educators with regular access to the hardware, software, and connectivity to use digital learning platforms regardless of their physical location. *Is it thus ethical that all learners and educators do not have access to the hardware, software, and connectivity necessary to engage with digital learning platforms?*

Despite decades of support from governments, philanthropy, and industry, universal access among learners and educators has not yet been realized, falling short of the goal of educational equity in which every learner has access to the resources they need (Council of Chief State School Officers, 2018). The initial U.S. National Education Technology Plan acknowledged the existence of a digital divide in education (U.S. Department of Education, 1996), a phenomenon that persists. From an analysis of 2018 American Community Survey data, Chandra and colleagues (2020) found that 15 to 16 million of the 50 million U.S. K–12 public school students (~30%) and about 300,000 to 400,000 of 3.8 million K–12 teachers (~10%) live in households either without an Internet connection or without a device adequate for distance learning at home. Additionally, about 17% of K–12 public school students live in households with neither an adequate connection nor an adequate device for distance learning at home.

More recently, researchers at LearnPlatform (2021) conducted an analysis of daily K–12 student usage of educational technologies used by 2.5 million students in 17 states from February through December 2020. Their analysis, represented in Figure 9.2, illustrates the access and usage divide between more affluent districts (i.e., districts with up to 25% free and reduced-price lunch student populations) and less affluent districts (i.e., districts with 25%–100% free and reduced-price lunch student populations). The y-axis is LearnPlatform's educational technology usage index, which is based on the number of visits to different tools per 1,000 users. The index provides standardization across different user groups, while also

Figure 9.2. Daily K–12 Student Usage of Educational Technologies from February through December 2020 by More Affluent and Less Affluent Districts

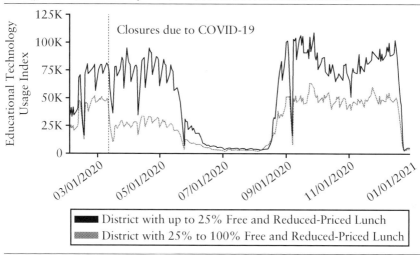

Note: LearnPlatform. (2021). *Edtech engagement & digital learning equity gaps.* Reprinted with permission by K. Rectanus, November 29, 2020.

adjusting for the breadth of different tools used. After school closures due to COVID-19 in the spring of 2020, more affluent districts recovered quickly and increased engagement, while less affluent districts did not return to pre-pandemic engagement levels until the fall of 2020.

To increase access and mitigate the divide, many schools and districts developed plans to ensure that all students have access to the Internet and devices. Of the 106 school districts in the Center on Reinventing Public Education's reopening database, 45% have plans to ensure that all students have access to the Internet, and 75% have plans to get student devices (Makori & Dusseault, 2020).

When on campus, higher education students have access to hardware and connectivity resources universities provide through libraries and computer labs. Obtaining access at home or off-campus, however, presents challenges. An April 2020 EDUCAUSE Quick Poll found that, of the 267 institutions surveyed internationally, more than one-quarter to more than one-third reported that students were having moderate or extreme difficulty with connectivity or getting access to the hardware they needed to continue their academic work (Grajek, 2020).

Associated with this lack of Internet access is a lack of Internet use. Although cost is a family's primary barrier to adequate connectivity, millions of Americans cannot access broadband at any price because it is not available where they live (Laeeq Khan et al., 2020). This lack of access affects learners and educators across the United States but is more frequently present in rural communities and among households with Black, Latinx, and Native American students (Hampton et al., 2020).

When significant numbers of learners do not have access to the hardware, software, and connectivity necessary to access and engage with digital learning platforms, they are prevented from generating data used to develop and validate algorithms that inform instruction. When those learners systematically come from vulnerable subpopulations (e.g., rural learners, learners with special needs, learners in low-income families), the access divide creates a data divide.

The Data Divide

Data are the lifeblood of digital platforms. When learners and educators engage with these platforms in combination with other data sources, extraordinarily large amounts of micro, meso, and macro formats of big educational data result, varying in quality, quantity, and variety. The data collected from learning platforms contain not only summative evaluations of students' knowledge, ability, and skills, but also the processes of their learning and acquisition of relevant skills and knowledge (Ercikan & Pellegrino, 2017).

When considering how this lifeblood feeds the platforms, however, educational leaders need to consider the implications of the access divide. *Is it ethical that a lack of learner and educator access means those with access contribute to a learning platform's data sets and are therefore considered in subsequent models, algorithms, and interpretations based on that data, whereas those without access do not contribute?* Additionally, researchers need to modify and reduce data to what can fit into a mathematical model; when taken out of context, these data can lose their meaning and value (Boyd & Crawford, 2012).

While no data set is perfect, sets with duplicated, outdated, incomplete, inaccurate, incorrect, inconsistent, or missing records have the potential to create *data bias*, which is the systemic distortion in data that compromises representativeness (Marco & Larkin, 2000; Olteanu et al., 2019). The lack of representation in data plays out in otherwise well-intentioned technologies. For example, investigating the racial, skin type, and gender disparities embedded in commercially available facial recognition technologies, Buolamwini and Gebru (2018) revealed how those systems largely failed to differentiate and classify darker female faces while successfully differentiating and classifying white male faces. The poor classification for darker female faces stemmed from the data sets used to develop the algorithms, which included a disproportionality large number of white males and few Black females. When researchers used a more balanced data set to develop the algorithm, it produced more accurate results across races and genders.

The Algorithmic Divide

If data are the lifeblood of the platforms, algorithms are the brains that result from the application of statistics and computer programing to data to realize relationships, predict outcomes, and automate procedures and decisions. Personalized learning, a powerful application of algorithms to support learning and teaching (Pane et al., 2015; Pane et al., 2017b), is "focused on, demonstrated by, and led with the learner . . . rooted in the idea that learning happens both in the classroom and beyond, and is connected meaningfully to peers, mentors, and the community" (Herbert, 2016, p. 1). Dede (2019) describes this kind of learning and teaching as having at least four characteristics:

- Developing multimodal experiences and a differentiated curriculum based on universal design for learning principles
- Enabling each student's agency in orchestrating the emphasis and process of his or her learning, in concert with the evidence about how learning works best and with mentoring about working toward long-term goals
- Providing community and collaboration to aid students in learning by fostering engagement, a growth mindset, self-efficacy, and academic tenacity
- Guiding each student's path through the curriculum based on diagnostic assessments embedded in each educational experience that are formative for further learning and instruction (p. 3)

To develop the algorithms that support personalized learning and underpin digital platforms, researchers and designers from the educational data mining and learning analytics communities have developed and applied advanced statistical and computational methods to model big educational data (e.g., Blikstein et al., 2014; Levy, 2019; Niemi et al., 2018). Researchers have developed algorithms that measure and enhance disciplinary knowledge and understanding (Heffernan & Heffernan, 2014; Ritter et al., 2007); predict standardized test scores (Adjei et al., 2017) and academic achievement (Baker et al., 2004; Cocea et al., 2009; Fancsali, 2014, 2015; Kostyuk et al., 2018; Pardos et al., 2014); and measure student engagement and boredom (D'Mello et al., 2017), creativity (Shute & Ventura, 2013), persistence (Wang et al., 2020), inquiry skills (Sao Pedro et al., 2013), and problem solving (Shute & Wang, 2017).

Research has also shown the psychometric value of process data to detect rapid guessing in assessments (Guo et al., 2016), understand test-taking strategies (Stadler et al., 2019), improve test design (Lee & Haberman, 2016), and improve score reliability (van Rijn & Ali, 2017), all of which are important considerations in designing and delivering assessments through digital learning. Despite its relatively brief history compared to other scholarly disciplines, these research communities have built a solid knowledge base and described the kinds of challenges associated with generalizability, interpretability, applicability, transferability, and effectiveness needed to advance the field (Baker, 2019).

For an education community continually doing more with less, these algorithmic insights can be a welcome information source. *However, is it ethical that the algorithms that inform teaching and learning may not fully represent the learners they are designed to educate or that the algorithms absorb and reflect human biases during their design, development, and evolution when humans interact with them?* Algorithms that seek to replicate existing conditions can embed existing biases. As Metz (2019) explains, large social data sets feed systemic bias into algorithms, and unchecked algorithms can result in systemic discrimination that favors certain individuals or groups over others (Friedman & Nissenbaum, 1996).

Examples of algorithmic bias abound in the criminal justice system (Angwin et al., 2016; Završnik, 2021), social services (Eubanks, 2017), and job recruitment (Caliskan et al., 2017). While education algorithmic bias is well documented (Regan & Jesse, 2018), a timely example developed during the 2019–2020 school year involving International Baccalaureate (IB) students and a system constrained by the realities of COVID (Boland & Cogley, 2020; International Baccalaureate, 2020). When IB lacked the capacity to monitor and administer students' final exams remotely, the organization used an algorithm to predict students' final scores. More than 700 schools requested a second review after claims that the algorithm was systematically biased and mis-scored thousands of students, robbing them of university acceptances and college scholarships.

Educators and policymakers have a responsibility to avoid overly relying on any single algorithm to make important decisions because educational issues are far more complex than a single algorithm can capture (Daniel, 2019). They also have a responsibility to understand the basics of algorithmic development and how designers mitigate bias (Kirkpatrick, 2016; Shah et al., 2020). While a machine-developed algorithm might be able to make accurate predictions, ethical questions arise about whether those predictions can and should be trusted when the solution relies on black-box systems about which stakeholders have no information or insight. By asking critical questions regarding a learning platform's underlying data sources, algorithm development, and ongoing testing, educational leaders can elicit the transparency from developers and vendors that students deserve. Three essential questions follow.

First, how did the developer ensure that the underlying data feeding the platform's algorithms represent the diversity of the students? Developers need to document and address inclusivity, stakeholder awareness, and potential ethical risks during the design and testing of algorithms to ensure that all populations are represented and protected from harm (Mitchell et al., 2020; Yapo & Weiss, 2018).

Second, how did the developer protect against algorithmic bias in its learning platform? To date, algorithm development has largely occurred with minimal oversight or deep consideration of ethics and bias (Luckin et al., 2016). For organizations that create learning platforms, mitigating algorithmic bias begins with the staffing of the team responsible for developing and validating an algorithm. Mitigating bias requires a diversity of disciplines, research questions, life experiences, cultures, races, religions, ages, sexes, sexual orientations, and disabilities (Nielsen et al., 2018). To be successful in their work, the team individually and collectively must practice *reflexivity* by reflecting on their beliefs, practices, and judgments during and after the research process, acknowledging how these may have influenced the research (Finlay, 2016). When outside teams incorporate data that they did not collect directly, it can drastically diminish the value of their reflexivity and potentially compromise the validity of their research outcomes (Daniel, 2019).

Third, how does the developer continue to monitor the platform for bias? The threat of bias requires constant review and audits of equity, quality, and fairness (see Educational Testing Service, 2014; Shute et al., 2020), as well as policies and markets that incentivize iterative improvements in the accuracy, fairness, reliability, and accountability of these algorithms.

The Interpretation Divide

When we reach the interpretation divide in the cycle, educators and learners excluded through the access and data divides have not contributed to the data sets used to develop learning platform algorithms. As classroom instruction and education policy has increasingly relied on data-based decision-making, educators, researchers, and policymakers use and point to data to justify and guide decisions at the student and classroom level, scaling up to entire populations and subpopulations of students in schools, districts, states, and countries (Schildkamp et al., 2013). Learning platform data provides yet another data source to support decision-making. The legendary engineer W. Edwards Deming claimed that, "without data, you're just another person with an opinion." *However, is it ethical for educators to use data and the outputs of algorithms to make decisions without having received training on how to interpret or use them?* Users' knowledge of data-based decision-making can be (1) *missing*, they never learned how to interpret it in the first place; (2) *inert*, they know how to interpret the data but do not know when or how to apply it; (3) *routinized*, they apply an interpretation technique without thinking through whether it is the right technique for the given situation; (4) *surface*, they are familiar but not proficient with an interpretive technique; or (5) *perishable*, they knew something at one point but have lost it because they have not applied it recently (based on the fragile knowledge construct developed by Perkins, 1992).

An additional risk to interpreting data from learning platforms and other sources comes from *confirmation bias*, which occurs when individuals or groups search for or interpret data in a way that confirms their experiences and preconceptions, leading to biased decisions. MacLean and Dror (2016), in their summary of research on confirmation bias, note that an inaccurate, initial understanding of a situation can compromise an individual's or group's attempts to reach correct decisions. They further note that individuals working alone or in groups tend to seek out and give greater weight to information consistent with their expectations while ignoring, discrediting, or trivializing information that is inconsistent with their working theory.

To counteract the interpretation divide, Mandinach and Schildkamp (2021) make several recommendations that education decision-makers can enact, including prioritizing and supporting data interpretation education for teachers. Additionally, they recommend that those analyzing data refrain from relying on a single data source, such as assessments or that generated from a learning platform, instead considering it along with other classroom data sources. Contextualizing the data to add context regarding a student's environment is also critical: "Educators need data, such as demographics, attendance, health, transportation, justice, motivation, home circumstances (i.e., homelessness, foster care, potential abuse, poverty), and special designations (i.e., disability, language learners, bullying) to contextualize student performance and behavior" (p. 2).

Educational leaders can also support the design of thoughtful frameworks that take and make sense of data from a variety of sources. For example, Mandinach and Miskell (2018) studied the affordances of technologies used in blended learning environments and how they affected teaching and learning activities. The study used mixed methods to examine whether the blended learning environments provided enhanced access to and more diverse data for teachers and students from which to make educational decisions. The study found that the technologies provided more diverse data to administrators, teachers, and students and allowed for flexible adaptations to virtual and face-to-face learning to meet students' needs. The blended environments helped to create data cultures within the schools where educators used data to communicate and have an impact on instructional activities.

Schildkamp and colleagues (2019) identify five key building blocks for educational leaders wanting to cultivate effective teams that use data and mitigate confirmation bias in their school: (1) discussing and establishing a vision, norms, and goals of data use with educators; (2) meeting educators where they are by providing individualized technical and emotional support; (3) sharing knowledge across the team and providing autonomy; (4) creating a safe and productive climate within the team that focuses on data use for improvement rather than accountability; and (5) brokering knowledge and creating a network that is committed to data use.

The Citizenship Divide

Through learner and educator engagement with digital platforms and other technologies that generate massive amounts of data come creating new mechanisms for advancing what is known about how people learn, developing new administrative procedures on how best to use scarce resources, discovering novel relationships and patterns, increasing the accuracy of predictions, and improving the automation of low-level tasks and decisions. Coupled with these opportunities are technical, ethical, and logistical challenges that will grow more complex over time.

Though many early researchers and scholars associate the digital divide with unequal access to technology hardware and the Internet, sociologist Paul Attewell (2001) defined it as the "technology gap between the 'information haves' and information 'have-nots'" (p. 252). In this chapter, we present the cyclical effects of ethical decisions involving big data and digital learning platforms. The disparity among the haves and have nots not only precludes learners and educators from accessing information and collaborating over distance and time but also diminishes their ability to accumulate social capital and prepare for success in a knowledge-based economy. Across life outcomes such as health, wages, and indicators of civic engagement and trust, adults with higher levels of literacy, numeracy, and 21st-century skills, as well as technology access, fare better than their counterparts with lower skill levels and less connectivity (Kirsch et al., 2021; Ramsetty & Adams, 2020). *Is it ethical that without intervention, each cohort of learners is poised to perpetuate structural stigmas and preserve the trends of the past, with some subgroups unduly benefiting and others not?* As Zwitter (2014) warns, the more that the lives of learners and educators become mirrored in the data they generate through digital learning platforms and other media, the more their present, past, and future potentially become more transparent and predictable.

LOOKING FORWARD

Unwise technology use for learning and teaching through digital learning platforms and other tools further magnifies the structural disparities already inherent in society. To take an ethical approach to addressing the divides described in the cycle and increase opportunity and equity while mitigating bias, educators, designers, and policymakers must constantly reflect on the ethical questions raised in this chapter and a constellation of investments and actions. The following is based on Dede (2015):

1. Empower communities of researchers, funders, policymakers, practitioners, and other stakeholders to use new forms of evidence to puzzle through and answer questions together. Investigations

should focus on the purpose of the study, prior research, and research questions before selecting data and methods for answering those research questions.

2. Infuse evidence-based decision-making continuously with constant reflection on issues of equity, quality, and fairness.
3. Use new and traditional forms of micro, meso, and macro data to develop new ways of measuring learning and impact for formative, summative, and administrative purposes.
4. Work to reconceptualize how data are generated, collected, stored, accessed, analyzed, interpreted, and acted on by different categories of users (e.g., educators vs. research) for different purposes.
5. Develop new types of analytic methods to enable rich findings from complex forms of educational data and new forms of visualizations to identify useful patterns in educational data that may not be obvious and help educators more easily navigate, interpret, and act on data (Daniel, 2019).
6. Build human capacity through professional development and degree programs to better integrate pedagogical and ethical uses data science into the design, development, and use of digital learning platforms and digital tools.

By addressing the ethical questions associated with each segment of the cycle and by addressing these recommendations, we can begin to realize the potential of a lifelong education and improve life outcomes.

REFERENCES

Adjei, S., Ostrow, K., Erickson, E., & Heffernan, N. (2017). Clustering students in ASSISTments: Exploring system and school-level traits to advance personalization. In X. Hu, T. Barnes, A. Hershkovitz, & L. Paquette (Eds), *Proceedings of the 10th international conference on educational data mining* (pp. 340–341). International Educational Data Mining Society.

Angwin, J., Larson, J., Mattu, S., & Kirchner, L. (2016). Machine bias: There's software used across the country to predict future criminals. And it's biased against blacks. *ProPublica*.

Attewell, P. (2001). Comment: The first and second digital divides. *Sociology of Education, 74*(3), 252–259.

Baker, R. S. (2019). Challenges for the future of educational data mining: The Baker Learning Analytics Prizes. *Journal of Educational Data Mining, 11*(1), 1–17.

Baker, R. S., Corbett, A. T., Koedinger, K. R., & Wagner, A. Z. (2004). Off-task behavior in the cognitive tutor classroom: When students "game the system."

In *Proceedings of the SIGCHI Conference on Human Factors in Computing Systems* (pp. 383–390). Association for Computing Machinery.

Blikstein, P., Worsley, M., Piech, C., Sahami, M., Cooper, S., & Koller, D. (2014). Programming pluralism: Using learning analytics to detect patterns in the learning of computer programming. *Journal of the Learning Sciences*, 23(4), 561–599.

Boland, H., & Cogley, M. (2020). The inside story about how an algorithm created A-level chaos. *The Telegraph*. https://www.telegraph.co.uk/technology/2020/08/20/inside-story-algorithm-created-a-level-chaos/

Boyd, D., & Crawford, K. (2012). Critical questions for big data: Provocations for a cultural, technological, and scholarly phenomenon. *Information, Communication & Society*, 15(5), 662–679.

Buolamwini, J., & Gebru, T. (2018). Gender shades: Intersectional accuracy disparities in commercial gender classification. *Proceedings of the 1st Conference on Fairness, Accountability and Transparency. Proceedings of Machine Learning Research, 81*, (77–91).

Caliskan, A., Bryson, J. J., & Narayanan, A. (2017). Semantics derived automatically from language corpora contain human-like biases. *Science, 356*(6334), 183–186.

Chandra, S., Chang, A., Day, L., Fazlullah, A., Liu, J., McBride, L., Mudalige, T., & Weiss, D. (2020). *Closing the K–12 digital divide in the age of distance learning.* Common Sense Media; Boston Consulting Group.

Clark, D. B., Tanner-Smith, E. E., & Killingsworth, S. S. (2016). Digital games, design, and learning: A systematic review and meta-analysis. *Review of Educational Research*, 86(1), 79–122.

Cocea, M., Hershkovitz, A., & Baker, R. S. (2009). The impact of off-task and gaming behaviors on learning: Immediate or aggregate? In V. Dimitrova, R. Mizoguchi, B. du Boulay, & A. Graesser (Eds.), *Proceedings of the 2009 conference on artificial intelligence in education: Building learning systems that care: From knowledge representation to affective modelling* (pp. 507–514). IOS Press.

Council of Chief State School Officers. (2018). *States leading for equity: Promising practices advancing the equity commitments.*

D'Angelo, C., Rutstein, D., Harris, C., Bernard, R., Borokhovski, E., & Haertel, G. (2014). *Simulations for STEM learning: Systematic review and meta-analysis.* SRI International.

Daniel, B. K. (2019). Big data and data science: A critical review of issues for educational research. *British Journal of Educational Technology, 50*(1), 101–113.

Dede, C. (2015). *Data-intensive research in education: Current work and next steps.* Computing Research Association.

Dede, C. (2019). Improving efficiency and effectiveness through learning engineering. In C. Dede, J. Richards, & B. Saxberg (Eds.), *Learning engineering for online education: Theoretical contexts and design-based examples* (pp. 1–14). Routledge.

Díaz, P., Ioannou, A., Bhagat, K. K., & Spector, J. M. (Eds.). (2019). *Learning in a digital world: Perspective on interactive technologies for formal and informal education*. Springer.

Dieterle, E. (2010). Video games for teaching and learning science. In A. Hirumi (Ed.), *Playing games in school: Video games and simulations for primary and secondary education* (pp. 89–119). International Society for Technology in Education.

D'Mello, S., Dieterle, E., & Duckworth, A. (2017). Advanced, analytic, automated (AAA) measurement of engagement during learning. *Educational Psychologist, 52*(2), 104–123.

Educational Testing Service. (2014). *ETS standards for quality and fairness.*

Ercikan, K., & Pellegrino, J. W. (Eds.). (2017). *Validation of score meaning for the next generation of assessments: The use of response processes*. Routledge.

Eubanks, V. (2017). *Automating inequality: How high-tech tools profile, police, and punish the poor*. St. Martin's Press.

European Economic and Social Committee. (2017). *The ethics of big data: Balancing economic benefits and ethical questions of big data in the EU policy context*. Publications Office of the European Union.

Fancsali, S. (2014). Causal discovery with models: Behavior, affect, and learning in cognitive tutor algebra. In J. Stamper, Z. Pardos, M. Mavrikis, B. M. McLaren (Eds.), *Proceedings of the 7th International Conference on Educational Data Mining* (pp. 28–35). International Educational Data Mining Society.

Fancsali, S. (2015). Confounding carelessness? Exploring causal relationships between carelessness, affect, behavior, and learning in cognitive tutor algebra using graphical causal models. In *Proceedings of the 8th International Conference on Educational Data Mining*, (pp. 508–511). International Educational Data Mining Society.

Finlay, L. (2016). Negotiating the swamp: The opportunity and challenge of reflexivity in research practice. *Qualitative Research, 2*(2), 209–230.

Fischer, C., Pardos, Z. A., Baker, R. S., Williams, J. J., Smyth, P., Yu, R., Slater, S., Baker, R., & Warschauer, M. (2020). Mining big data in education: Affordances and challenges. *Review of Research in Education, 44*(1), 130–160.

Fishman, B., & Dede, C. (2016). Teaching and technology: New tools for new times. In D. H. Gitomer & C. A. Bell (Eds.), *Handbook of research on teaching* (5th ed., pp. 1269–1334). American Educational Research Association.

Friedman, B., & Nissenbaum, H. (1996). Bias in computer systems. *ACM Transactions on Information Systems (TOIS), 14*(3), 330–347.

Grajek, S. (2020). EDUCAUSE COVID-19 QuickPoll results: Help for students. *EDUCAUSEreview.*

Guo, H., Rios, J. A., Haberman, S., Liu, O. L., Wang, J., & Paek, I. (2016). A new procedure for detection of students' rapid guessing responses using response time. *Applied Measurement in Education, 29*(3), 173–183.

Hampton, K. N., Fernandez, L., Robertson, C. T., & Bauer, J. M. (2020). *Broadband and student performance gaps: Lack of broadband and dependence on cell phones for home internet is leaving rural Michigan students behind*. Michigan State University.

Hatzenbuehler, M. L., & Link, B. G. (2014). Introduction to the special issue on structural stigma and health. *Social Science & Medicine, 103*, 1–6.

Heffernan, N. T., & Heffernan, C. L. (2014). The ASSISTments ecosystem: Building a platform that brings scientists and teachers together for minimally invasive research on human learning and teaching. *International Journal of Artificial Intelligence in Education, 24*(4), 470–497.

Herbert, B. (2016). *The LEAP learning framework: Personalizing learning in the classroom.* LEAP.

International Baccalaureate. (2020). *IB update on May 2020 diploma programme and career-related programme results.*

Kirkpatrick, K. (2016). Battling algorithmic bias. *Communications of the ACM, 59*(10), 16–17.

Kirsch, I., Sands, A., Robbins, S., Goodman, M., & Tannenbaum, R. (2021). Buttressing the middle: A case for reskilling and upskilling America's middle-skill workers in the 21st century. https://www.ets.org/s/research/pdf/buttressing-policy -report.pdf

Kostyuk, V., Almeda, M. V., & Baker, R. S. (2018). Correlating affect and behavior in reasoning mind with state test achievement. In *Proceedings of the 8th International Conference on Learning Analytics and Knowledge,* (pp. 26–30). Association of Computer Machinery.

Laeeq Khan, M., Welser, H. T., Cisneros, C., Manatong, G., & Idris, I. K. (2020). Digital inequality in the Appalachian Ohio: Understanding how demographics, internet access, and skills can shape vital information use (VIU). *Telematics and Informatics, 50.* https://doi.org/10.1016/j.tele.2020.101380

LearnPlatform. (2021). *Edtech engagement & digital learning equity gaps.* https:// learnplatform.com/insights/infographic/2020-digital-equity-in-review

Lee, Y.-H., & Haberman, S. J. (2016). Investigating test-taking behaviors using timing and process data. *International Journal of Testing, 16*(3), 240–267.

Levy, R. (2019). Dynamic Bayesian network modeling of game-based diagnostic assessments. *Multivariate Behavioral Research, 54*(6), 771–794.

Luckin, R., Holmes, W., Griffiths, M., & Forcier, L. B. (2016). *Intelligence unleashed: An argument for AI in education.* Pearson.

MacLean, C. L., & Dror, I. E. (2016). A primer on the psychology of cognitive bias. In C. T. Robertson & A. S. Kesselheim (Eds.), *Blinding as a solution to bias: Strengthening biomedical science, forensic science, and law* (pp. 13–24). Academic Press. https://doi.org/10.1016/B978–0-12-802460-7.00001-2

Makori, A., & Dusseault, B. (2020). Students experiencing homelessness are largely invisible in school reopening plans. *The Lens: Bringing vision and clarity to education policy.* Center on Reinventing Public Education.

Mandinach, E. B., & Miskell, R. C. (2018). Blended learning and data use in three technology-infused charter schools. *LEARNing Landscapes, 11*(1), 183–198.

Mandinach, E. B., & Schildkamp, K. (2021). Misconceptions about data-based decision making in education: An exploration of the literature. *Studies in Educational Evaluation, 69,* 1–10. https://doi.org/10.1016/j.stueduc.2020 .100842

Marco, C. A., & Larkin, G. L. (2000). Research ethics: Ethical issues of data reporting and the quest for authenticity. *Academic Emergency Medicine, 7*(6), 691–694.

Metz, C. (2019, November 12). We teach A.I. systems everything, including our biases. *The New York Times.* https://www.nytimes.com/2019/11/11/technology/artificial-intelligence-bias.html

Mitchell, M., Baker, D., Moorosi, N., Denton, E., Hutchinson, B., Hanna, A., Gebru, T., & Morgenstern, J. (2020). Diversity and inclusion metrics in subset selection. In *Proceedings of the 2020 AAAI/ACM Conference on AI, Ethics, and Society* (pp. 117–123). Association of Computing Machinery.

National Academies of Sciences, Engineering, and Medicine. (2018). *How people learn II: Learners, contexts, and cultures.* The National Academy Press. https://doi.org/10.17226/24783

Nielsen, M. W., Bloch, C. W., & Schiebinger, L. (2018). Making gender diversity work for scientific discovery and innovation. *Nature Human Behaviour, 2*(10), 726–734.

Niemi, D. M., Pea, R. D., Saxburg, B., & Clark, R. E. (Eds.). (2018). *Learning analytics in education.* Information Age Publishing.

Olteanu, A., Castillo, C., Diaz, F., & Kiciman, E. (2019). Social data: Biases, methodological pitfalls, and ethical boundaries. *Frontiers in Big Data, 2.* https://doi.org/10.3389/fdata.2019.00013

Pane, J. F., Steiner, E. D., Baird, M. D., & Hamilton, L. S. (2015). *Continued progress: Promising evidence on personalized learning.* RAND Corporation.

Pane, J. F., Steiner, E. D., Baird, M. D., Hamilton, L. S., & Pane, J. D. (2017a). *How does personalized learning affect student achievement?* RAND Corporation.

Pane, J. F., Steiner, E. D., Baird, M. D., Hamilton, L. S., & Pane, J. D. (2017b). *Informing progress: Insights on personalized learning implementation and effects.* RAND Corporation.

Pardos, Z. A., Baker, R. S., San Pedro, M., Gowda, S. M., & Gowda, S. M. (2014). Affective states and state tests: Investigating how affect and engagement during the school year predict end-of-year learning outcomes. *Journal of Learning Analytics, 1*(1), 107–128.

Passey, D., & Higgins, S. (2011). Learning platforms and learning outcomes—insights from research. *Learning, Media and Technology, 36*(4), 329–333.

Perkins, D. (1992). *Smart schools: Better thinking and learning for every child.* Free Press.

Ramsetty, A., & Adams, C. (2020). Impact of the digital divide in the age of COVID-19. *Journal of the American Medical Informatics Association, 27*(7), 1147–1148.

Regan, P. M., & Jesse, J. (2018). Ethical challenges of edtech, big data and personalized learning: Twenty-first century student sorting and tracking. *Ethics and Information Technology, 21*(3), 167–179.

Richards, J., & Dede, C. (2012). Opportunities and challenges of digital teaching platforms. In C. Dede & J. Richards (Eds.), *Digital teaching platforms: Customizing classroom learning for each student* (pp. 1–6). Teachers College Press.

Ritter, S., Anderson, J. R., Koedinger, K. R., & Corbett, A. (2007). Cognitive tutor: Applied research in mathematics education. *Psychonomic Bulletin & Review, 14*(2), 249–255.

Sao Pedro, M. A., Baker, R. S., Gobert, J. D., Montalvo, O., & Nakama, A. (2013). Leveraging machine-learned detectors of systematic inquiry behavior to estimate and predict transfer of inquiry skill. *User Modeling and User-Adapted Interaction, 23*(1), 1–39.

Schildkamp, K., Lai, M. K., & Earl, L. M. (Eds.). (2013). *Data-based decision making in education: Challenges and opportunities.* Springer.

Schildkamp, K., Poortman, C. L., Ebbeler, J., & Pieters, J. M. (2019). How school leaders can build effective data teams: Five building blocks for a new wave of data-informed decision making. *Journal of Educational Change, 20*(3), 283–325.

Shah, D. S., Schwartz, H. A., & Hovy, D. (2020). Predictive biases in natural language processing models: A conceptual framework and overview. In *Proceedings of the 58th Annual Meeting of the Association for Computational Linguistics* (pp. 5248–5264). Association for Computational Linguistics.

Shute, V. J., Rahimi, S., Smith, G., Ke, F., Almond, R., Dai, C. P., Kuba, R., Liu, Z., Yang, X., & Sun, C. (2020). Maximizing learning without sacrificing the fun: Stealth assessment, adaptivity and learning supports in educational games. *Journal of Computer Assisted Learning, 37*(1), 127–141.

Shute, V. J., & Ventura, M. (2013). *Stealth assessment: Measuring and supporting learning in video games.* The MIT Press.

Shute, V. J., & Wang, L. (2017). Assessing and supporting hard-to-measure constructs in video games. In A. A. Rupp & J. P. Leighton (Eds.), *The handbook of cognition and assessment: Frameworks, methodologies, and applications* (pp. 535–562). John Wiley & Sons.

Stadler, M., Fischer, F., & Greiff, S. (2019). Taking a closer look: An exploratory analysis of successful and unsuccessful strategy use in complex problems. *Frontiers in Psychology, 10,* 777.

U.S. Department of Education. (1996). *Getting America's students ready for the 21st century: Meeting the technology literacy challenge. A report to the nation on technology and education.*

van Rijn, P. W., & Ali, U.S. (2017). A comparison of item response models for accuracy and speed of item responses with applications to adaptive testing. *British Journal of Mathematical and Statistical Psychology, 70*(2), 317–345.

Wang, Y., Kai, S., & Baker, R. S. (2020). Early detection of wheel-spinning in ASSISTments. In I. I. Bittencourt, M. Cukurova, K. Muldner, R. Luckin, & E. Millán (Eds.), *Artificial intelligence in education. AIED 2020. Lecture Notes in Computer Science* (Vol. 12163, pp. 574–585). Springer International Publishing.

Yapo, A., & Weiss, J. (2018). *Ethical implications of bias in machine learning* [Conference presentation]. Hawaii International Conference on System Sciences 2018, Waikoloa Village, HI.

Završnik, A. (2021). Algorithmic justice: Algorithms and big data in criminal justice settings. *European Journal of Criminology, 18*(5), 623–642. https://doi.org/10.1177/1477370819876762

Zwitter, A. (2014). Big data ethics. *Big Data & Society, 1*(2), 1–6.

CHAPTER 10

When Data Use Raises Equity and Ethical Dilemmas in Schools

Amanda Datnow, Marie Lockton, and Hayley Weddle

INTRODUCTION

The use of data in schools is intended to lead to fairer, evidence-based decision-making that supports the improvement of education for all learners (Lai & Schildkamp, 2013). At the same time, prior research has shown that using a frame of equity is important in data use, as otherwise data can be used to limit rather than expand opportunities for students (Datnow & Park, 2018). Data-informed decision-making can also raise ethical issues, particularly with respect to the education of students who have historically been disenfranchised. In this chapter, we draw on qualitative data gathered in schools engaged in an instructional improvement project that involved data use in order to examine various school scenarios in which data use, equity, and ethics intersect.

Equity issues are central to questions of ethics, and vice versa. Here we examine ethical dilemmas through the lens of equity. While many authors have raised ethical issues with respect to the use of big data (Herschel & Miori, 2017; Puaschunder, 2019; Zimmer, 2018), that is not our interest here. Our focus is on instances in which ethical and equity issues arise as educators make data-informed decisions in schools. There is a paucity of research that focuses on the ethics of data use in K–12 education (for an exception, see Flores & Gunzenhauser, 2016). Thus, to ground this investigation, we examined pertinent literature on ethical issues faced by educators grappling with equity and ethical issues, especially when related to issues of data and accountability, as well as research on data use and equity more generally.

ETHICS, EQUITY, AND DATA USE

Several authors examine the equity and ethical dilemmas that professionals, particularly those in the field of education, encounter in their work (Chabon & Morris, 2004; Dawson, 2014; Flores & Gunzenhauser, 2016;

Johnson, 2007; Shapiro & Stefkovich, 2001). The ethics of access and in-clusion are discussed (Dawson, 2014; Johnson, 2007). Johnson's (2007) study, for instance, discusses the ethics of access in teaching for equity, and Dawson (2014) explains that "access, equity and inclusion/exclusion ought to be understood as complex, interconnected and multifaceted issues" (p. 235). Frameworks are also offered for understanding issues of equity and ethics (Chabon & Morris, 2004; Dawson, 2014). Chabon and Morris's (2004) framework poses questions to consider, including what is the ethi-cal question, what do we need to know, who is involved, and what are the possible actions. They also ask, "What evidence, legal and ethical guidance, and/or personal, social, and professional insights support/contradict this ac-tion?" (p. 1). This last question is perhaps most pertinent to the work educa-tors engage in with respect to data-informed decision-making.

The preceding framework addresses important questions regarding ethical dilemmas but does not delve specifically into the intersection of eth-ics and equity. Shapiro and Stefkovich's (2001) framework introduces an equity dimension. The authors propose a framework with four dimensions, one of which is the ethics of critique, which has roots in critical theory and critical pedagogy and is focused on

> awakening educators to inequities in society and, in particular, in the schools. The ethics of critique asks educators to address questions regarding social class, race, gender, and other ways in which status differentials come into play, such as: Who makes the laws? Who benefits from the law, rule, or policy? Who has the power? Who are the silenced voices? (p. 15)

Applying the ethics of critique to various ethical dilemmas, the authors point out that, "in all these dilemmas, the administrators and teachers in charge want to do the right thing. However, what is right for one person or group may not be right for others" (p. 114). In one case the authors discussed regarding a situation involving special education inclusion, the educators involved tried to balance the goals of equality versus equity. In another set of dilemmas focused on accountability versus responsibility, teachers were faced with directives to "do what it takes" in order to avoid state sanction based on state test results.

Flores and Gunzenhauser (2016) examine some of the ethical issues that arise as school leaders take action on the basis of data revealing opportunity gaps in their schools. These authors use a language of justice when examin-ing equity issues. They explain how "principals' positionalities also contrib-ute to their dispositions and ethics," with some principals seeking justice in addressing opportunity gaps and others denying the presence of opportunity gaps, leading to inaction (p. 20). The authors acknowledge that more needs to be learned about data use, ethics, and equity so that data are not misused and inequalities are not exacerbated.

While the intersection of data use and equity in K–12 education received scant attention in the past, there is a growing body of research in this area. A special issue of the *Journal of Educational Administration* was devoted to this topic (Datnow et al., 2017), and several of those articles illuminate important issues for consideration. Numerous authors note that even when equity is ostensibly a goal of system and school reform efforts, it can go unacknowledged in data use practices (Gannon-Slater et al., 2017; Huguet et al., 2017). This can be because cultures of accountability dominate data conversations and imperatives (Braaten et al., 2017; Gannon-Slater et al., 2017) or because leaders miss opportunities to provide an equity frame to data use efforts (Huguet et al., 2017). The use of narrow forms of data in making decisions that are consequential for students' education can also close doors for them rather than open them (Datnow & Park, 2018).

While well intended, the use of benchmark assessment data has raised some ethical and equity issues in schools. Many districts adopted benchmark assessments during the high-stakes accountability era ushered in by No Child Left Behind (NCLB; Datnow & Park, 2014; Hamilton et al., 2009; U.S. Department of Education, 2010). The goal of such assessments has often been to gauge student progress toward state standards and provide teachers with data to guide instructional decisions accordingly (Bulkley et al., 2010; Goertz et al., 2010; Oláh et al., 2010; Young & Kim, 2010). Some benchmark assessments are created by external developers to map closely to state assessments so that students can be prepared in both content and format (Andrade et al., 2012). In other cases, districts develop their own benchmark assessments that are tied to district and state curriculum, or teacher teams are asked to create benchmark assessments drawing from item banks of questions. The belief is that interim assessments can pinpoint areas for student growth so that teachers can address learning gaps, which is an ethical aim.

At the same time, the use of benchmark assessments has also led some districts to narrow instructional improvement efforts around tested subjects (Braaten et al., 2017). This raises ethical and equity issues as students may not receive full access to other important subject areas such as science. Some teachers also report a misalignment between the content tested on the benchmark assessment and what they covered in class (Cosner, 2011), which creates stress for students and teachers. These concerns are compounded by teachers reports that data from benchmark assessments are often not examined in great depth (Hoover & Abrams, 2013), which can raise ethical and equity concerns.

Equity issues also arise in data use when data are used to confirm assumptions about students rather than question them (Lachat & Smith, 2005; Oláh et al., 2010). Whereas data can be used to challenge existing beliefs about student ability, they can also be used to reinforce low expectations for students who have typically been underserved in school systems, including students of color or students in special education (Bertrand &

Marsh, 2015). Leaders can play an important role in shifting the dialogue so that student data are framed in terms of growth and assets rather than deficits (Park, 2018). An additional challenge is that many educators lack the data literacy to use data effectively (Mandinach & Gummer, 2016), and thus may unwittingly make ill-informed decisions on the basis of data that are not in students' best interests.

On a related note, the placement of students into classes has long raised equity concerns as racialized tracking patterns have resulted in Black and Latino students being disproportionately placed into lower track classes as compared to their white peers (Lewis & Diamond, 2015; Oakes, 2005). Data often play an important role in this process. In recent years, educators have used benchmark assessment data for class placement, which is not their intended purpose (Davidson & Frohbieter, 2011; Shepard et al., 2011). Very few assessments have been validated for class placement purposes, and thus schools commonly turn to assessments that are designed for other reasons, meanwhile closing doors for students in the process (Datnow & Park, 2018). Prior research has documented how organizational regularities have dictated tracking decisions in schools as well (Oakes & Guiton, 1995). At times, educators predetermine how many students will have an opportunity to take advanced classes based on teacher availability and/or class size restrictions. Test score cutoffs are sometimes shifted to accommodate these organizational constraints, meanwhile limiting opportunities for students.

In sum, as prior literature reveals, there are a host of equity and ethical issues that arise in data use, and they are often commingled. Based on research cited earlier with respect to equity and ethics (e.g., Chabon & Morris, 2004; Shapiro & Stefkovich, 2001), we find the following set of steps/questions to be a helpful frame in examining issues that educators commonly encounter in the use of data:

First, pose the dilemma as a question so that different responses can be considered. Then consider the following:

What are the possible actions?
What evidence supports an action?
Who has the power?
Who are the silenced voices?
Who/what will benefit and how? Who/what will lose and how?
Given this analysis, what is the best course of action?

Figure 10.1 provides a flowchart to illustrate how these questions could be used in a decision-making encounter.

In this chapter, we present two vignettes gathered in a study of middle schools under pressure to improve student achievement in mathematics. We briefly describe the methods of our study before examining the dilemmas

Figure 10.1. Flowchart for Data-Informed Decision-Making with Ethics and Equity in Mind

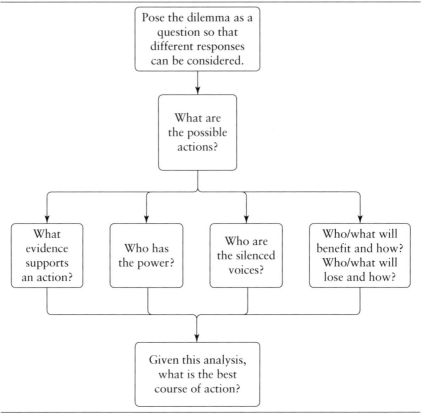

educators faced when grappling with how to balance equity and ethics in different aspects of data use.

METHODS

This chapter draws on extensive qualitative data gathered in four urban middle schools. These schools had been selected by the district to participate in a 4-year math instructional improvement project due to patterns in student performance in math that were below district and state averages. The project aimed to promote students' math achievement by supporting teachers' collaborative efforts to improve instruction through coaching, professional development, and joint teacher reflection data to inform practice. As part of these efforts, math teachers met regularly in department-wide and grade-level structured collaboration meetings to plan instruction, review student data, and discuss pedagogical approaches.

As qualitative researchers on the project, we developed a deep understanding of how teachers navigated efforts to collectively improve instruction. We used case study methods to explore how teachers built capacity for data-informed instructional improvement as this process unfolded in context (Yin, 2018). Case study methods are advantageous for highlighting the complexities of real-world situations and pushing the boundaries of existing theory (Eisenhardt, 1989; Yin, 2018). Each school constituted a case, as did each teacher team within schools. Having this nested case study design allowed us to examine data in different ways for varied kinds of analysis in the broader study.

The four middle schools included in this study are geographically close to each other in the same school district in the United States. The schools ranged in size from 364 to 1,092 students, and each served students in grades 6 to 8. The schools were composed primarily of Latinx students with smaller numbers of Black, Asian, White, and Multiracial students. The percentage of English learners ranged from 15% to 43% across the schools. The schools served a majority of low-income students, with 73% to 98% of students at each school qualifying as socioeconomically disadvantaged. The schools consistently performed lower than their district's average on their state's math assessment, that is, 15% to 31% of students meeting or exceeding standards in math.

Data for this study were collected over a period of 4 years from 2015 to 2019. During this time, we conducted 165 interviews with math teachers, school administrators, and the math instructional coach, who were interviewed annually. Interviews were semi-structured and focused on a range of topics related to instructional improvement efforts, data use, and collaboration. All interviews were taped and transcribed verbatim. In addition to conducting interviews, we also conducted 235 hours of observations of a total of 200 teacher collaboration meetings and workshops. We captured many direct quotes, often documenting entire conversations verbatim. Finally, we collected or took photos of documents used in collaboration meetings.

We began analyzing data with a set of a priori codes developed as part of the broader improvement project. To establish reliability of our coding scheme, we coded selected interviews and observations and then compared results among members of the research team. We used MAXQDA, a qualitative coding software tool, to facilitate the coding of the data. Detailed findings from our analyses of teachers' data use are reported in published articles (Datnow et al., 2019; Lockton et al., 2019). In this chapter, we highlight vignettes from our data that demonstrate ethical and equity issues that arise in the process of data use. We integrate direct quotes from our study participants in those vignettes, and it is important to note that while they highlight individual voices, the quotes we selected were representative of the opinions of many.

ISSUES OF EQUITY AND ETHICS IN DATA USE

Educators make many daily decisions that require using the lenses of equity and ethics. Because data use was a priority in the schools we studied, we had an opportunity to examine the ways in which they grappled with these kinds of dilemmas in the context of data use efforts. We present two issues that educators struggled with, and we interrogate them using the series of questions raised above. Before doing so, we provide a brief background of how data use fit into instructional improvement at the schools.

The instructional improvement project began with an explicit focus on helping teachers use data to support instruction geared around students' needs. The project implemented a biannual math diagnostic assessment. The district also implemented benchmark assessments annually in a process that shifted through the years in response to teacher feedback. In two grades, students also had to take math placement tests. While teachers understood the potential of data use, they struggled with the fact that assessments felt misaligned, data were not nuanced enough, or not enough time was spent connecting data to classroom practices. Teachers also felt constrained by the pacing guide and other district requirements (Lockton et al., 2019). Because the state's annual state assessment was foremost in administrators' minds, it tended to receive the most attention in data use discussions in schools (Datnow et al., 2019).

Issue 1: Ethical Issues in Benchmark Assessments

In one middle school we studied, educators found themselves faced with an ethical dilemma related to benchmark assessments. This largely stemmed from needing to produce data for the district while at the same time recognizing that students had been tested frequently. School administrators felt compelled to present the most updated data to the district. One administrator was frustrated that teachers had not given the district interim assessment they were supposed to administer, reminding the teachers, "Maybe I wasn't clear enough. I told you guys to give the test before we went on break."

Teachers explained their concerns about giving an interim assessment so close to the state's annual assessment. One teacher explained, "We have field trips, professional development, and I'm stressed about the amount I have to cover. Do we want to take another instructional day out for testing?" Another teacher noted that they had already administered a practice state test, which took 4 days. The administrator noted, "we need to have some gauge at the school level to see where you guys are at. [The interim assessment is] supposed to test the standards that you're teaching in class." Another goal was to "practice taking the test with the state test practice."

The teachers continued to push back, as for them, planning for and administering the interim assessment presented an ethical dilemma. Relative to the intent of the administrator, one teacher got to the heart of the matter: "I feel like improving test scores and giving [the principal] data right now are not compatible." Another teacher added: "It's not what's best for kids."

The administrator insisted on giving an interim assessment, even if it was modified and the data were not an accurate reflection. A teacher raised another ethical issue. She felt that the test results were demoralizing for her lower-performing students. She explained that those students "always have rotten data. They're so beaten down after taking any of these tests. I feel bad for them. And I don't want it to reflect on me either. And I feel so bad for them."

The administrator validated the teachers' concerns and said, "I'm on your side. I hear your concern. But I'm facing other pressure saying I need to have some data to present to the upper people. Whether we like it or not, we're judged by our test score. That's all the community and the upper management sees. They don't understand all the constraints we're dealing with."

The teachers continued to push back, asking if they could give the interim assessment after the state test, but the administrator explained that this would defeat the goal of data use "because you're supposed to look at it and use it to improve instruction." However, it was clear that the teachers did not believe the test would provide useful data to inform instruction.

Reflection on Issue 1: Applying the Framework. Let us reflect on the ethical dilemma described in the preceding paragraphs and consider the possible courses of action by applying the proposed framework that intersects ethics and equity in data use.

First, it is important to pose the dilemma as a question so that different responses can be considered. The question in this case is, *should teachers administer an assessment that takes valuable instructional time, especially when it is clearly just for administrative purposes?*

Second, *what are the possible actions?* The possible actions are to administer the assessment or use existing data.

Third, *what evidence supports an action?* Although data were not specifically brought to the table, the teachers referred to evidence that the students had performed so poorly on a prior assessment that the data were demoralizing for them and not useful for the teachers.

Fourth, *who has the power?* In this case, the administrators have the power, as they can require the teachers to administer an assessment.

Fifth, *who are the silenced voices?* The silenced voices in this case are the students. The teachers attempt to speak on their behalf, noting that they have been tested too often, but they do not have an opportunity to speak for themselves, which is not uncommon.

Finally, *Who/what will benefit and how? Who/what will lose and how?* If the teachers administer the test, the site administrators will show

compliance with district demands. The district requires benchmarks in order to consistently measure how students across schools are progressing
in mastering the state standards, and thus having data are useful. If low-
performing schools are allowed to opt out, the district could be seen as
neglecting care for students' education and lowering expectations. From
the teachers' perspective, however, administering an additional assessment
results in a loss of valuable instructional time. They do not believe the assessment is likely to benefit students. If the teachers do not administer it,
students could benefit from the increased instructional time and less testing
time. The site administration stands to lose, though, due to a lack of compliance with district demands, and the district has less data to track student
performance.

Given this analysis, what is the best course of action? Examining the
situation, the most ethical and equity-guided action would be to not administer the assessment. This would protect students from another assessment that would not lead to positive consequences for improving teaching
and learning, given the circumstances. It also feels unethical to prioritize
another interim assessment when state testing will ultimately be the method
of evaluating effectiveness of the school and success of the students. Ideally,
the teachers' concerns about over-testing and the timing of the assessment
could be communicated to district administrators so that future adjustments
could be made that accomplish both the district- and classroom-level goals.

We now turn to an examination of ethics and equity issues in the use
of data for class placement. Again, this vignette relates to use of data from
assessment results, as the project we were engaged in had this as a central
feature of instructional improvement.

Issue 2: Using Data for Class Placement

Using data for class placement decisions raises a host of equity and ethical concerns that also deserve attention. We will discuss several issues that
we observed in the middle schools we studied and then present a vignette
for deeper investigation. First, in several schools we studied, we learned
that achievement levels in math were low overall, but not uniformly low as
some students scored at high levels. However, ethical and equity issues arose
when there were not enough students who qualified for advanced classes
to form these classes. Thus, the students were denied an opportunity to
have the more rigorous instruction available to students in other schools.
Taking regular-level classes also meant that advanced math pathways were
not available to the students in the future. It seems unethical not to act on
data that suggest action is appropriate, particularly in this case as it was
in keeping with district guidelines. An alternative might have been to push
other students into an advanced class who may have not qualified based on
their test results. This would at least open doors to higher-level instruction

for more students, but support would need to be provided so that the students could all be successful.

Schools used data not just for advanced math class placement but also for placement into remedial math classes for students entering middle school. This was initially based on students' scores on a newly created district placement test. In a subsequent year, using multiple sources of information to inform advanced math class placement became a policy requirement. Transparency in the placement process was strived for, but it wasn't always maintained. One school we studied discussed what language to post clearly on their website to limit the potential for parents to appeal placement decisions, as managing too many appeals could become onerous. Meanwhile, it is arguably unethical to discount input from families as advocates and as a possible source of valuable data that could be pivotal in students' academic trajectories. Research has also documented that middle-class or more affluent parents are likely to advocate on their students' behalf and receive attention from school personnel, whereas lower-income parents are less likely to feel welcomed or comfortable engaging in such advocacy, assuming that educators will make sound decisions on behalf of their children (Horvat et al., 2003).

In one middle school with low student performance in both reading and math, educators believed that students would be best served if they could be grouped in classes according to their reading achievement. The school served a large number of English learners and felt this approach would best meet their needs. Thus, educators used data on students' reading assessments when students entered 6th grade to determine class placement. As one teacher explained, some students came in with *very* low reading levels: "We have a lot of non-readers, a lot of Pre-K, K [Kindergarten] level students." She also estimated that more than half of the students received special education services, and a proportion had newly arrived in the United States.

Students with the lowest reading scores were grouped in separate classes. A teacher explained: "I think the philosophy behind it was to be able to slow down for an entire group of students and really focus in on them through small group instruction, through slowing things down, and really, really getting in and being able to work with those students who typically get left behind." Although the instructional approach was to slow things down, the goal was to get them closer to grade level by the end of the year.

However, because of the logistics of the master course schedule that partnered English and math teachers, students were also de facto grouped for math, regardless of whether their achievement level in math supported this decision. The math instruction varied in the two types of classes, as one teacher explained: "I go a lot slower, I do a lot of review of basic skills, and I spoon-feed it to them little bits at a time, and we use a lot more manipulatives, like we make fraction kits. The other group, I would maybe demonstrate once with manipulatives, and we go much faster." While according to several teachers, students' achievement in reading often overlapped with their achievement in math, they did admit that there were some outliers who could have perhaps benefited from more challenging math instruction or a faster pace.

Reflection on Issue 2: Applying the Framework. Let us step back from this ethical dilemma and consider the possible courses of action by applying the proposed framework that intersects ethics and equity in data use. First, it is important to *pose the dilemma as a question* so that different responses can be considered. The question in this case is, *what are the consequences of de facto grouping students for math based on their reading achievement?*

Second, *what are the possible actions?* The possible actions are to (1) use reading achievement data to group students for both math and reading, given the school's scheduling model; (2) use math achievement data to group students for math and separately for reading, thus disrupting the scheduling model that teachers found useful; or (3) heterogeneously group the students, aiming for a mix of students with a range of prior achievement levels in math and reading.

Third, *what evidence supports an action?* Assessments in reading were relied on as evidence for class placement. Faced with a pattern of low achievement in reading, educators felt that they could better address students' reading needs by grouping them by level. Math assessment data were not accounted for.

Fourth, *who has the power?* In this case, the administrators and teachers at the school level have the power to make decisions regarding class placement. It appears that decisions were primarily made by the administration but were supported by teachers.

Fifth, *who are the silenced voices?* The silenced voices in this situation are the students and the parents. They were not consulted about class placement, and there were references to putting a process in place to minimize parent appeals.

Finally, *Who/what will benefit and how? Who/what will lose and how?* The decision to de facto group students for math based on their reading achievement levels has possible benefits for the organization and for teachers. It was easier for the school to keep students together rather than to organize a schedule in which they have separate groupings for math and reading. Teachers believed that this model allowed them to better address the learning needs of students. This was deemed especially critical in reading, and teachers did not find it exceptionally challenging to deal with the outliers in math. The students lose in two ways. First, grouping students into low-track classes has shown negative effects (Oakes, 2005). Second, students' math achievement is disregarded in this model of class placement, and their access to rigorous math instruction is limited.

Given this analysis, what is the best course of action? Examining the situation, the most ethical and equity-guided action would be to abandon the policy of placing students into classes based on prior achievement in reading and group them heterogeneously in math. District policy required schools to determine whether students qualify for accelerated math, but during the time of our study, not enough students qualified for accelerated math to justify forming a class. It would be worthwhile to revisit this policy in light of research showing that students do not benefit from tracking in math. Ultimately, tracking itself is inequitable and raises a host of equity and ethical concerns.

DISCUSSION AND CONCLUSION

As an examination of these vignettes reveals, the use of data in schools raises a host of ethical and equity concerns that are closely linked. On a daily basis, educators are faced with challenging decisions that have varied consequences for administrators, teachers, and students. While one might expect that when using data to inform decisions, choices may be clearer, in fact a host of ethical and equity concerns remain to be addressed. In some cases, what serves administrative or organizational purposes may not serve students or teachers well. Moreover, what serves one group of students well may not be good for another. For example, as we explained in the first vignette, administering an assessment may provide administrators with data to examine student progress, but when students have been over-tested and teachers are short on instructional time, it doesn't benefit students or teachers. In the second vignette, it was organizationally simpler to group students for remedial reading and de facto group them into low-level math; however, this limited students' opportunity to learn in math. A common feature in both vignettes is that students' and parents' voices were not included. This is not uncommon in schools serving underserved communities, yet it is a critical equity issue that needs to be considered. The set of questions we posed helps to illuminate the power differentials that are often apparent in school decision-making structures. These questions are useful in data use dilemmas, but they could also be applied to other difficult decisions faced by educators.

As previously noted, there is a dearth of research that examines the ethics of data use decisions in schools. Yet as this exploration makes clear, there are good reasons to pursue further investigation in this area. Researchers who have studied data-informed decision-making may find that the data they have gathered in prior studies could be interrogated with an ethical lens. Research of this variety could be more impactful if results are shared with educators. Although educators commonly apply an ethical frame in an implicit manner, it would be useful to explicitly use this concept when inquiring into data use processes in schools. Another idea would be to plan an improvement project in which educators were provided with the set of questions posed in this chapter and supported in applying them to decision-making. Researchers could then examine the impact of these questions on decision processes. It is important to note, however, that many schools operate within a set of accountability frameworks, policies, and expectations that themselves create tensions with respect to equity and ethics. That said, as the vignettes we discussed here reveal, there are key decisions made at the school level even within broader constraints.

The questions in the framework could also help educators be more reflective about data use. With the many demands on educators' time in schools, decision-making can be reactive as opposed to proactive. In the schools studied, teachers and leaders faced several competing demands for their time, including responding to multiple district-level reform priorities, navigating accountability pressures, and developing instructional strategies to meet the needs of their students. Understandably, conversations about data were often short. Further, many teachers expressed uncertainty about how to meaningfully make sense of and act on student data. The framework outlined in this chapter could serve as a tangible tool for guiding purposeful and equity-centered discussion about the use of data to inform decision-making.

An important limitation to this chapter is that we as researchers made decisions, albeit based on a framework, about what is ethical, who benefits, and so on. The collaborative and longitudinal nature of the project likely afforded us insights into the dilemmas, as we developed authentic and trusting relationships with the teachers included in this study. However, it is essential to acknowledge that we are not living the daily realities of educators in the schools we studied or struggling with ethical implications of data-informed decisions. Engaging district leaders, school administrators, and teachers together in a collaborative research design process could prove fruitful in teasing out how decisions in one domain (e.g., the district office) may inadvertently raise ethical and equity tensions in another (e.g., the classroom).

REFERENCES

Andrade, H., Huff, K., & Brooke, G. (2012). *Assessing learning: The students at the center series.* Jobs for the Future. http://studentsatthecenter.org/topics/assessing-learning

Bertrand, M., & Marsh, J. A. (2015). Teachers' sensemaking of data and implications for equity. *American Educational Research Journal, 52*(5), 861–893.

Braaten, M., Bradford, C., Kirchgasler, K. L., & Barocas, S. F. (2017). How data use for accountability undermines equitable science education. *Journal of Educational Administration, 55*(4), 427–446.

Bulkley, K. E., Christman, J. B., Goertz, M. E., & Lawrence, N. R. (2010b). Building with benchmarks: The role of the district in Philadelphia's benchmark assessment system. *Peabody Journal of Education*, 85(2), 186–204.

Chabon, S. S., & Morris, J. F. (2004). A consensus model for making ethical decisions in a less-than-ideal world. *The ASHA Leader*, 9(3), 18–19.

Cosner, S. (2011). Teacher learning, instructional considerations and principal communication: Lessons from a longitudinal study of collaborative data use by teachers. *Educational Management Administration & Leadership*, 39(5), 568–589.

Datnow, A., Greene, J. C., & Gannon-Slater, N. (2017). Data use for equity: Implications for teaching, leadership, & policy. *Journal of Educational Administration*, 55(4), 354–360.

Datnow, A., Lockton, M., & Weddle, H. (2019). Redefining or reinforcing accountability? An examination of organizational routines in U.S. schools. *Journal of Educational Change*, 21, 109–134. https://doi.org/10.1007/s10833-019-09349-z

Datnow, A., & Park, V. (2014). *Data driven leadership*. Jossey Bass.

Datnow, A., & Park, V. (2018). Opening or closing doors for students? Equity and data use in schools. *Journal of Educational Change*, 19(2), 131–152.

Davidson, K. L., & Frohbieter, G. (2011). *District adoption and implementation of interim and benchmark assessments* (Report No. 806). National Center for Research on Evaluation, Standards, and Student Testing (CRESST). https://cresst.org/publications/cresst-publication-3175

Dawson, E. (2014). Equity in informal science education: Developing an access and equity framework for science museums and science centres. *Studies in Science Education*, 50(2), 209–247.

Eisenhardt, K. M. (1989). Building theories from case study research. *Academy of Management Review*, 14(4), 532–550.

Flores, O., & Gunzenhauser, M. G. (2016). *Justice in the gaps: School leader ethics and the use of data to address the opportunity gap* (ED596648). ERIC (AERA Online Paper Repository). https://eric.ed.gov/?id=ED596648

Gannon-Slater, N., La Londe, P. G., Crenshaw, H. L., Evans, M. E., Greene, J. C., & Schwandt, T. A. (2017). Advancing equity in accountability and organizational cultures of data use. *Journal of Educational Administration*, 55(4), 361–375.

Goertz, M. E., Nabors Oláh, L., & Riggan, M. (2010). *From testing to teaching: The use of interim assessments in classroom instruction* (CPRE Research Report No. RR-65). Consortium for Policy Research in Education. https://www.cpre.org/sites/default/files/researchreport/832_testing-teachingfinal-report-cpre-website.pdf

Hamilton, L., Halverson, R., Jackson, S. S., Mandinach, E., Supovitz, J., & Wayman, J. (2009). *Using Student Achievement Data to Support Instructional Decision making*. IES Practice Guide. NCEE 2009-4067. National Center for Education Evaluation and Regional Assistance.

Herschel, R., & Miori, V. M. (2017). Ethics & big data. *Technology in Society*, 49, 31–36.

Hoover, N. R., & Abrams, L. M. (2013). Teachers' instructional use of summative student assessment data. *Applied Measurement in Education, 26*, 219–231.

Horvat, E., Weiniger, E.B., & Lareau, A. (2003). From social ties to social capital: Class differences in the relations between schools and parent networks. *American Educational Research Journal, 40*(2), 319–351.

Huguet, A., Farrell, C. C., & Marsh, J. A. (2017). Light touch, heavy hand: Principals and data-use PLCs. *Journal of Educational Administration, 55*(4), 376–389.

Johnson, A. S. (2007). An ethics of access: Using life history to trace preservice teachers' initial viewpoints on teaching for equity. *Journal of Teacher Education, 58*(4), 299–314.

Lachat, M. A., & Smith, S. (2005). Practices that support data use in urban high schools. Special Issue on transforming data into knowledge: Applications of data-based decision making to improve instructional practice. *Journal of Education for Students Placed At-Risk, 10*(3), 333–349.

Lai, M., & Schildkamp K. (2013). Data-based decision making: An overview. In K. Schildkamp, M. Lai, & L. Earl (Eds.), *Data-based decision making in education: Challenges and opportunities* (pp. 9–21). Springer.

Lewis, A., & Diamond, J. (2015). *Despite best intentions: How racial inequality thrives in good schools.* Oxford University Press.

Lockton, M., Weddle, H., & Datnow, A. (2019). When data don't drive: Teacher agency in data use efforts in low performing schools. *School Effectiveness and School Improvement, 31*(2), 243–265. https://doi.org/10.1080/09243453.2019.1647442

Mandinach, E. B., & Gummer, E. S. (2016). What does it mean for teachers to be data literate: Laying out the skills, knowledge, and dispositions. *Teaching and Teacher Education, 60*, 366–376.

Oláh, L. N., Lawrence, N. R., & Riggan, M. (2010). Learning to learn from benchmark assessment data: How teachers analyze results. *Peabody Journal of Education, 85*(2), 226–245.

Oakes, J. (2005). *Keeping track: How schools structure inequality* (2nd. ed.). Yale University Press.

Oakes, J., & Guiton, G. (1995). Matchmaking: The dynamics of high school tracking decisions. *American Educational Research Journal, 32*(1), 3–33.

Park, V. (2018). Leading data conversation moves: Toward data-informed leadership for equity and learning. *Educational Administration Quarterly, 54*(4), 617–647.

Puaschunder, J. M. (2019). Big data ethics. *Journal of Applied Research in the Digital Economy, 1*, 55–75.

Shapiro, J. P., & Stefkovich, J. A. (2016). *Ethical leadership and decision making in education: Applying theoretical perspectives to complex dilemmas.* Routledge.

Shepard, L., Davidson, K., & Bowman, R. (2011). *How middle school mathematics teachers use interim and benchmark assessment data* (CSE Technical Report). University of California, National Center for Research on Evaluation,

Standards, and Student Testing (CRESST). https://cresst.org/publications /cresst-publication-3176/

U.S. Department of Education, Office of Planning, Evaluation and Policy Development (2010). *Teachers' ability to use data to inform instruction: Challenges and supports.* Author.

Yin, R. E. (2018). *Case study research and its applications: Design and methods* (6th ed.). Sage.

Young, V. M., & Kim, D. H. (2010). Using assessments for instructional improvement: A literature review. *Educational Policy Analysis Archives, 18*(19), 1–37.

Zimmer, M. (2018). Addressing conceptual gaps in big data research ethics: An application of contextual integrity. *Social Media+ Society, 4*(2), 2056305118768300.

What Does the Future of Data Ethics Look Like?

Ellen B. Mandinach and Edith S. Gummer

This volume contains chapters that address contributing components to data use in education. Before moving to a synthetic overview, we acknowledge that there are some concerns about data-driven decision-making that impact responsible data use. Mandinach and Schildkamp (2021) review these concerns, but here we focus on and address ways that data use can be made more effective and appropriate by extrapolating from the chapters in this volume and our understanding of the landscape of educational data use. The focus must be on building educational professionals for whom data ethics become a foundational skill set and disposition. We recognize data ethics are complex. Educators are increasingly faced with a plethora of diverse data sources and even incomplete data from which interpretations are drawn with possible unintended consequences. And there may not be just one interpretation or actionable step from any decision. We therefore posit that data use is not a panacea. It is a challenging enterprise with the potential for positive impact but also for inappropriate data use despite educators' positive intentions.

One of the challenges of writing about the unethical use of data in education is the fact that unethical decision-making in any field may be made or justified with or without data. We did not intend this book to focus on malfeasance in education, but to illuminate the use of data, explicitly or implicitly, that supports decisions that are not ethical. These include deliberate attempts to sway judgments and perceptions by misrepresenting the findings from data or twisting the interpretations to fit a particular perspective, political influence, or belief system. Any decision in education can have unintended consequences, even with the best intent. Hindsight and identifying where a particular decision may have either privileged some groups over others or harmed particular groups of students, teachers, and other groups is part of the uncertainty in applying research findings to educational problems and engaging in improvement in education. Ignorance of effective data practices is not an excuse for making decisions that turn out to be unethical, but professionals in education have a mandate to seek out the best data and evidence and use it appropriately.

Clearly, using data in education has had multiple positive effects in improving educational institutions and practices. Lupton and Williamson (2017) have identified multiple benefits that can result from collecting detailed information about students. They discuss the positive ways students can engage in self-surveillance and using their own data as they increasingly develop control over themselves (Lupton, 2016) and use data to present themselves in virtual social contexts (Sauter, 2014). Expanding datafication of students has the potential to contribute to the strategies that adults—parents and teachers—use to identify and refine to provide care for children. But Lupton and Williamson (2017) clearly identify many of the potential misuses of data, and the key issues to be considered reflect the important canons indicated by the *Forum Guide to Data Ethics* (National Forum on Education Statistics [NFES], 2010) referenced multiple times in this volume. Education researchers have begun to address the issues (National Academy of Education, 2017), but the rights of students to the potential invasive collection of data and its unethical use is still underexamined in the United States.

That we emphasize the unethical decisions based on data use is largely due to space constraints of this book. Grounding the discussion of unethical decision-making across social contexts and professions is intended to illuminate the common issues that we face. This book has a dominant focus on ethical uses of data in education in the United States. It is not intended to suggest that other countries do not have many of the same issues or that they are exempt from them. The social sciences community in Europe has a substantive history, such as the adoption of the General Data Protection Regulation (GDPR). We hope that this volume will expand the conversations beyond the technical discussions of data use into a wider one that addresses both the nature of the decisions being made and the use of the data that ethically support them.

This concluding chapter attempts to address the emerging landscape of data use through a lens that balances educational professionalism, data literacy, the context in which decisions are situated, and appropriate levels of skepticism. All of these are intended to meet the objective of making the soundest possible decisions to inform educational practice. It is incumbent on educators to inform their decisions through the use of the widest possible data sources, including contextual information from which to determine what may be the most appropriate action steps.

We firmly believe that data literacy is fundamental to responsible data use. The construct must be fully integrated and sustained throughout educators' learning trajectories (Mandinach & Gummer, 2013, 2016), with attention given to ethical data use. Until data literacy is recognized as an essential set of knowledge and skills, there will continue to be a problem with educators who are not adequately prepared to use data effectively and responsibly. Thus, data literacy goes to the heart of the data ethics issue.

Correspondingly, there is limited awareness of and attention to addressing knowledge development among educators specific to the ethics of data use (Mandinach & Wayman, 2020). As noted in prior chapters, few stakeholder groups are taking responsibility for ensuring that educators have adequate knowledge of the topic. Is it the responsibility of the individual, educator preparation, districts, state education agencies, or professional organizations? We believe it is the responsibility of all the above. But we also believe that ethical use of data involves more than understanding the Family Educational Rights and Privacy Act (FERPA); instead, data ethics are about responsible data use, which fundamentally embraces data literacy. As an initial step, WestEd (Mandinach et al., 2020; Mandinach et al., 2021) has been working with the Future of Privacy Forum (FPF) to develop materials for educators that deal mostly with data privacy but also engage in the broader discussion of data ethics. And FPF has developed resources on its website that are available to educators (https://studentprivacycompass.org /resources/educatortraining/#reducingrisk).

REVIEW OF THE CHAPTERS

We review the preceding chapters to highlight the key messages we hope you will consider. It is our hope that you will learn about and become aware of data ethics and the importance of using data responsibly. In the introduction, we (Mandinach and Gummer) cover a focused landscape of literature in psychology and elsewhere that pertains to sound decision-making. There is a long history that can inform our thinking about the topic. The field of education must build on and fully understand how cognitive fallacies occur and how they impact decision-making. Education is not alone. The chapter provides an overview of how data ethics play out (not well) in other fields. It also explores why denial and skepticism exist and their impact on education.

In the first chapter that starts off Part I of the book, we extend the examination of ethics to education, a profession in which ethical violations may be less blatant than in other fields but in which such violations nevertheless occur despite good intent. The chapter addresses the need for educators to be data literate and links data literacy skills to data ethics.

In Chapter 2, Vance and Waughn review the privacy regulations that impact educational data in their review of the history of FERPA and how privacy is defined by the regulation. Similarly, in Chapter 3, Parton and Hochleitner provide an important landscape view of how privacy is viewed across the country and the policies that states have implemented to oversee data privacy. These three opening chapters provide a foundational overview of both data ethics and data privacy, but we must be cognizant that data privacy is only one component of data ethics.

In Chapter 4, Nichols focuses on how accountability continues to impact responsible data use. She recounts the history of accountability pressures that continue to constrain educators' adoption of a full range of data beyond student assessment data. As the chapter notes, accountability accounts for much of the unethical behavior observed in education, as educators feel pressured to game the system in some way in order to have their schools and districts look better.

The next six chapters make up Part II and are considered use cases, how data ethics play out in various components of education. In Chapter 5, Mandinach and Jimerson explore use cases of how data ethics occur in different areas of districts. They acknowledge how complex ethical decisions on data use can be, especially with the often-competing priorities of data for accountability and continuous improvement. The chapter provides several examples of ethically charged decisions that educators face and concludes with recommendations that are practical and implementable.

In Chapter 6, Mandinach and Nunnaley focus on how professional development deals with data ethics, both by data-related providers and providers in general. The fact that data use providers do not directly address data ethics is telling, and the chapter calls for a concerted focus on data ethics training. The chapter lays out 10 recommendations for how professional development can incorporate data ethics in practice.

In Chapter 7, Gummer, Gibbs, and Dorn move from the prior chapter's focus on professional development to educator preparation. The chapter reviews the realities of preparing educators for data literacy, finding that, while data literacy is underemphasized due to a focus on the narrower area of assessment literacy, data ethics fall victim both to the underemphasis on data literacy as well as to the paucity of focus on ethics more generally throughout educator preparation. The authors introduce practical strategies for introducing data ethics into preparation programs.

Chapter 8 focuses on the role of testing companies in ethical data use. Camara, Croft, and van Davier address how major testing companies address issues of data ethics in large-scale testing programs. The chapter considers the role of artificial intelligence as well as the collection, access to, and release of assessment data from testing companies. The chapter also addresses issues around equity in assessment data.

In Chapter 9, Dieterle, Holland, and Dede address the need to consider how educational technologies impact data use. Because data use relies on technology to support such use, platforms must be protected and educators must know how to use them properly. This chapter presents a framework from which to examine the concerns of educational technology and ethical issues of its impact on educational practice.

Concluding Part II of the book, Chapter 10 describes the importance of data ethics in terms of equity in schools. Datnow, Lockton, and Weddle provide salient examples of equity and ethical dilemmas and then raise looming questions and reflect on how ethics and equity apply in the particular situations. The authors challenge educators to ask better questions and researchers to examine ethics in education.

Here in the concluding chapter, we pose several recommendations to stimulate change in the field of education to ensure that data ethics becomes an embedded and integrated part of practice.

These chapters provide a rich landscape of how data ethics impact components of educational practice. Intent is typically positive, yet sometimes the outcomes are less so. We now address salient recommendations that are drawn from the chapters.

RECOMMENDED NEXT STEPS

We now turn to a set of recommended steps that those in education can consider and take to ensure that data ethics become enculturated parts of practice. We recognize that this will be no easy task for a number of reasons, much of which has to do with the hierarchical and systemic structure of education. Change may come slowly, but there must be change with respect to the need to address responsible data use across the various levels of the education system.

Consider Frameworks

We draw on the work of Project Evident (2020), which has developed a framework for the use of data and evidence. The Project Evident guide notes five components of its framework: (1) a culture of learning about how to use data and evidence, (2) a theory of change that addresses the systemic needs for using data appropriately, (3) having effective data systems, (4) data collection that is continuous with the goal to ensure that data collected address underrepresented groups, and (5) evaluation and data use that examines differential impact with an objective of equitable results. As Datnow and Park (2018) note, equitable data use is foundational to ethical data use.

We also draw on Raffaghelli (2020) who provides a representation of data literacy in social justice that includes four dimensions: critical data literacy, data in the society or personal/ethical data literacy, civic data literacy, and the ethical use of educational data or pedagogical data literacy. It is the final dimension that is particularly relevant as Raffaghelli (2020) focuses heavily on the ethical component of using data to support pedagogy.

In Chapter 2, we review the nine canons of data ethics laid out in the *Forum Guide* (NFES, 2010). Bringing the discussion full circle, we highlight the first two canons as we believe they most closely address the dispositions of responsible data practice, in contrast to the technical skills (NFES, 2010, p. 7). The first canon is "Demonstrate honesty, integrity, and professionalism at all times." The second canon is "Appreciate that, while data may represent attributes of real people, they do not describe the whole person." Professionalism is a necessity in education and can be found in most codes of ethics and includes many of the data literacy skills and knowledge we have discussed. As the *Forum Guide* states, "staff who consistently demonstrate honesty, integrity, and professionalism are the foundation of ethical behavior in an education organization" (NFES, 2010, p. 9). The second canon reflects the need to recognize that data use has limitations; it does not and cannot comprehensively reflect everything an educator needs to know about a student or a situation. The canon addresses the use of personal judgments, assumptions, prejudices, confirmation biases, and inappropriate interpretations. Therefore, the limitations of data use must be recognized and considered.

There are important guidelines that inform the design of data collection focus, processes, and use in the education research arena that have applicability here. Guidelines around considering the relationships among research and practice questions, design of investigations, and justifications of inferences that can be made are addressed by federal education agencies in multiple guidelines. In particular, the *Common Guidelines for Education Research and Development* (Earle et al., 2013) represents an interagency effort to create "a common understanding of the nature, strengths, and limitations of various genres of research and fostered appreciation and respect for context when judging whether, and if so, how evidence should count" (Maynard, 2018, p. 139). A supplement to the *Common Guidelines* emphasizes the need for multiple lines of data or evidence required in education and points to the importance of replication studies that are needed to strengthen or contest initial studies to create a strong base of evidence in education (Institute of Education Sciences and National Science Foundation, 2018). These sets of guidelines are at the heart of what types of data become evidence in educational decision-making.

Appropriate Consensus Messaging—Broad View of Responsible Data Use

Data ethics mean different things to different people. When the term *data* is mentioned, most educators provide similar responses. Data are test results, quantifiable numbers, and student performance indices. As we have enumerated across this volume, this is a narrow view that handicaps educators into making myopic decisions. A broad view of what constitutes evidence is needed—evidence that considers "context, data quality, and systemic drivers of inequities" (Bauer & Fitzsimmons, 2002, p. 4). Correspondingly, a broad view of data ethics is also needed. But we suspect that when the term *data ethics* is mentioned, people most likely think of FERPA and the protection of privacy and confidentiality. This is an essential component of data ethics, but it is also narrowly focused. We laid out the argument in prior chapters to think broadly about not just data ethics but also responsible data use. As such, data literacy must focus on effective and responsible data use. Thus, we strongly recommend a broad view of what it means to use data ethically and responsibly, which means educators must be data literate and ethically focused. Messaging within the field of education and beyond should adopt this broad perspective.

Awareness

Following from the first recommendation, there is a pressing need to build awareness about the importance of data ethics. It is unclear how aware educators are about the topic, even about FERPA. They may have a passing knowledge, but most likely it is inadequate. Helping educators to more fully understand FERPA and other related regulations is essential. Then expanding on this knowledge, we need to build awareness of the broader notion of responsible data use. The field needs to understand why data ethics are important, what their roles are in terms of using data responsibly, how data ethics will impact their daily practice, and the location of resources to support knowledge and skill acquisition. Thus, we recommend that policymakers and education leadership seek ways to increase awareness of and messages about the importance of data ethics. We also recommend that education policymakers and administrators change the frame from a perspective of top-down data use to a more co-constructed, locally relevant focus. The issues in ethical uses of data in the education policy arena are largely couched in terms of "evidence-based" policies and practices, with frequent references about how education should be more like medicine. However, even in evidence-based medicine, there are disagreements about how evidence should be used and about the differences in the ways that scientists and politicians couch their discourse and justifications for conclusions. A recent synthesis based on systematic reviews of evidence in medicine with a focus on critical analysis and policy theory emphasizes these differences with inferences that are substantively relevant to education (Cairney & Oliver, 2017). They point out that "actors are influential when they 'frame' their evidence in simple, manipulative and/or emotional terms to generate policymaker attention" (p. 2) and question whether researchers should do the same and whether that would abrogate some of the objectivity that scientists seek. They also raise the question about the value of researchers being explicit about scientific uncertainty when presenting findings. Cairney & Oliver (2017) also raise questions about the complexities of multilevel systems where various contexts and stakeholder interests may influence the focus of hierarchies of evidence that range from causal to correlational to context-specific findings. The authors conclude that it is not enough just to insist that policymakers (and practitioners) adopt a scientific perspective on examining evidence, but that scientists and researchers should consider engaging in a more collaborative process of evidence dissemination that more directly involves policymakers and practitioners in both identifying what evidence to collect and how it might be used. Cycles of such collaborative practice are very evident in the improvement science efforts that are rising in education (LeMahieu et al., 2017).

Considerations

We pose several steps to being a good consumer of data drawn from Bergstrom and West (2020). First, consider the source of information when examining a report, an article, or other resources. Second, beware of unfair comparisons in reading documents or in your reporting. Third, consider the orders of magnitude in reporting, and consider if small differences are meaningful and impactful. Fourth, avoid confirmation bias. At all stages of data use, entering into an activity with preconceived perceptions is problematic at best. Fifth, consider multiple hypotheses or explanations for results. Outcomes are never simple and rarely confirm to a single explanation. Finally, if a result appears to be too good to be true, question the result, and invoke an appropriate level of skepticism.

Build Capacity

Capacity building around responsible data use is essential. Many agencies and organizations have responsibility for and roles in helping educators develop their skills and knowledge around data literacy and responsible data use. And as noted earlier, this enterprise is systemic (Mandinach & Gummer, 2013, 2016). It requires the collaboration and coordination among several kinds of entities. We examine the recommended steps for each of the agencies.

The primary player in capacity building is educator preparation (Mandinach & Gummer, 2013). Emphasizing the importance of both data literacy and, more specifically, data ethics, must begin early in educators' careers. Bringing awareness first and then building foundational knowledge and skills is what educator preparation programs do, for both teachers and administrators. For novices and college students, data ethics may seem like an abstraction; appropriate topics must be introduced and infused in a practical way throughout the curriculum and students' clinical experiences.

Educator preparation must help prepare educators to find coherent ways to knit together the ethical values on which both data use and professional practice overall are grounded. While professional codes of ethics are critical components of teacher preparation, many gray areas of practice fall outside the lines of normative codes of ethics. Professional codes of ethics are rich in far-reaching ethical language with implications for a host of as-yet unmet moral challenges. Terms such as "just," "fair," or "equitable" get to the heart of why many educators decide to enter the profession. Codes of ethics provide an essential starting point for reflection on and co-construction of educators' and future educators' personal ethical frameworks. This reflection must extend beyond a single classroom or a collection of isolated lessons. Infusing ethics throughout classrooms, campuses, and clinical experiences is essential to preparing educators who enter the field equipped to interpret the new and unexpected ethical challenges of the profession through the clarity of their own personal beliefs.

Professional development is a second major support. Providers that specialize in data use are a natural fit, but they must evolve their focus on ethics in data use. For other professional development topics, it is possible to integrate the concepts into professional development processes.

The local education agencies make up the third player. Districts may not be able to afford the major professional development providers, so they must resort to homegrown, in-service sessions. They must develop the internal capacity. They must recognize data ethics as a priority, not a peripheral topic. Further, districts must consider data ethics important for all staff members who touch data, from data clerks to transportation and cafeteria directors, to teachers and administrators. We strongly advocate for district onboarding to include data ethics to circumvent many bad practices. Such onboarding could then be sustained and reinforced over time for staff.

State education agencies can play a role in establishing the importance of data ethics through explicit messaging and including the topic as part of licensure and credentialing processes. If data ethics play a larger role in standards and requirements, educators, districts, and educator preparation will have to pay attention as the message will be explicitly communicated that the topic is important. Further, states can modify their codes of ethics to include responsible data use, using more explicit messaging than what currently exists (Mandinach & Wayman, 2020).

Professional organizations have a key responsibility. The organizations for teachers, administrators, school boards, and state standards can acknowledge the importance of data ethics and integrate the topic into standards, requirements, and messaging. Perhaps most essential is for the National Association of State Directors of Teacher Education and Certification (NASDTEC) to work with its state representatives to incorporate data ethics into state standards with common and understandable language. Thus, organizations have the power to push the envelope by explicitly communicating the need to build educators' capacity.

A related topic is incentivizing educators to learn about data ethics to expand their practices to deal with ethical uses of data. These incentives may be internal, improving student learning and educator performances, or it might be external, through badges and new areas of advance certifications (A. Wenzel, personal communication, January 21, 2020). If educators take courses or learn about data ethics on their own, through the Privacy Technical Assistance Center (PTAC), the Future of Privacy Forum (FPF), the materials developed by Mandinach and colleagues (2020), or other means, they can earn a badge for which their districts can give them credit, enhance evaluations, or provide other perks.

Develop Resources and Materials

Capacity building depends on having resources to which educators can turn for information. The PTAC (https://studentprivacy.ed.gov) of the U.S. Department of Education provides training, materials, assistance, and FAQs, but these resources focus on FERPA. As noted earlier, FPF provides guidance, but again with the limited scope of privacy and confidentiality. We see a real need for resources that more broadly address data ethics as responsible data use. These materials could be used in educator preparation, professional development, and by district in-service trainers and human resources departments. They can also be used by individuals interested in learning more about data ethics. The materials should incorporate scenarios, case studies, and vignettes based on authentic situations from which lessons learned can be easily understood and contextualized (Warnick & Silverman, 2011).

Learn from Good and Bad Examples in Other Disciplines

This volume contains a multitude of examples, mostly of inappropriate data use that may not violate FERPA, but surely reflect inappropriate or irresponsible data use. We tend not to hear about positive examples, which may well be the norm. In an earlier book, our editors provided feedback to us asking why most of the examples about data-driven decision-making focused on the negative rather than the positive. We talked of attending to problems of practice and remediating learning deficits. But with an asset-based model, we now can highlight the positive, talk of strengths, and capitalize on assets.

What Does the Ideal Look Like?

In the ideal world, all educators would (1) be aware of the importance of using data responsibly, (2) have been trained to understand data-driven decision-making and have an appropriate level of data literacy based on their specific roles, (3) exhibit culturally responsive data literacy, and (4) know how to use data and base their decision-making on facts and evidence to avoid denial and skepticism.

FINAL THOUGHTS

This volume has covered a great deal of territory. As we noted earlier in the book, data ethics issues do occur, but there is no way to know how pervasive they are. Most educators are well intentioned and do not intend to use data inappropriately. In providing insights into places where data have been used inappropriately, we hope to avoid future misuse or at least develop awareness. We hope that the contents of this volume will help the education field become more aware of the many complexities that relate to ethical data use. The issues are embedded in a highly complex and deeply entrenched system of interrelated components. Each component has a major part to play and can influence how the others react and behave. Each component is affected by its unique pressures and roles. Enhancing the dialogue about the importance of ethical and responsible data use is a first step. This includes the most foundational issue that undergirds the majority of ethical transgressions: the emphasis on accountability and compliance pressures that consciously and unconsciously influence educational practice.

However, improving awareness will go only so far. The field must also build capacity through knowledge and skill development so that educators know how to use data responsibly. Knowing and doing are two different things. There must be clear messaging not only of the importance of ethical data use but explicit expectations, with consequences when educators and others do not adhere to good practice. We have seen the impact when people have been unethical, cheated, or made mistakes either intentionally or unintentionally. It is incumbent on all educators to be data literate and to be ethical users of information. This next step is to ensure that such responsible practices become enculturated throughout education. We must give educators the proper tools to be better data users and consumers of information. We must help them identify and adopt larger ethical frameworks that will equip them in navigating the as-yet uncharted reaches of data ethics. We must address and change the underlying root causes and pressures that have created the situations that perpetuate poor practices. Educators must be armed with data and evidence and use them effectively and responsibly. Ethics must undergird the field.

We leave you with two final sources of wisdom from Dilbert (Adams, 2020a, 2020b). In the first panel: Dilbert says, "Yesterday someone disagreed with me, and I changed his mind using data and reason." In the second panel: Wally says, "That isn't possible." Dilbert then replies, "I didn't think so either. But it happened." In the final panel: Wally responds, "Smells like a trap." Dilbert concludes, "I couldn't sleep all night." Using data is not a trap. Data are necessary in education and other fields. In the second strip, the Boss says, "You are all required to complete a class in ethics." Dilbert responds, "Wouldn't that make us the only ethical organization in our industry and create a competitive disadvantage that leads to our demise?"

The Boss counters, "Stop your worrying. The class is required, but I'm not expecting any of it to stick." Ethical data use must stick; it is not the demise of education but improved practice. Educators must be armed with diverse sources of data from which to make informed decisions. The data must be used responsibly and ethically. Now is the time for educators and all citizens to recognize the importance of sound data use in all decisions.

REFERENCES

Adams, S. (2020a, November 21). *Dilbert.* https://dilbert.com/search_results?month =11&year=2020

Adams, S. (2020b, December 22). *Dilbert.* https://dilbert.com/search_results?month =12&page=3&sort=date_asc&year=2020

Bauer, T., & Fitzsimmons, K. (2020, November 13). Five strategies for advancing to the next generation of evidence. *Project Evidence.* https://www .projectevident.org/updates/2020/11/13/five-strategies-for-advancing -to-the-next-generation-of-evidence

Bergstrom, C. T., & West, J. D. (2020). *Calling bullshit: The art of skepticism in a data-driven world.* Random Books.

Cairney, P., & Oliver, K. (2017). Evidence-based policymaking is not like evidence-based medicine, so how far should you go to bridge the divide between evidence and policy? *Health Research Policy and Systems, 15,* 1–11.

Datnow, A., & Park, V. (2018). Opening or closing doors for students? Equity and data use in schools. *Journal of Educational Change, 19*(2), 131–152.

Earle, J., Maynard, R., & Neild, R. (2013). *Common guidelines for education research and development.* Institute of Education Sciences; National Science Foundation. http://ies.ed.gov/pdf/CommonGuidelines.pdf

Institute of Education Sciences, U.S. Department of Education and National Science Foundation. (2018). *Companion guidelines on replication & reproducibility in education research.* https://www.nsf.gov/pubs/2019/nsf19022/nsf19022.pdf

LeMahieu, P. G., Bryk, A. S., Grunow, A., & Gomex, L. M. (2017). Working to improve: Seven approaches to improvement science in education. *Quality Assurance in Education, 25*(1), 2–4.

Lupton, D. (2016). *The quantified self: A sociology of self-tracking.* Polity Press.

Lupton, D., & Williamson, B. (2017). The datafied child: The dataveillance of children and implications for their rights. *New Media & Society, 19*(5), 780–794.

Mandinach, E. B., Cotto, J., Wayman, J. C., Rastrick, E., Vance, A., & Siegl, J. (2020). *User's guide for data privacy and data ethics scenarios.* WestEd.

Mandinach, E. B., & Gummer, E. S. (2013). A systemic view of implementing data literacy into educator preparation. *Educational Researcher, 42*(1), 30–37.

Mandinach, E. B., & Gummer, E. S. (2016). *Data literacy for educators: Making it count in teacher preparation and practice.* Teachers College Press.

Mandinach, E. B., Jimerson, J. B., Cotto, J., Vance, A., & Siegl, J. (2021). *User's guide for data privacy and data ethics scenarios for leaders*. WestEd.

Mandinach, E. B., & Schildkamp, K. (2021). Misconceptions about data-based decision making in education: An exploration of the literature. *Studies in Educational Evaluation*, 69, 1–10. https://doi.org/10.1016/j.stueduc.2020.100842

Mandinach, E. B., & Wayman, J. C. (2020). *Survey of curriculum: First deliverable in privacy training resources project*. WestEd; Future of Privacy Forum.

Maynard, R. A. (2018). The role of federal agencies in creating and administering evidence-based policies. *The ANNALS of the American Academy of Political and Social Science*, 678(1), 134–144.

National Academy of Education. (2017). *Big data in education: Balancing the benefits of educational research and student privacy: Workshop summary*. http://naeducation.org/wp-content/uploads/2017/05/NAEd_BD_Booklet_FINAL_051717_3.pdf

National Forum on Education Statistics. (2010). *Forum guide to data ethics* (NFES 2010–801). U.S. Department of Education, National Center for Education Statistics. https://nces.ed.gov/pubs2010/2010801.pdf

Project Evident. (2020). *Data & evidence equity guide*. https://static1.squarespace.com/static/58d9ba1f20099e0a03a3891d/t/5f3d3dcd2988f13d2b7f816b/1597849038367/The+Data+%26+Evidence+Equity+Guide.pdf

Raffaghelli, J. E. (2020). Is data literacy a catalyst of social justice? A response from nine data literacy initiatives in higher education. *Education Sciences*, 10, 1–20.

Sauter, T. (2014). 'What's on your mind?' Writing on Facebook as a tool for self-formation. *New Media & Society*, 16(5), 823–839.

Warnick, B. R., & Silverman, S. K. (2011). A framework for professional ethics courses in teacher education. *Journal of Teacher Education*, 62(3), 273–285.

About the Contributors

Wayne Camara, Law School Admission Council, is the Distinguished Scientist for Measurement Innovation, and served as senior vice president for research at ACT and the College Board for more than 25 combined years. He is a former president of NCME and was elected to leadership positions in APA, AERA, ATP, and SIOP. His research focuses on admissions testing, validation evidence, subgroup differences, and professional standards and practice.

Michelle Croft, Iowa City Community School District, is a research and data analyst. She was previously a principal research scientist at ACT, where she specialized in K–12 policy research and education law. Her recent projects have included the use of college entrance exams under ESSA, student data privacy, testing opt-outs, and test security.

Amanda Datnow, University of California, San Diego, is a professor in the Department of Education Studies and associate dean of the Division of Social Sciences at the University of California, San Diego. Her research focuses on educational reform and policy, with a particular interest in issues of equity and the professional lives of educators. Her recent work has involved studies of data use, teacher collaboration, and school transformation.

Chris Dede, Harvard University, is the Timothy E. Wirth Professor in Learning Technologies at Harvard's Graduate School of Education. His fields of scholarship include emerging technologies, policy, and leadership. In 2007, he was honored by Harvard University as an outstanding teacher. He is currently a member of the OECD 2030 Scientific Committee and an advisor to the Alliance for the Future of Digital Learning.

Edward Dieterle, Educational Testing Service, leads ETS's Center for Strategic Research & Development Alliances to develop, deepen, and sustain strategic alliances to help advance quality and equity in education. Earlier in his career, he was a senior program officer for research at the Bill & Melinda Gates Foundation, where he developed and administered the Foundation's personalized learning research portfolio, and was a researcher of educational technologies at SRI International, a high school chemistry teacher, an instructor at Johns Hopkins University, and a curriculum developer for public television and the National Park Service.

Sherman Dorn, Arizona State University, is a historian of education policy and professor at Mary Lou Fulton Teachers College, Arizona State University. As a university administrator between 2011 and 2021, he supervised and supported educational leadership programs at both the master's and doctoral levels and supported the redesign or design of more than a dozen degree programs.

Norman Paul Gibbs, Arizona State University, is a PhD candidate for Educational Policy and Evaluation at Arizona State University. He has research interests in migrant education, participatory pedagogies, and the ethical use of data in educational administration. He has held teaching and administrative positions in K–12 and higher education institutions, both in the United States and internationally.

Edith S. Gummer, PNW EvaluAnd Consultants, is currently founding a nonprofit organization to provide evidence-based services in research and evaluation. She previously served as the executive director for the Office of Data Strategy at the Mary Lou Fulton Teachers College at Arizona State University where she worked with faculty and staff to innovate information systems into longitudinal, research-enabled data systems. With data as a foundation, Gummer also worked as a program officer at the National Science Foundation and the Ewing Marion Kauffman Foundation.

Beth Holland, The Learning Accelerator, is a partner at The Learning Accelerator and leads the organization's research and measurement efforts. For the past several years, she has been examining the challenges of equity and communication within K–12 public school systems for her dissertation, as a postdoctoral research fellow at the University of Rhode Island, where she worked on a project funded by the U.S. Department of Education's Ready to Learn Initiative, and at the Consortium of School Networking (CoSN) where she led their Digital Equity and Rural initiatives.

Taryn A. Hochleitner, Data Quality Campaign, associate director for policy and advocacy, identifies, advocates for, and supports changes to state policy and practice that make data work for students. She tracks the changing landscape of state policies that govern education data, and shares resulting insights and recommendations with policymakers and the field. Before joining DQC in 2014, Taryn was a research associate for Education Policy Studies at the American Enterprise Institute.

Jo Beth Jimerson, Texas Christian University, is an associate professor of Educational Leadership at Texas Christian University. Following more than a decade of work teaching and leading in Texas PK–12 public schools, she joined the College of Education faculty at TCU, where she works with aspiring campus, school district, and higher education leaders. Her research focuses on educational data use, instructional leadership, and principalship. She received her PhD in Educational Policy and Planning from the University of Texas at Austin in 2011.

Marie Lockton, University of California, San Diego, is a researcher and educator. She studies equity-driven educational change efforts in schools and school districts with the goal of assisting leaders and teachers in making meaningful changes to policy and practice. Her work focuses on educator learning and collaboration and on aligning educational contexts to better draw on the diverse strengths of students and educators. As a teacher, she aims to increase students' agency in their own learning and to promote productive collaboration between and among students and teachers.

Ellen B. Mandinach, WestEd, is a senior research scientist at WestEd and a leading expert in data-driven decision-making in education. Mandinach developed the constructs of data literacy for teachers and culturally responsive data literacy. She has served on many advisory boards around data use, created the AERA Special Interest Group on Data-Driven Decision making in Education, and has published widely on the importance of using data in educational practice.

Sharon L. Nichols, University of Texas, San Antonio, is professor and chair of the Department of Educational Psychology at the University of Texas at San Antonio. She teaches graduate and undergraduate classes in learning theory, motivation, development, and research methods, and she has authored more than three dozen books, journal articles, and book chapters related to youth development, motivation, and education policy. Her current work focuses on the impact of test-based accountability on teachers, their instructional practices, and adolescent motivation and development.

Diana Nunnaley, Using Data Solutions, is the CEO and director of Using Data Solutions. For the past 20 years, her work has been totally dedicated to providing leaders with the learning needed to help them create the data systems, teacher preparation, and support needed to create a culture of evidence-based decision-making and continuous learning leading to improvements. She taught middle school math and supported teachers, teacher leaders, and administrators for 30 years by providing professional development and technical assistance to aid their efforts to increase student growth and achievement.

Brennan McMahon Parton, Data Quality Campaign, vice president of policy and advocacy, leads DQC's strategy to ensure that state leaders enact policies and practices that get individuals across the P–20W spectrum the data they need for every student to excel. She joined DQC in 2011 to advance the organization's mission to ensure that data are used in service of student learning. Before joining DQC, she worked at the State Collaborative on Reforming Education, in Nashville, Tennessee, as a research and policy analyst.

Amelia Vance, Future of Privacy Forum, is the director of Youth & Education Privacy. As a lawyer, she advises policymakers, academics, companies, districts, and states on child and student privacy law and best practices. She also convenes stakeholders to ensure the responsible use of student data and education technology in schools. Her research interests include the unintended consequences of privacy legislation; how to communicate about privacy, data use, and data sharing in education; and how to build privacy guardrails around school safety measures and surveillance.

Alina von Davier, Duolingo, is a chief of assessment with Duolingo and founder and CEO of EdAstra Tech, LLC. Her research interests include computational psychometrics, automatic item generation, and scoring and assessment science in general.

Casey Waughn, Armstrong Teasdale, LLP, is an attorney whose practice focuses on data privacy, security, and litigation matters. She was previously a Policy Fellow at the Future of Privacy Forum.

Hayley Weddle, University of Pittsburgh, is an assistant professor of Education Policy. Her research examines the equity implications of policy implementation across state and local levels. She is particularly interested in the role of school, district, and state leaders in fostering equity for multilingual learners. Across her work, Weddle also examines strategies for developing meaningful and reciprocal partnerships among researchers, practitioners, and policymakers.

Index